THE WHISTLEBLOWER'S DILEMMA

The Whistleblower's Dilemma:
Confronting Fraud at AIG

By Gordon S. Massie

The Whistleblower's Dilemma: Confronting Fraud at AIG

Copyright © 2010 by Gordon S. Massie

Revised Edition
Printed in the United States of America

ISBN 978-0-9830676-1-0

Designed and Produced by
Kingsley Literary Services
www.kingsleybooks.com

This book may have never happened without the consistent prodding of my dear brother-in-law and prolific author, Daniel Matt. "Danny" never failed to see the potential of this book and the pressing need for me to tell my story.

Many thanks to Joel Segel of Needham, Mass. who became my writing coach, ghostwriter, mentor, and friend. Joel contributed significantly to the writing of many key chapters in this book.

I can never express enough love and thanks to all of my extended family and especially my beloved wife, Barbara. They never questioned the wisdom of my actions, they stood by me during my ordeal at AIG, and they have all strongly supported my decision to publish this book.

I also wish to give special thanks to my son, Hunter, for his work in designing both the front and back covers of this book.

Finally, to our many special friends, to numerous former co-workers from American General and AIG, and to the many who encouraged me throughout this project: Thank You.

Gordon S. Massie

v

For more information please log on to
www.aigwhistleblower.com

Contents

Chapter 1: The Shock of Deceit

We heard about bad guys while growing up. I watched Westerns on TV and heard tales of cruel and godless kings in our occasional visits to church. My father told me about fighting the Japanese on a Naval battleship in World War II. But knowing the good guys from the bad was never something a boy needed to trouble himself about in the leafy innocence of Orinda, California, a suburb just east of Berkeley. I was a child of the baby-boom Fifties. My father, a respected local businessman, was president of the Rotary Club. My mother tended the three kids, played tennis, and volunteered in the community. We lived only a few hundred yards from Del Rey Elementary School, and when the final bell rang, I would race my pals down the sidewalk to snag the best spots in our family room for "Leave it to Beaver."

The "rumpus room," as my parents called it, was a big, comfortable space with a wall of floor-to-ceiling windows looking out on a backyard filled with massive redwood trees. The other three walls were covered with cheap wooden paneling that splintered and sagged as the years passed. The furnishings were all rejects from other rooms or the comfortable castoffs of departed relatives: dog-eared sofas and mismatched chairs, stained carpets, and lamps that worked only on their own terms. Armed by my mother with two Oreo cookies and a glass of whole milk each, we would watch our ancient black-and-white TV from "forts" constructed from sofa cushions, mismatched pillows, and stray blankets, all strategically deployed around the room. The trials and tribulations of the "Beav" and his brother Wally were ours. Oh, the trauma of an errant baseball hit through a crabby neighbor's window! The dastardly manipulations of the oily Eddie Haskell! We loved "Leave it to Beaver" because its plots and dramas mirrored our own lives perfectly. My parents seemed just like Ward and June Cleaver. My father issued edicts from behind his newspaper while sitting in his favorite easy chair, just like Ward did. As if to cement the connection, the Beaver himself—actor Jerry Mathers—would become a classmate of mine years later at the University of California at Berkeley.

One day, though, my father put down his newspaper to talk to me. I remember our conversation as one of my first stepping stones into the disquieting world of moral choices.

I'm almost embarrassed to admit it, given the amount of suffering in the world, but by the time I entered high school I can honestly say I had never experienced any real pain or trauma. I spent my early years immersed in family, friends, sports, school, and part-time jobs. Drugs and alcoholism, divorce or teen pregnancy were unknown in my sheltered and wholesome world—at least to me. Smoking in the boys' room was the most dastardly crime ever committed at Miramonte High School. I had no reason for fear or distrust, no reason to doubt anyone's integrity, until I was hired for my first real job.

In my hometown back in the '60s, working at a gas station was cool, and my father, who knew everybody, got me a job at Billy Knox Chevron, five miles down the road from Orinda in the fast-growing town of Moraga. Billy Knox himself, a small man with curly dark hair and a heavy smoking habit, agreed to hire me to pump gas and help out with fixing cars at a dollar and forty cents an hour. I was in heaven from day one. The main job of the gas station attendants—maybe three of us per shift—was pumping gas, but when the pumps were idle, Billy and his manager, John Williams, would let us help them out repairing customers' cars. The station had two garage bays, each with a hydraulic auto lift. Wrenches and power tools lay around every-where. The air was filled with the pungent odors of solvents and gasoline. An AM radio in a nearby corner blared *Light My Fire* by the Doors or the Monkees' *I'm a Believer*.

The military's influence in that post-War era was still so perva-sive that everybody—the milkman, the mailman, even the gas station attendant—seemed to wear a uniform. Each day I was given freshly laundered white shirts and pants to wear over my clothes, and each day I would besmear them with grease stains and road grime, badges of distinction for me among my less fortunate friends who pushed lawnmowers for their spending money. My buddies would cruise by and we would chat as I filled up their tanks. "Yeah, I've been work-ing with Billy on a brake job for this Chevy Nova," I'd say casually, pretending that I actually knew something about it. Pretty girls drove in regularly for fill-ups, and I was always ready with my best smile before popping the question. "Check your oil, Miss?"

Best of all, Billy would let me put my own 1965 Mustang up on the lift after operating hours. Cars needed more regular maintenance then, especially the older models. They had points and plugs and con-densers to change, carburetors to adjust, timing that needed to be reset. The richer kids in our middle-class community might get new cars for their sixteenth birthdays, but most of us bought old clunkers for a few hundred bucks and prayed they'd keep running. Learning to maintain my own car, I saved myself the cost of constant tune-ups and covered myself with grease and glory. I loved my job. I loved my life.

Then things started to change. Billy Knox Chevron had been the only station in town, but as the region grew other stations opened up nearby, and Billy must have started feeling the pressure. I didn't under-stand that then. All I knew was that Billy and John began acting in a way that seemed—well, sort of secretive. Billy would be hard at work, toiling underneath an auto on one of the lifts, and when I popped in to the service bay with a question he would jump, as if I'd startled him, or move to block what he was doing from view. Sometimes what he and John were doing didn't square with what I had learned.

"Why are you spraying WD-40 on these shock absorbers?" I'd ask innocently, eager for my next bit of lore on the mysteries of auto maintenance.

"Oh, I just like to clean 'em up for the customer."

"I never knew that was necessary."

"Sure is. Helps 'em last longer," Billy said, but his confident reassurance was oddly undermined by the almost too-casual tone in his voice. It was all very strange. Some of the other guys and I began to wonder: What the heck was going on?

A mechanically inclined friend reacted incredulously to this notion of shock absorber cleaning, so the next morning I took a look at the final work order for the car Billy had been tinkering with. "Replace four leaking shocks," Billy had written. Wait a minute, I thought. Billy had supposedly been cleaning the original shocks for this customer—then had turned around and sold the guy four new shock absorbers? I waited until Billy was busy elsewhere, then I went to the dumpster and rooted around. Sure enough, there were the customer's four shocks. None of the hydraulic fluid from inside the shocks had leaked out. The only sign of "leakage" was the WD-40 sprayed all over them. Was it possible that Billy, my employer and mentor, was a con man?

I started to watch Billy and John more closely. I wasn't so much troubled as curious. Just how are these guys ripping customers off? I soon learned. Repairable flat tires were slashed or gouged and the customers were sold new ones. Service work was charged and never performed. Oil filters were not replaced but wiped clean to look new. John Williams had even constructed a peep hole to give himself a personal view of the ladies' restroom. This seemed vulgar to me, but I was not involved and I did not consider any of this my problem. At least not until Mr. Thiele came in for car service.

Mr. Thiele was a man of modest means who washed and waxed his precious 1956 Mercury sedan every Saturday morning. His son, Rob, had been my best friend since the sixth grade, building many a fort in my rumpus room. Rob sometimes had to opt out of ball games or other weekend activities that required admission tickets, and I knew that money was often tight at the Thiele's house. I cringed as kindly Mr. Thiele drove into our service bay at Billy Knox Chevron. How would Billy and John take advantage of Rob's gentle and trusting dad?

"That ol' Merc still looks brand new!" I told him, hoping to head off what I feared might be coming.

"Thanks, Gord. You know she's my baby."

"Just getting her serviced today?" I asked desperately.

"That's all, I hope!"

I gulped. The daily dishonesty at Billy Knox Chevron suddenly felt more like my problem. Sure enough, Mr. Thiele drove his baby home that day with four new shock absorbers, at a cost of almost $100. Big money back then. Billy had sold him on the need for new shocks to replace his "leaking" ones and ensure a safe ride for his family. Safety first! Billy knew how to prey on his customers' weaknesses and I had done nothing to prevent it.

Now I felt like the accomplice to a crime. This was not the Beaver Cleaver world I knew. For days I tried to persuade myself that this wasn't my problem. I wasn't doing anything wrong, was I? Billy and John weren't asking me to take part, were they? But this was very different behavior than my mother and father had modeled at home. They treated everyone, regardless of race or cultural background, with honesty and dignity, while I had treated Mr. Thiele with callousness and indifference. I had received nothing but love and goodwill for all of my seventeen years. This was the first real challenge I had known. Why was I afraid to do the right thing? What kind of person was I?

Since my father had landed me this job, I decided to ask for his advice. When he heard my tales of dirty tricks at Billy Knox Chevron, he looked disturbed. "I certainly wouldn't want *you* to treat any one that way," he said, and left it at that. This wasn't the clear direction I was looking for, though, so later that day I tracked him down to his easy chair.

"Dad, what do you think I should do about my job?"

"Well, Gord," Dad said from behind his newspaper. "What do *you* think is the right thing to do?"

I had come to him for answers, and all I was getting were more questions. "If I knew that, I wouldn't be asking you," I said grumpily.

My father stood up, folded his paper methodically, and came over to sit directly in front of me. The look on his face was stern, his furrowed brow framed by traces of gray at each temple. His eyes looked straight into mine.

"But this isn't my decision. I know what I would do. But you have to ask yourself what your *own* values are."

"I don't know! I've never had to deal with this kinda thing before."

My father was so much older and wiser, so much surer of himself. I wanted him to make the decision for me.

But he didn't back down. "What are your values?" he repeated. "What are your ethics, Gord? I know you love your job, and that finding another one won't be easy. But, sooner or later, you have to decide. What do you stand for—not just now, but for the rest of your life? Values are not something you change to fit the situation. They have to be constant."

Two days later I dutifully reported for work, put on my freshly laundered Chevron uniform in the back storage room, and went out to the garage bays. The first thing I noticed were four empty shock absorber boxes in the garbage can and only a late-model Chevy on the lift. I walked slowly back into the storage room. They ripped off another customer, I thought. I stripped off my uniform for the last time, walked out of the station, and drove home. I never did tell Billy the real reason I had quit. I wasn't man enough for that kind of confrontation. The next day I simply called the station and told him I'd found another job. The deception at Billy Knox Chevron might continue, but I would no longer be a part of it. I had answered my father's questions—for now, anyway. Only many years later would I realize that walking away was not always enough.

Chapter 2: "Bidness" in the Tank

It was a humid July morning in 1985, and the winding and forested roadway through the Great Smoky Mountains of East Tennessee was flowing back under our spinning wheels. The leader of our six man motorcycle group was somewhere out ahead of me. A string of other guys rode behind as we all snaked along the asphalt through the woods. Beneath me, my V-Twin engine was purring like a kitten in the dense morning air. All of us savored the twisting and undulating back roads of the Smokys which closely tracked the surrounding mountainous topography. Racing through the thick, eastern hardwoods at 60 miles per hour, crystal clear lakes would magically appear, then a vast open meadow, soon to be eclipsed by more grand vistas of forested hillsides. Up ahead, a broad sweeping curve veered to the left. I leaned into the curve, accelerated, and shifted up a gear. I heard that sweet exhaust note and felt the power of the engine. A tight, twisting bend swerved to my right. Then I had to slow down, brake gently, down shift and lean right. Endless curves for miles and miles. With the wind blasting at my chest and the motorcycle responding to my every input, I felt just as though I was flying. This was motorcycling at its finest to me. Great weather, great roads, and great friends.

We did this every year. I had a wife and two young children at home back in Houston. We enjoyed our vacations together, but family trips demanded almost constant management of two needy and opinionated youngsters, hardly conducive to true rest and relaxation. It was more like controlled chaos. The five other guys and I were all just beginning to gain momentum in our early professional careers. Like me, they were married and had young and active children. Life was good, life was sweet—but busy and hectic. When we were not at the office, reaching for the next rung on our corporate ladders, our lives seemed ruled by soccer games, piano lessons, and ballet recitals. Riding with my buddies, on the other hand, was a *real* vacation. Thanks to them and to my wife, Barbara, I had no demands, no one else's schedule, no diaper changes, no little league practice, just a great opportunity for three full days of fun and freedom on the open road.

My first "motorcycle" had been a mini-bike with a 4 horsepower lawnmower engine. The entire machine, with its two tiny wheels, rose all of two feet off the ground. Maybe on a good day it was good for twenty miles an hour. But I didn't care. It was early fun and freedom to me. I used to ride it through the endless pear orchards around our California home when I was twelve years old. Since then, and many full sized motorcycles later, a little speed, a little risk, and a new and curving road in any part of the country had always spelled magic for me. Add to that a bunch of like-minded guys, men who could ride for a whole day in any conditions with nary a complaint, and you've got my idea of heaven. On our stops we'd joke around and rib each other, keeping it light. But the teasing was constant and brutal:

"When ya gunna learn to ride that thing?"

"Maybe a scooter is more your style!"

"How many years has it been since you cleaned your Honda?"

"In case you forget, try to keep the rubber side down."

There was much to be said about the camaraderie of this group, but I had no idea back then how much I would need their help and support one day. For now, my gloves were on, my visor was down, I was flying down these mountain roads, and I didn't have a care in the world.

This vacation was especially sweet for me, since I had no work-related responsibilities to mull on while I rode. I'd left one job behind and was about to start another. It was a good time to switch. In 1985, as the Houston locals would drawl, "the awl bidness [oil business] was in the tank." The halcyon days of $35 per barrel oil were gone, replaced by the brutal and cold reality of oil priced now in the mid-teens. Houston and much of southeast Texas was mired in a deep economic slump. So was the overall economy throughout the entire marketing area that had been assigned to me by the Prudential Insurance Company. Demand for oil drove everything in the energy business, of course. But it also indirectly drove demand for office space, housing, retail stores, bank loans and a whole lot of other enterprises. My Texas marketing region was clearly plagued by all the signs of recession: closed stores, home foreclosures, high unemployment, and minimal business activity.

I had taken a job with Prudential three years before with the responsibility for marketing loans directly to medium-sized businesses throughout Houston and East Texas. These loans were called private placements. They were usually 10+ years in maturity, carried a fixed rather than adjustable rate of interest, and were negotiated directly between the borrower and the lender, rather than being subject to a public bond offering. My job was to hit the road, make the sales calls, close the transactions, and develop long-term relationships with my customers. There was only one problem. In 1985, most of the companies that Prudential had loaned money to in this region were struggling. Most of the companies on my list of loan prospects couldn't come close to Prudential's lofty credit quality standards. My loan production was also "in the tank," and I was beginning to worry that staff cuts weren't far off. As they say, it's better to get a job while you already have a job. So, I went looking.

Given the economic downturn in East Texas, home prices in Houston had plummeted as much as fifty percent from their highs in 1980. The prospects of putting my home on the market, taking a financial loss, and moving were not appealing at all, and so my first order of business was to see what financial jobs might be available in the Houston area. One prospect that quickly caught my eye was American General Corporation (AGC), a fast-growing, multi-line insurance company that had been established back in the 1920s by a Houston native. As luck would have it, AGC's annual shareholders' meeting was scheduled to take place in downtown Houston in early May of 1985. I was a stockholder myself—owned all of 200 shares—and I planned to attend. While there, I would be on the lookout for Julia Tucker. Julia and I had met once before, when she was in charge of private placements for Equitable Insurance in Houston. She and I had made loans to some of the same companies. Now she was the newly-appointed Head of Private Placements at AGC. If I liked what I heard at the annual meeting, I planned to accidentally "bump into" Julia during the post-meeting hobnobbing.

Sure enough, I liked what I heard from management. AGC was growing by leaps and bounds, gobbling up other insurance companies. At the time, this practice was almost unheard of in the insurance sector, but AGC had recently completed two of the largest insurance company acquisitions on record, buying NLT of Nashville and Gulf Life Insurance of Jacksonville, Florida. They had the reputation of somehow assimilating other companies successfully and making the mergers work. By the end of the decade, they would quadruple their assets. This buying spree catapulted AGC onto the national stage, a significant participant in the U.S. life insurance, annuity, and property casualty insurance businesses. Most important to me, all of AGC's invested assets were going to be managed by the company's investment staff in Houston, which I had heard was only a small group and very much in need of experienced investment people.

I wasn't sure I remembered exactly what Julia looked like, and of course I had absolutely no assurance that she would even attend the annual meeting. But I got lucky. There she was, right across the hotel lobby. Julia was an attractive, professionally attired woman in her middle thirties with shoulder length brown hair. She looked much as I had vaguely remembered. I approached my target casually.

"Julia! How have you been?"

Julia got that *Uh, help me out here* look on her face, so I reintroduced myself.

"Gordon Massie, with Prudential. We met several years ago…"

"Oh, yes." She remembered. Julia had been Phi Beta Kappa at the University of Texas and had an MBA from Columbia. She was charming, engaging, and exceptionally bright. After a few minutes of general chit-chat, I let drop that after three-plus years at Prudential I was looking for "new opportunities." Julia was an extrovert, even with a semi-stranger. She didn't hide herself behind any aura of coolness. "You are? When can we meet again?" We quickly set a lunch date for the following week in American General's executive dining room.

The dining room was richly furnished with solid mahogany walls, plush carpet, and freshly pressed white table clothes with linen napkins. Impeccably uniformed waiters darted about. I could tell that this was where the American General brass dined on a daily basis. It seemed like a very formal and somewhat serious place to meet Julia, who soon came bounding in with her fresh smile and ever pleasant disposition. I was soon very comfortable in her presence.

Have you ever had one of those job interviews when you knew from very early on that the job was yours if you wanted it? This was one. Julia was drowning in work. She and her very small staff were still trying to assimilate AGC's recent acquisitions and their combined investment portfolios. She was sorely in need of experienced private placement people. Since I had that on my résumé and didn't drool or walk on all fours, I was a natural candidate, and Julia spent most of our time together trying to sell me on American General. "It's the land of opportunity!" she said repeatedly.

She did a good job. We had a very pleasant lunch together. AGC was profitable and growing fast, and—since the company invested in the securities of companies throughout the U.S.—a job with them would significantly reduce my economic exposure to the faltering Houston economy. By the time the waiter brought our coffee I had only one question left, something I'd heard about in researching the company.

"What is this thing called Modelnetics?"

Julia sat back in her chair for a moment, and I could see her shifting gears, carefully mulling over her next response. Her ever present smile seemed to disappear. Modelnetics, she said carefully, was simply a management system created by Harold Hook, Chairman and CEO of American General Corporation. It consisted of 150 or so models, or pictographs, each of which conveyed a basic concept of management. AGC employees were expected to learn these models and to use them in their work.

"Can you give me an example?"

Well, said Julia, one of her favorite models was called the "Tomato Plant." The pictograph of this model conveyed a simple plant figure. The lesson behind the pictograph was that one should not plant more tomato plants than one can carry water to. If you as an employee were told by your supervisor at AGC that you had a "Tomato Plant Problem," it simply implied that you were a poor planner or had problems with time management. So in a sense Modelnetics was just our own code or language at AGC. It really was no big deal, she said.

I bit my lip, trying to look serious. Would I be analyzing private placements or farming tomatoes? But okay, I thought. Sounds harmless enough to me. I felt very enthusiastic about AGC and told Julia so. I also felt very comfortable with Julia. She was open, engaging, and very witty. She was also an accomplished professional who knew her business well and had a great reputation. She seemed like a great person to work for at American General. Within a few weeks, a job offer was made and I accepted with only a minimum of haggling, part of it to get a little time off between ending one job and beginning the next. In two weeks I would begin my new position with AGC, a newly minted Second Vice President of Private Placements, but there was time enough for that later. First I had some motorcycle riding to do with my buddies.

Chapter 3: Junk Bonds and Predator Balls

What I didn't fully realize until after joining AGC in August of 1985, was that Modelnetics was, to a large degree, representative of how AGC was managed. Harold Hook had actually created and implemented a comprehensive management system entitled "Main Event Management" (MEM). Modelnetics was merely the language or system of building blocks for MEM. MEM truly defined the culture of AGC in Houston. Mr. Hook had been an officer in the US Navy and later entered the insurance business where he quickly rose through the ranks of several smaller, regional, life insurance companies before joining AGC in 1975. It was during these pre-AGC years that he personally developed Modelnetics and MEM which, from my point of view, were clear evidence of the personality of Harold Hook and how he saw the need within corporate America to create order out of chaos.

Mr. Hook was a firm believer in management organization and systems. Everything should be documented and all employees should participate in this documentation and use it to enhance their own efficiencies, as well as the collective efficiencies of AGC. For example, every employee from Mr. Hook down to the newest mailroom intern had to have and maintain a "Desk Manual," usually a very thick three ring binder which in theory was supposed to fully document every task that a particular employee was responsible for completing. In effect, this was an extraordinarily detailed job description which went on to describe how each employee's tasks should be done. In fact, AGC employed a cadre of "Consulting Analysts" whose jobs, in part, consisted of reviewing employee Desk Manuals to make sure that they were current and reflected the standards of MEM. The idea behind a Desk Manual was that if you left your job someone new could come along and learn your job very quickly. In a somewhat less than affectionate way, these Consulting Analysts often were referred to by the Investment Department staff as "the new Hitler Youth."

MEM required loads and loads of documentation. We used to joke that AGC had single-handedly cornered the market in three ring binders. MEM stipulated that additional reference manuals be maintained throughout the organization for every conceivable topic or inquiry imaginable. Remember these were pre-intranet days and everything was put on paper. If you wanted to send flowers to a grieving employee, sure enough, there was an MEM manual which contained a section on this topic. Some poor soul, probably a Consulting Analyst, had spent days writing a memo and getting it approved so that I would fully understand all the flower rules and regulations before I acted. MEM manuals dictated virtually every system and procedure at AGC. Company memos had to follow a predetermined format. The form and layout of all presentations were carefully stipulated. Organization charts were continuously revised. Annual Salary Reviews had to follow a very strict format and, among other things, required a "Modelnetics Checklist" whereby each employee's performance and character traits were systematically compared with the standards suggested by various models from Modelnetics. Here is where I came to truly appreciate "Tomato Plants." And, of course, all approvals and approval processes were subject to many memoranda, which after creation were subsequently entombed in these three ring binders.

In effect, Modelnetics and MEM were administrative burdens which permeated much of what was done at AGC. Management time was heavily diverted to the almost constant classes, reviews, and systems updates. Every employee had to take a twenty-week course (1.5 hours/week) on the basics of Modelnetics. More senior folks took extended classes on how to teach Modelnetics and then became committed to teach twenty-week sessions for new employees. Top management seemed forever lost in "Advanced MEM Training," often to the point of compromising their "real" job performance. Some employees embraced all this and became true believers. Most rolled their eyes, sucked it up, and went with the program. Others griped openly and chafed at the system, and they didn't stay long.

As you can imagine, form often triumphed over function within this environment at AGC. Desk Manuals were hurriedly updated to please a Consulting Analyst rather than used on a daily basis. People showed up for Modelnetics classes only to become totally distracted or sleep. Many people only used Modelnetics when it made them look the part for top management. In a true triumph of form over substance, I presented an Investment Committee Memorandum to Mr. Hook and the senior management of AGC recommending an investment in a particular company. In spite of the facts that this was an important investment and that we were subject to some time constraints in obtaining internal approvals, Mr. Hook summarily rejected my memo because it did not appropriately adhere to the required MEM memorandum format.

But the facts were that Harold Hook wanted things his way and he was the Big Boss. He wanted to know that we followed procedures before committing millions of dollars on behalf of AGC. He understood that a company the size and complexity of AGC needed something to hold it together and make it work. He believed in systems, procedures, controls, and the need for a common culture; all of which I grew to appreciate over the span of my career. I could either take it or leave it and I chose to stay. And as the perpetually upbeat Julia would always say, "let's make it fun."

But don't get me wrong, I was happy at AGC. It was a conservative, very ethical, tightly run organization that was still assimilating its recent acquisitions. I found my co-workers to be smart, hardworking, honest, focused, and fun to be around. AGC's cash flow for investments was increasing and we were seeing a steady flow of new and interesting investment opportunities. The recent growth of AGC allowed us to compete for investments on a grander scale. The investment bankers from Wall Street had taken notice and it was great fun to be part of this effort. Another important point was that I very much enjoyed working for Julia Tucker, who really did her best to help shield us from some of the demands of MEM.

Upon joining AGC my focus was going to be Private Placements. Unlike Prudential where I was out beating the bushes for deals, at AGC most of our deal flow came to us from Wall Street investment bankers. We would receive a thick private placement offering book describing the major aspects of a company and the terms of the offering. As potential investors we were given the opportunity to meet top management, tour the company's important facilities, run our projections, ask a load of questions, and to generally and methodically assess all the risks of lending to this particular company, often with a group of other insurance companies. It was a genteel world of investing featuring close relationships, predictable routines, long lead times and loads of documentation. All of this fit well with AGC's style of a plodding and bureaucratic approval process which required (in addition to all the fundamental credit analysis) the preparation of an extensive (8-10 page) Investment Committee Approval Memorandum, as per MEM, of course.

The Investment Committee, chaired by Harold Hook, felt like military inspection. What seemed to matter most was not what we said (the substance of our presentation), but how the material was presented. Did we look the part and pay proper homage to MEM? There was rarely lively debate and the meetings tended to feel more ritualistic, again more of a triumph of form over substance. Very simply, if you were well spoken and your presentation materials followed MEM protocol you tended to sail right through the meeting, without a whole lot of discussion about the underlying risks of the recommended investment.

Looking back on my early days at AGC, I remembered that sometimes the most tedious of assignments can blossom into the richest of opportunities. In December 1985, after giving me a few months to settle into my new job at AGC, Julia Tucker asked me to compile some statistics on AGC's portfolio of private placement bonds that were rated as "below investment grade." This made sense. Like any financial company, we needed to monitor our holdings of these risky assets and keep tabs on our financial health. This was especially important since we had recently swallowed up two other large insurance companies and a pile of smaller ones, some thirty companies in all. A big part of American General's success was due to our ability to integrate other companies into our own, and we needed to know exactly the conditions of all these companies' investment portfolios. We also had a government regulatory incentive. In order to protect the consumer, states limit the amount of lower-quality, speculative-grade bonds an insurance company can hold.

Bonds have their risks and rewards, just like any other investment vehicle, and the market has developed a bond rating system to help investors know what they're getting into. The world's most prominent bond rating agencies are Moody's and Standard & Poor's. They use slightly different designations, but both rating systems range from "Triple-A" to D. Bonds of the highest quality, with the smallest risk of default, merit a Triple-A rating. Bonds rated AA and A—high grade and upper medium grade, respectively—still reflect companies with strong financials and with very low risks of default. One step lower on the ratings ladder, bonds rated Triple-B—lower medium grade—will typically reflect companies with higher levels of debt and/or lesser earnings available to pay interest obligations. BBB is still considered investment grade, but things begin to get dicier, with more sleepless nights for investors, once you fall into the "below investment grade" categories of BB, B, and CCC, designating bonds which are in increasingly risky and speculative categories. The final rating category, the dreadful D, is reserved for bonds that are in default and not paying interest.

Companies whose bonds are assigned the more speculative ratings are generally suffering from some degree of financial stress. Maybe their earnings have been weak or volatile. Maybe they've taken on a lot of debt relative to their shareholders' equity. Maybe they are simply smaller companies which face intense competition in their industries. Sometimes they simply haven't been operating for very long, making their credit worthiness difficult to ascertain with any certainty. Often their bonds' higher-risk rating reflects a combination of these factors. Detractors of these speculative-grade instruments, disdainful of their risky ratings, referred to them as "junk bonds." Those more inclined to see their potential emphasized the higher interest yields with which companies compensate investors for taking on this added level of risk—hence the term "high-yield bonds."

These ratings were generally assigned to publicly-issued bonds, but companies like AGC generally assigned private placements internal ratings of their own, using rating standards that more or less complied with Moody's and Standard & Poor's. Each of our insurance companies had a massive printout of all their holdings; the acquired bond, the issuing company, the rating, our cost, current market value, interest rate on the security, etc. And each company was supposed to update the information on those printouts using data feeds from our accounting department and from the rating agencies. But every insurance company we purchased seemed to have their own way of doing it. They'd own the same bond as we did but with different ratings, and the records weren't current or accurate. My job was to herd them all into line and this to me was not the most exciting of tasks.

So I was off on assignment for Julia, dutifully leafing through the endless paper accordions that computers printed out in those days, compiling my stats. The size of AGC's portfolio of below-investment-grade *private* placements turned out to be modest. I noticed almost immediately, however, that we had a rather extensive portfolio of speculative-grade *public* bonds. These publicly traded bonds were scattered throughout the portfolios of other departments of the insurance companies we'd acquired, such as the Common Stock or Investment Grade Bond departments. When all was said and done, they added up to some four hundred million dollars worth: only about four percent of our total holdings, but still a hefty chunk of change.

In each case I would check the bond's rating, substantiate that it was below investment grade, then start asking around. "Anybody know anything about this?" In some cases these were once-healthy companies whose credit ratings had since been downgraded. In others the reason for the purchase was less clear. When I inquired, for example, why we were holding a large bond position from company ABC, whose performance in recent years gave us little reason to be confident about their future, a typical answer was, "I don't know anything about ABC. That was probably bought by that idiot, Smith"— or any other name of a long-departed employee.

In other words, our public speculative-grade bond holdings were orphans. The high-grade bond managers—mostly middle-aged, conservative men—wanted nothing to do with them. Until the mid-1980s, the world of investment-grade bonds was a stodgy and conservative place. It was not a very demanding area of finance. Market prices traditionally didn't fluctuate much. Credit analysis was not that involved. Nearly every issue was of a very high quality, and investments very rarely defaulted. Widows and orphans who invested in this market could easily sleep comfortably at night.

The term "junk bond" (coined well before Drexel and their ilk) referred to that rare investment-grade bond that the rating agencies had demoted to below investment grade. The old-school managers of our other departments wanted no part of these bonds. "Junk," to them, meant "beneath my dignity to even look at." In their minds, and in the minds of many others at the time, junk bonds were simply an undesirable asset class. They were not only unsafe; they had recently taken on an immoral quality as well. They had become the tools of corporate raiders, endorsed by Michael Milken and his evil empire at the investment banking firm of Drexel Burnham Lambert. What Drexel had created in the early 1980's was a new issue market for high yield bonds which had not really existed before. Companies with bonds rated below investment grade could now issue new bonds with low ratings as long as the interest rate was deemed adequate by investors. As a result, AGC's $400 million portfolio consisted of bonds which had been downgraded to below investment grade, as well as some new issues of bonds rated below investment grade at the time of issuance.

But one guy's undesirable is another guy's opportunity. This to me was like finding treasures in your attic. Fresh on Julia's desk several days later was a complete statistical summary of AGC's total public, speculative-grade bond holdings, complete with an urgent recommendation that AGC immediately appoint someone to take responsibility for the direct management of these risky assets. "You can't just ignore these risky bonds," I warned Julia. Lo and behold, the very next day Julia called me into her office. "Congratulations, Gordon," she said. "You are now AGC's new public high-yield bond portfolio manager."

Julia was right. American General was truly the "Land of Opportunity."

My promotion was emblematic of a staid world—publicly-traded investment-grade corporate bonds—that was suddenly being turned upside down. High-yield bonds were the brave new asset class of the 1980s. They gave young, upstart companies access to capital heretofore reserved only for the highly rated elite. Supposedly stodgy management teams of large public corporations were being cast out by corporate raiders who now had access to massive amounts of cash via the high yield bond market. New industries such as gaming and telecommunications were also surging. And all this shakeup was being fueled with high-yield financing by the likes of Drexel Burnham.

Now here I was, at the grand old age of 34, running a $400 million, high-yield bond portfolio for a fast-growing institution that had recently become a real player in the financial markets. I was truly on top of the world. I felt pretty well prepared for this new position. Public and private high-yield issues had similar risk characteristics.

But the two forms differed in important ways. The issuing of new private placement bonds was conducted at a stately pace. They involved the exchange of private information. As a prospective lender, you'd visit the company, talk to the management, scour the whole company at a somewhat leisurely pace. Private placements were also subject to rigid and complicated trading restrictions. Publicly traded bonds, on the other hand, were traded freely and fast. Public bond issues tended to be larger than private ones, meaning that, on average, there was more money involved. Public bonds involved only publicly available information and gave investors much less time to analyze the issuing company. So I would need to trade a lot more actively than I had previously, making quick investment decisions, sometimes without as much information as I would like.

I had only one problem. How could I move quickly enough to both manage and grow this high-yield bond portfolio while dragging the ball and chain of Modelnetics and MEM?

High-yield bonds trade much like stocks, with buyer and seller negotiating transactions through a bond broker. "Buy and hold" is not an option—not if you want to make money. High-yield bonds are also high risk, their market prices volatile. They must be traded freely and fast. New high-yield bond issues could come and go in a matter of minutes. Bids and offer prices, especially for larger issues, could fluctuate every minute. You have to keep your ear pretty close to the ground. If you hear any news that might affect a company's bond price, you need to make your move before that news is widely disseminated, selling at the highest price you can or buying at the lowest.

AGC's slow, methodical, private placement investment style did not extend to the Jack-be-nimble world of high-yield bonds. My phone flashes. It's my contact at Drexel Burnham. "Gordon," he says, "I have 5 million Farley 7's at 63. I am seeing a bid of 62.5 away. Can you top?" In other words, "Please decide right away whether you'd like to pay $630 dollars a bond for a five million dollar par value offering of Farley Corporation seven-percent bonds."

The classic AGC answer would be, "Okay, I have to write the memos and go through all the investment committee approvals. I'll get back to you in two weeks."

"But you're already holding Farleys?"

"Doesn't matter. Same process. Two weeks."

No one in the high-yield world waited two weeks for anything. By that time, Drexel would have shopped the bonds to other potential buyers. If they needed to, they'd lower the price, but in two weeks, under any normal circumstance, that offering would be long gone. My challenge, then, was to bridge the gap between the staid and bureaucratic world of Harold S. Hook's AGC and the gun slinging, fast-paced, capitalism-gone-wild style of the new high-yield bond market as exemplified by Drexel Burnham.

That world truly opened up to me when I attended my first of what later became known as Drexel's predator balls. The 1986 Drexel Burnham Lambert High Yield Bond Conference was held at the opulent Beverly Hilton Hotel in Los Angeles, only a few blocks away from Drexel's headquarters. Hundreds of company CEOs, tycoons, and corporate raiders had come to rub elbows with thousands of high yield bond investors, actual and potential. Tucked away in different conference rooms in the hotel's labyrinthine basement, four or five company presentations were going on simultaneously. Lavish lunches and dinners were served in the Grand Ballroom where prominent guest speakers sang the praises of high-yield bonds, or hyped their own company's glowing prospects. The crowd was studded with some of the heaviest hitters of the day: Ted Turner, chairman of Turner Broadcasting; Ron Perlman, chairman of Revlon; Carl Lindner of the American Financial Group; Carl Icahn, multibillionaire financier and corporate raider extraordinaire. Various Hollywood celebrities were also prominent throughout the crowds. Evening entertainment was from the likes of Frank Sinatra, Diana Ross, or Dolly Parton.

Finally, of course, there was "Mike"—Michael Robert Milken, the man who developed and championed this seemingly "miraculous" new way of financing. Milken was a charismatic and innovative promoter who challenged the wisdom of the conventional bond market. He woke up the old establishment, slapped them around, and derided them for being too closed-minded. He had a gift for finding companies—or whole sectors—that needed capital, didn't have investment grade ratings, but had stories compelling enough to persuade investors to take the risk of funding them. These companies deserve access to public markets, he said—and we're going to put a big fat yield on the bond so investors will buy 'em. For below-investment-grade bonds the rate would not be eight percent as was typical for the safer ratings, but twelve percent which will more than compensate for the added risk of default.

Maybe it was a company with an acquisition and turnaround story. Maybe it was a whole new growth industry like telecom or gambling. The gambling industry, for example, had an odor of ill-gotten gain that wrinkled the noses of conservative investors. None of their bond issuers had been rated investment grade. Milken talked back. Look at Circus Circus, he said. They have a dominant market position in Las Vegas. They have a fantastic cash flow. Their casinos are mobbed! They can easily pay down their debt—and *you* can own their debt and make four percent more a year than you could with an investment-grade bond.

Milken was scheduled to speak at breakfast, which started as early as 6 a.m. The turnout was huge. Mike, as they say in investment-speak, "talked up his book," waxed eloquent on the virtues of high-yield bonds in general and of Drexel's client companies in particular. High-yield bonds, he said, could free our economy from the economic drag of bloated, inefficient corporate managements. Corporate takeovers thus financed would enhance asset valuations and cut costs, give smaller and less established companies access to capital, and allow new industries to flourish. The longer he talked, the more miraculous these new debt instruments appeared. The world was suffering from a debt crisis, he said. High-yield bonds could help there. We had an international drug trade problem. Perhaps high-yield bonds might fund payments to Bolivian farmers for not growing coca leaves. That was certainly "out of the box" thinking!

The cult of personality at the conference was intense. People idolized Milken. They worshipped at his feet. They hung on his every word, applauding till their hands were red. I, on the other hand, felt dumb and confused. I wanted to believe all this new hype, but my eight prior years of investment experience and training were waving a cautionary flag. True, I was only 34, but by the standards of the room I was a middle-aged veteran. Looking around me, I saw an awful lot of people in their twenties, investors fresh out of school who were lapping this stuff up with no sense of perspective or counter-argument. There was nothing wrong with the prudent use of high-yield bonds, but wasn't Milken overselling their prospects a bit? High-yield bonds were simply a newly developed form of risky corporate debt. They had no magical or mystical qualities. What mattered was not the bonds themselves but how they were used and for what purpose. Could you really make a company more efficient by loading it up with piles of new debt? Could a corporate raider with no experience in that particular industry do a better job than existing, more experienced managers? I had a lot of questions, and I wasn't hearing too many solid answers. But to argue these points was to suggest that the king had no clothes.

At one point I decided to approach the king myself. What did I have to lose? My purpose wasn't to pay homage. I just wanted to look him in the eye and try to measure the sincerity of this larger-than-life being close up. Milken was normally surrounded by an entourage of admirers, but I walked up to him in one of the conference hallways during a rare moment of solitude. He was thin, almost gaunt, wearing a white shirt and black suit. He looked a bit disheveled. His dark, deep set eyes were those of a man who did not get a lot of sleep. I remembered my father's advice from when I was a young boy. "Gord," he'd say, "When you meet someone for the first time, make sure you look them in the eye. And give 'em an extra firm handshake." Milken had apparently not mastered either concept. The hand I was shaking felt like a warm piece of dead meat. Those eyes were darting about the room, looking for more important fish to fry. And up close, the king's dark, curly crown of hair turned out to be a toupee. (Later, in federal prison, they took his toupee away from him.) We exchanged brief greetings and Mike asked about AGC's high yield bond portfolio. Soon, after he realized that we were only a bit player in "his" market, Mike was off, tracking down heavier hitters. My moment in the sun was so brief.

Suddenly this whole world seemed like make-believe. Wasn't Hollywood just down the street? The entire purpose of this conference was to sell us on the unquestioned virtues of high-yield bonds and of Drexel Burnham in particular—and I was less than totally sold. Nonetheless, I had a job to do and this was my marketplace. My challenge was to find values and opportunities in the high-yield market that I could "sell" to the methodical, conservative world of Harold Hook and MEM. My task was to thoroughly study this new market, and to separate fact from fiction, myth from reality. Was there real value to AGC in continuing to invest in this market? At that point, I was not so sure.

Chapter 4: The Rise and Fall

My first order of business upon taking control of AGC's high-yield bond portfolio was to "review the cards I was dealt." I needed to quickly review the 30-odd companies that had issued public debt which were now represented in my portfolio. Recall that these bonds had been purchased by many different insurance organizations and because of the mergers and employee turnover much of the history of these bond acquisitions and the credit files on the respective companies had been forever lost. So, I rolled up my sleeves and went to work. I contacted the companies to obtain their recent publicly filed financial statements, contacted Wall Street analysts to pick their brains, researched industry data, and made appointments to visit company managements. After my initial review, I placed each of my 30-odd companies into one of three categories, as shown below:

Fallen Angels: These were large and legitimate companies that had previously issued publicly traded debt which at the time was rated investment grade by the two major bond rating agencies. Due to credit deterioration related to a downturn in their business or as a result of the company electing to take on increased levels of debt (more on this later), the debt of these companies had been downgraded to below investment grade. Examples included Hughes Tool which was impacted by the decline in demand for its oil drilling tools, and Holiday Inn which had recently taken on a boat-load of debt as part of their strategy to buy in their stock in order to fend off a corporate raider.

Emerging: This category also included legitimate compa-nies, however these were younger, smaller companies without extensive years of operation. Some examples included Telecommunication, Inc., a highly leveraged pioneer in cable television, and Circus Circus which was recognized as one of the up-and-coming casino companies in Las Vegas.

Garbage: These were the companies owned and controlled by men who used them as their personal piggy banks, with-out any regard whatsoever for the bondholders. Examples included Sharon Steel and Rapid American Corp.

As I recall, it was in April 1986 that I obtained a copy of Rapid American Corp's 10k, their annual financial statement for the year ending 12/31/85 filed with the Securities and Exchange Commission. Within about thirty minutes of cracking the cover of this document I was sitting in utter disbelief. The first eight pages of the all-important footnotes to these financial statements contained the information on "Insider Transactions." It was plain to see that Rapid American was truly a "family run" company because it was blatantly run for the sole benefit of the family of its Chairman and CEO, Meshulam Riklis. The company itself owned the chain of McCrory Stores, those mostly inner city, Woolworth-esque, variety stores, that to my way of thinking had long ago passed their prime. The company was highly leveraged and earnings were in a steady decline as this company was feeling the growing competition from stores like Wal-Mart. But the Insider Transactions were what really troubled me. The entire board consisted of Riklis' friends and fami-ly. His twenty-something daughter was on the Board and also employed as the Marketing Head at somewhere around $800,000 per year. A big chunk of Rapid American's assets consisted of "Receivables from Affiliates" which was code for "I (Riklis) sucked a bunch of money out of this company and it now holds my personal IOU." Unbelievable . . . and there were eight pages of this stuff!

I wanted to unload our $10,000,000 par value bond position in Rapid American immediately, but the bonds were trading around $85 (actually expressed as a percentage of par so the market price of each $1000 par value bond was $850). This meant that a sale of the bonds would generate about a $1.5 mm loss since AGC's original cost in the bonds was around par value. I was cautioned about taking this loss at this time and also decided to wait until I had the opportunity to hear Riklis speak at the upcoming Drexel High Yield Bond Conference. My contact at Drexel had tipped me off to the news that Riklis had some exciting new plans to invigorate the McCrory Stores and that I might get a better price after this news was revealed at the Drexel conference.

Whenever Michael Milken introduced a company CEO as the next speaker at his conference he would always put together a glowing set of accolades about this person and his company. Sometimes these intros would go on for many minutes and leave me feeling that ol' Mike was laying it on pretty thick. The best thing that Mike could apparently find to say about Meshulam Riklis was that he had known him for many years and that Riklis had never defaulted on his debt. WOW! Talk about damning with faint praise. Also, I had discovered earlier that Riklis was currently married to Pia Zadora, a semi-famous actress of that era who was some 40 years his junior. Well at least he could put "Sugar Daddy" on his résumé!

So out came Riklis onto the stage to share with us his vision of a revitalized chain of McCrory Stores. There were probably a thousand or more people in the room awaiting his arrival. Out came this heavy-set, balding, sixty-something, cherubic figure of a man who for the next twenty minutes or so told jokes to this crowd of financial analysts. Yes, jokes. . .I'm not kidding and some were pretty off-color. So, I was sitting there convinced that no one in their right mind would ever again pay anything close to 85 for my bonds. Finally, Riklis, after saying absolutely nothing about McCrory, introduced his new hire, a former big-wig with Montgomery-Ward, who delivered his presentation on the turnaround at McCrory. "Monkey Wards," those stores were horrible even in the 1980's and this guy was my savior? He gave his spiel about new inventories and signage at the stores but that was about it. Nothing in my mind that would do much of anything to prop up the market value of my bonds.

So, on first day back in Houston I went about selling my $10,000,000 of Rapid American 10% bonds. Drexel knew of my desire to sell and they had been leading me to believe that the best price they thought they could deliver was in the "low 80's." Kidder Peabody was a competitor of Drexel's at the time and they had actually been very helpful in helping me get information on Rapid American. They thought they could honestly get me $86 for the bonds (apparently someone missed Riklis' presentation), so I gave Kidder the bonds to sell at $86. Sure enough, I got a call back within an hour from Kidder announcing "you're done at $86 on all $10 mm." Wow, they sold them all at my price. I was so glad to see those bonds go, even at a sizable loss.

But wouldn't you know it, within an hour of the sale, my Drexel contact called back and said "we could have gotten you $90 and Michael is pissed." Well to this day I firmly believe that Drexel knew who bought the bonds and when. They only called me back when they knew the sale was complete and they did not have to make good on their fictitious bid of $90. Why were they quoting in the low 80's when a few hours later the price was 90? Anyway, what mattered to me was that I got the best price for AGC and it wasn't too long thereafter that Rapid American ran into cash flow problems and filed bankruptcy, leaving the bondholders with little more than pennies on the dollar. Surprise, Surprise!

So why do I bring this up? What is the significance of this sad tale about Rapid American? My point is that Drexel could not be trusted. They could not be trusted to perform adequate due diligence on Rapid American and Meshulam Riklis. Why would they even deal with such a low life? They misrepresented the turn-around at McCrory and they used intimidation after I traded with one of their competitors. I realized then and there that I had to be extraordinarily cautious when dealing with Drexel and their bond offerings. The big problem with my new revelation was that Drexel controlled somewhere around half of the new issue and secondary trading markets for high yield bonds at the time. Maybe I could keep Drexel at arm's length but I couldn't avoid some interaction with this firm. From 1986 through 1988 Drexel's issuance of new high-yield bonds on behalf of the customers was truly amazing. Often we saw as many as 2-3 new deals a day. These were complex, risky transactions which could take considerable time to understand and we passed on about 98% of these bond offerings.

What was really going on during this period was that Drexel was antagonizing numerous influential people, especially Fortune 500 CEO's and holders of public investment grade bonds. Drexel would go into partnership with a corporate raider, or takeover artist, and together they would identify their target company. Ideally, in their minds, this target had a bloated cost structure, sleepy management, little debt, a low stock price, and an established business with good cash flow. The corporate raider would then publicly announce a hostile takeover of the target company at some price above the stock's current trading level. These raiders were given some level of credibility by showing their "Highly Confident Letters" from Drexel. These letters were issued by Drexel explaining that Drexel was highly confident it could raise the money to finance the announced hostile takeover. So what was the management of the target company to do?

These corporate managers actually had a variety of choices, none of which was particularly attractive to them. These choices are summarized below:

Greenmail: Since the corporate raider usually had accumulated a large position in the target company's stock before announcing the hostile takeover, one option was for management to buy out the raider's stock position at a hefty premium. In other words, just a big payment to go away. Of course, the other shareholders became livid at the prospect of huge greenmail payments to minority shareholders. Why should company assets be used to pay "bribes" to these green-mailers? Carl Icahn was viewed as the poster child for the use of these greenmailing techniques. Another problem with greenmail was that a target company had absolutely no assurances that some other corporate raider wannabe wouldn't come along and try to play the same game.

Recapitalize: The idea here was to ugly-up your balance sheet while simultaneously putting cash into the hands of your shareholders. The standard technique employed by management was to go to their banks or the bond market and borrow huge sums in order to either buy in their stock or to pay a massive, one-time dividend to their shareholders. The idea here was that you could placate your shareholders with cash while turning your formerly investment grade rated company into something rated B because of all the added debt. Presumably this technique would also scare away your corporate raider.

White Knight: This was the term used to describe another potential buyer of the target company that could swoop in and out-bid the corporate raider. The "White Knight" was typically a competitor of the target company and generally was thought to be a more attractive, or friendly suitor than the corporate raider. The risk to existing management was that their jobs were in jeopardy.

Give In: Finally, the target company could give in to the corporate raider and agree to being acquired. Of course, the corporate raider, with Drexel's help, now had to create a new acquisition company, usually with about nine parts debt to every one part of equity. After the acquisition the new company's balance sheet had enormous amounts of debt and the company had no change in its earning power or cash flow, which was, of course, essential to service that mountain of new debt.

So perhaps you can imagine that if you were a Fortune 500 corporate chieftain at the time, Michael Milken and the folks at Drexel were not on your Christmas card list. But it wasn't just Drexel. The other major investment banks at the time, such as First Boston, Morgan Stanley, and Goldman Sachs, etc. were all seeing Drexel's early successes in this game and several chose to vigorously compete since the investment banking fees were enormous.

The other constituency that Drexel and others infuriated was the huge group of holders of investment grade bonds, such as insurance companies, mutual funds, banks, and pension funds. Remember when I mentioned all the documentation associated with doing private placement loans? A big part of this documentation involved financial covenants which were incorporated into the private placement loan agreement. These covenants regularly limited a company's ability to incur massive amounts of new debt or to pay huge dividends to its shareholders. Covenants were there to help protect the bondholders from self-inflicted credit deterioration. Only problem was very few public bond indentures (equivalent to a loan agreement) for these investment grade bond issuing companies had any such covenants. Who would have thought they would be needed? What company in its right mind would voluntarily trash its balance sheet to the point of losing its investment grade bond rating? Besides, if you as a bond buyer wanted these types of covenants in a public indenture, you would have been laughed at by the issuing company. The bottom line was that these re-capitalizations or hostile acquisitions were devastating to the staid world of public investment grade bonds. Market prices would fall precipitously as credit ratings regularly collapsed from Single A to Single B overnight, and there was very little that bondholders could do about the situation. AGC was holding a large position in Holiday Inn bonds that had been rated Baa1/BBB by the bond rating agencies. After Holiday Inn recapitalized in order to fend off a corporate raider the bonds were downgraded to B1/B and the market price fell 25-30%. Ouch!!

Drexel actually sowed the seeds of its own destruction because of the incredible number of poorly conceived and badly structured deals that it sponsored. In the acquisition fervor that developed, stock prices were bid up to silly levels and pro forma debt levels (adjusted to take into consideration all the new debt to be issued) reached ridiculous heights. One rather simplistic analytical tool that was used at the time was the EBITDA/Interest ratio. EBITDA stood for a company's Earnings Before Interest, Taxes, Depreciation, and Amortization. Interest was the total amount of interest that was due on all of the company's debt. For a typical investment grade rated company this ratio might have been at least 400% and probably a lot higher. As the acquisition fever took over, these pro forma ratios fell from around 200% to 150% or even lower. Think about it. You are a corporate CEO and your company generates $150 mm of annual EBITDA and now you have to look forward to an annual interest bill of $100 mm! So that still leaves a $50 mm margin, right? Wrong, that $50 mm will still need to be used for some taxes, debt repayment, capital expenditures, and increases in any working capital requirements (inventory, receivables, etc.). There was absolutely no margin for error and in many cases companies were so deprived of adequate cash flow that their business operations began to deteriorate immediately.

One of the most vivid examples of this craziness was the leveraged buyout of The Southland Corporation, the Dallas-based owner/operator of the ubiquitous 7/11 convenience stores. Now in fairness this was not a Drexel deal, but Drexel was still leading the charge for deals of this type. For various reasons, an acquiring group thought that Southland would be more valuable if it was acquired and then sold off in pieces or at least significantly reduced in size. Asset sales would be used to reduce a big chunk of the acquisition debt and, of course, operating costs would be cut in order to improve EBITDA, leaving the new company with plenty of margin to pay its obligations. Pro forma for its new capital structure, Southland's EBITDA/Interest ratio was a startlingly low 115%. Yes 115%. Anyone who bought this deal had to have unbridled optimism in the company's asset sales, planned operating efficiencies and cost cuts. Well, as luck would have it, Southland's asset sales didn't happen, at least not at the prices they expected. The Dallas real estate market was in a slump and the company's attempt to sell its corporate headquarters just didn't work. Some blocks of 7/11 stores were sold but it was really too little, too late. In the meantime, with an EBITDA/Interest ratio of 115%, what do you suppose happened to their store level capital expenditures and improvements? At the same time the major oil companies were all building their own modern, competing stores with large canopies over their gas pumps. By comparison the old 7/11 stores were outdated and down-right seedy. Maybe a merger with McCrory would have made sense! Anyway, before too long Southland ran out of cash and entered the world of Chapter 11 bankruptcy with bondholders having again to settle for pennies on the dollar.

Southland was just one example of the many deals that were falling apart at the end of the 1980's. Many were Drexel deals and many were not, but Drexel was the focus of much criticism because they were the poster child for the excesses of the high-yield bond market. Drexel also was a lightening rod for criticism because of the firm's perceived arrogance toward the traditional participants in the financial markets. Milken's public comments were often defiant towards regulators, investment grade bondholders, management teams and anyone who took issue with his fervent drive to spread the gospel of high-yield bonds. Drexel made no apologies for their many deals and their growing track record of shady and failing deals.

The ultimate downfall of Drexel began through the firm's association with Ivan Boesky, a prominent risk arbitrageur of the day. Risk arbitrageurs would speculate on stock prices of companies that were involved in acquisitions or were believed to be probable targets of potential acquirers. The safe way to play at this game was to buy the stocks of companies that were already the subjects of announced takeovers. There was usually a gap between the market price of the stock and the price that an acquirer had agreed to pay upon completion of the acquisition. An arbitrageur could capture this price differential if he owned the stock and the acquisition was then subsequently completed. His risk was that the acquisition failed and that the stock price fell back to its pre-merger announcement levels. A riskier way to play at this arbitrageur game was to speculate on which companies might become newly announced acquisitions, events which typically led to immediate spikes in companies' stock prices and lucrative profits to the arbitrageur. By the late 1980's, Ivan Boesky had acquired a reputation for being a very successful, and high profile risk arbitrageur. He had an established relationship with Drexel Burnham and when he wanted to raise capital to substantially increase his arbitrage activities he simply called his buddy, Michael Milken. So Drexel put together a complicated debt offering memorandum and scheduled a series of meetings with potential investors in Mr. Boesky's debt. We were contacted by our Drexel salesman and offered an opportunity to meet with Boesky and "get in early." What the heck. This guy was a big name at the time and they were coming to Houston. We had little to lose and it was a huge longshot that AGC would ever participate.

So into our conference room walked Ivan Boesky and his escorts from Drexel. Representing AGC were a number of senior investment people including Julia Tucker and myself. Ivan Boesky was of Russian descent and still spoke with a slight accent. He was a tall, slender, impeccably dressed, imposing figure. His hair was perfectly combed and slicked back and he wore the standard, Wall Street issue, pinstriped, black suit with an impressive "power tie." Boesky went on to try to convince us of his great powers in predicting acquisition targets and he showed us an impressive historical track record. The main problem that we saw with Ivan Boesky was that his success was only about his own "ability." He had no real organization behind him to supplement his talents. It was purely a bet on one man and we were uncomfortable with this one man and, of course, with Drexel's involvement. Upon Mr. Boesky's departure from our offices, Julia had a classic Julia comment: "He just smiled too much!" Boesky did in fact maintain a huge, ear-to-ear grin throughout his presentation. I added to this sophisticated form of credit analysis by suggesting that his suit was too shiny, a lot like a TV preacher might wear!

It wasn't long before our gut instincts proved true. Turned out that Mr. Boesky and Mr. Milken were both engaged in regular conversations and that the latter may have "accidentally" mentioned a few possible acquisition targets. Anyway, both gentlemen were subsequently accused and convicted of insider trading and sentenced to prison. The actual indictment of Milken also included an indictment of Drexel Burnham (the entire firm) for insider trading. This was the final spike into the heart of Drexel. No investment banking firm could ever survive a federal indictment for insider trading. Customers fled, banks pulled their lines of credit and soon Drexel discovered, first hand, the joys of Chapter 11 bankruptcy.

Drexel took a good idea and abused it. They approached their world with energy and enthusiasm but also an incredible degree of arrogance. They believed all of their own hype and never demonstrated the wisdom to question their own convictions. It was greed-gone-wild. At Drexel's funeral there were very few mourners.

Throughout all of this drama and trauma, what was going on at AGC? For the most part, we were drowning in a sea of fallen angels. Since AGC had a huge portfolio of investment grade bonds, we inevitably felt the impact of numerous downgrades as a result of all the leveraged acquisitions and re-capitalizations. By design, the senior management of AGC wanted to keep the ratio of below investment grade bonds to total invested assets at less than 5%. The constant flow of fallen angels into my portfolio left little time or capacity for added purchases of high yield bonds. We did nibble away at a few new and secondary high yield bond offerings and even some from Drexel, but by and large, AGC was only a bit player in this market. And the reality was that Mr. Hook was not at all a fan of Michael Milken and I was not about to risk my career by recommending 98% of the wacko deals of this era. I credit the structural limitations at AGC, the stodginess of AGC, the wisdom of Julia Tucker, and my own mistrusts for our collective ability to sidestep most of the carnage created between the years 1985 and 1990.

Watching the collapse of Drexel taught me volumes about the evils of greed, arrogance, and the callous disregard for the welfare of others. If wealth is your end game and you achieve it only through the abuse of your relations with others, you have paid far too high a price and truly achieved only a Pyrrhic victory.

Chapter 5: Recovery and Rationality

The bankruptcy of Drexel in 1989 produced a profound shock wave that effectively traumatized the entire high yield bond market. In spite of Drexel's sleazy dealings, this firm was still viewed as an investment banking powerhouse, even up to the day of its very demise. Dave Bergman was our salesman from Drexel and he had actually taken us to lunch in Houston on the day before Drexel announced their bankruptcy filing. Dave had confidently conveyed to us his staunch belief in Drexel and its ability to survive the federal indictments. Dave was a stand-up guy and he called back the next day to apologize for his ill-founded optimism and naivete.

In the aftermath of Drexel there were two overriding themes which hung over the high-yield bond market, a lot like a dark, smoky layer of Los Angeles' smog. First and foremost were the massive number of prior high yield deals that Drexel had structured and sold. Liquidity for these deals was totally gone. It was nearly impossible to find new secondary buyers without Drexel's sponsorship and market prices for these deals fell precipitously. Of course, every high yield deal suffered market price declines simply because the entire asset class had so completely fallen out of favor with investors. Just the sheer weight of all the high yield market's deals-gone-bad combined with all of the bad Drexel press put us bond buyers in no mood to hear any more sales pitches on new issues.

The secondary theme was the impending force of new government regulations. Savings and Loan Associations (S&Ls), Commercial Banks, and Insurance Companies comprised a large chunk of the then buyers and holders of high yield bonds. Almost overnight the S&Ls were regulated out of this market entirely. This actually made a lot of sense to me since the Savings and Loans had been using government guaranteed deposits to speculate on high yield bonds. We now call this a "moral hazard" because if the high yield bond market thrives the S&L's shareholders make a windfall on the large interest income above the cost of deposits, but if the high yield market collapses the government must absorb the losses as depositors are made whole. Banks and insurance companies were also subject to extensive new regulations pertaining to "Highly Leveraged Transactions," or HLT's. Banks and insurance companies were still permitted to hold some HLT debt but these new regulations severely limited the appetite that these institutions had for high yield bonds.

I remember feeling this eerie sense of peace at this moment in history. The chaotic frenzy had stopped. Sobriety took over. It was time to review the carnage in this marketplace and to quietly and methodically try to make sense of what had happened over the last five years. What about this market was worth saving and how could we collectively get it right next time?

To infer that American General completely sidestepped the high yield craziness of the time would be wrong. As I mentioned, AGC had its share of fallen angels and some of these holdings fell a bit too hard and fast, with disastrous consequences. Revco Drug Stores was an example of a retailer that went through a huge leveraged buyout. We had owned pre-buyout senior debt that actually became secured as a result of the buyout, but to no avail. Revco crashed and burned, a lot like Southland, and our investment in Revco ultimately was worth about 50 cents on the dollar.

Another very sad story involved American General's massive participation in the leveraged buyout of Brookstone, Inc. Brookstone was, and still is, a New Hampshire-based retail chain known for its unique collections of gifts, novelty items, and new product concepts, much like a Sharper Image store. Brookstone's stores were present in many of the country's upscale malls and in 1986 they were just beginning to consider opening additional stores in busy airports across the country. Brookstone, at the time, was owned by Quaker Oats, and the company had an excellent history of rising sales and profitability. Steve Cook, one of the principals of Duncan Cook, a Houston-based investment company, became aware of Quaker Oats' desire to sell Brookstone and he contacted us about assisting with the financing.

So, what made this deal attractive to us? Why should we approach this deal with more enthusiasm than we did the many Drexel deals crossing our desks at the time? Two reasons: we knew and trusted the people at Duncan Cook, and we had the ability to obtain an equity participation in the financing of this leveraged buyout (LBO). My biggest and loudest gripe when looking at virtually all of the Drexel deals was that there was no equity upside to the bondholders. It's that moral hazard thing again. If the buyout company is successful, the equity holders walk away with a huge windfall (sometimes returns of 5- or 10-to-1) because of all the financial leverage, while the bondholders get their original principal and the interest and nothing more. If the buyout company fails the equity holders are wiped out but the value of the bonds may be off 70-90% and the bondholder investment is much larger than the thin sliver of common equity in most LBO's of the day. If a company has 9 parts debt to 1 part equity on its balance sheet, isn't some of that debt actually equity, or quasi-equity? To me it was a sucker's bet to buy this quasi-equity, to take almost as much risk as the equity beneath you in the capital structure, and only receive your principal and interest in a best case scenario. In fact, one of the magic tricks used by the Drexels of the world at the time involved what I called "disappearing equity." A new acquisition company would be capitalized with say 40% senior bank debt, and underneath that was 50% subordinated debt (high yield bonds), and finally, under that a 10% layer of common stock. But then, hidden in the fine print of the offering prospectus, we would find that the equity holders (often the investment firm that put the deal together) were paying themselves an investment banking or deal origination fee that could effectively return to them a huge chunk of their original equity investment. So in some cases these deals were done effectively with close to 100% debt and no equity. Heads I win, tails you lose. The sponsors of the deal had nothing to lose and all the risk was on the bondholders.

Sure we would be taking lots of risk in the Brookstone deal, but we had done our due diligence on Brookstone, its management, and its industry. We liked the growth story and we felt that the purchase price was reasonable. We felt that the company would have a reasonable debt structure going forward and Duncan Cook and others were putting in real equity. If Brookstone could maintain its growth trajectory in the years ahead we felt comfortable that AGC's $35 mm investment in the subordinated debt of Brookstone would generate an attractive debt return, plus we would enjoy the returns from owning as much as a third of the common stock of Brookstone. Sounds reasonable, right? So the deal closed in the Fall of 1986.

The Brookstone deal started out fine and the company had a decent, all-important Christmas season, showing an attractive increase in comparable store sales. We were confident that Brookstone's management was buying the right inventory for their stores and that they were constantly looking for new and innovative product ideas to feature in their stores. This was essential at Brookstone since they charged a premium for their products and relied on their reputation for having a unique type of inventory. Once Brookstone products became commonplace and could be found at mass merchants at half the price, these products were quickly dropped and hopefully something new would be added. Rick Chalet had been the President of Brookstone when it was owned by Quaker Oats, and Rick was staying on as the Chairman of Brookstone after our buyout. Rick had been a key figure in Brookstone's history of keeping their store inventory "fresh and exciting." American General also maintained two seats on Brookstone's Board and, while I was not a board member, I did much of the leg work for the two AGC people on the Board.

Then slowly and methodically the troubles began to appear in the all-important same store's sales figures. Instead of following their historic trend of rising 5-10% in each comparable period, sales began to flatten. Why? All kinds of answers were offered up: Economic softness in key markets, delayed new product introductions, and new competitors in their markets. Regardless, the softness in sales continued. Same store sales went from flat to slightly negative. Christmas in 1987 was mildly disappointing and in early 1988, Brookstone began to run into cash flow problems. AGC and the other equity participants put in more equity and, in spite of the rosy forecasts, sales continued to drift lower. New store openings were delayed due to dwindling cash reserves. Employee morale began to suffer. What was going on in this company? What had changed from the happy times at Quaker Oats? The best conclusion that I could come up with was that Brookstone management was simply not up to the task of running a stand-alone, private, highly-leveraged company. Working for a deep pocketed Quaker Oats was a different challenge than relying only on your own skills. Also, several of the Brookstone managers, including Rick Chalet, were made semi-wealthy through the Quaker buyout and perhaps they had simply lost their collective drives.

I was asked to attend a Brookstone Board meeting in the Fall of 1989. Again, more bad news. Same store sales were negative, the company needed more cash, and there was absolutely no strategy or plan for a turnaround. Brookstone seemed like the corporate equivalent of a sidewalk panhandler, always asking for money, but not willing to take the steps needed to fix themselves. It was after the Board meeting that Rick Chalet gave me a ride to the airport for my flight back to Houston and we started discussing in vivid details the woes at Brookstone. Rick seemed to me to be withdrawn and aloof. The more I probed, the less real information I got from Rick and the angrier I became. This deal was a horrible reflection on me and the Investment Department of AGC. You could be sure that Mr. Hook knew what was going on with this failing company and I was worried about my credibility and my job. In my mind and the minds of others, Rick was not doing his job and I told him so. New products were not being introduced and the company lacked direction and leadership. We had counted on Rick to fill these important roles and he seemed to not care. What made matters worse was that he offered no explanation. In no uncertain terms, I gave Rick a firm piece of my mind, slammed the car door shut, and ran off to catch my plane.

On the plane flight home, I calmed down and began to reflect on my behavior with Rick. Yes, I had spoken my mind and I said what needed to be said. After all, this was business and things were not going well at all. I convinced myself that, while I could have certainly been more courteous to Rick, I had to get angry in order to get his attention concerning the gravity of the situation. Sometimes those who are facing potential disaster are the last ones to see the perils ahead.

So the next day I was in one of those never ending staff meetings when I was handed a note from Julia Tucker asking me to meet her in her office immediately. As I walked into Julia's office I could read her body language. After you work for someone for a while, you sometimes can just sense when things are not right. Julia's first question to me was "What did you say to Rick Chalet yesterday?" I went through an explanation of what I had said to Rick, but tried not to convey to Julia how angry I was at Rick at the time. Julia sat and reflected. I could tell that she was choosing her words carefully. After an awkward few moments she spoke. "Gordon, Rick committed suicide yesterday." I dropped my head into my hands and said nothing for what seemed an eternity. Julia knew that I had been angry at Rick and she also knew that I felt terrible about the news. She offered the explanation that apparently Rick had been depressed for some time and that I should not hold myself personally responsible for this tragedy. Regardless, I continued to feel awful. How could I have been so insensitive? How could I have stomped on this poor man's ego with such callous disregard? Were my job and my credibility so important to me that I would destroy whatever was in my way? Was I any better than the folks at Drexel who raped and pillaged their way to riches?

These had been crazy times both professionally and personally. Emotions had been running high and out of control greed had been replaced by out of control fear. I could rationalize my treatment of Rick as being reasonable, but the reality was that I too was out of control, just like the high yield market had been out of control. Just as we were trying to collectively salvage the remains of the high yield bond market, I had to salvage my own emotions and to focus on how I could approach my work with a greater respect for those in my world. People were what really mattered and I had let my own ego and greed run my emotions. To this day, I still have deep regrets for my treatment of Rick.

Fortunately, the decade of the 1990's began as a time of recovery for the high yield market as well as the participants who had fought so energetically in its trenches. The Resolution Trust Company bought up most of the high yield bonds owned by the S & L's. Deals were quietly restructured. Companies emerged from bankruptcy. Drexel disappeared. Wounds healed and the essence of a new high yield market began to appear, a market that was far more orderly and rational than its predecessor. Even Brookstone was able to right itself with the help of new owners and new management. Soon after Rick Chalet's death, AGC had completely run out of patience with Brookstone, just as Brookstone had completely run out of cash. We ended up throwing in the towel by selling our entire investment to a private equity group at a sizable loss.

The Brookstone Board had recently hired a new Chairman and CEO, Hank Kamenstein, and he was kept on by the new shareholders that purchased AGC's investment. And wouldn't you know it, Mr. Kamenstein, with the help of his new investors, was able to turn Brookstone around within a couple of years. Brookstone got back to the basics of keeping their inventories fresh and innovative and Hank Kamenstein proved an able leader and manager. But what was frustrating to me and others at AGC was that the basic Brookstone concept had not changed at all. It was just better executed by the right management. Another important lesson learned.

What emerged from the ashes of the high yield bond market was a new market that was more driven by fundamental credit analysis and not senseless hype. Deals were better structured with less leverage and much more reasonable EBITDA/Interest ratios. Wall Street investment bankers also took much more seriously their responsibility to perform comprehensive due diligence on the companies that they would choose to represent in the high yield market. Also, the market itself was accessed much more by companies with legitimate needs for long term debt rather than the slash and burn tactics of the Drexel era. Industries with honest growth prospects began to see this market as a viable source of long term capital very different than the banks, which typically had a short term horizon and demanded a rapid amortization of their term loans. High yield debt, on the other hand, was long term (usually 10-15 years), required little amortization, was fixed rate, and was often subordinated to the bank debt (a junior claim in bankruptcy), which kept a company's bankers happy.

Perhaps one of the most interesting industries to flourish during this period was the gaming or gambling industry. Formerly confined within the borders of the state of Nevada, gaming was now expanding into multiple new jurisdictions during the 1990's. Atlantic City, Colorado, Mississippi, Louisiana, Missouri, and Iowa were some of the areas that had legalized gambling, primarily for the purpose of creating jobs and a new industry to tax. Las Vegas, of course, was always considered the mecca for gambling in the U.S. and it was seeing tremendous growth of its own, with new casinos sprouting continuously on the Las Vegas strip. An interesting debate that was brewing at the time was whether the growth in new gaming jurisdictions outside of Nevada was a good thing or a bad thing for Nevada casinos, especially in Las Vegas. Some saw the new jurisdictions as taking away the need for people to travel to Las Vegas, whereas others saw the new jurisdictions as legitimizing the gaming experience and encouraging people to later "trade up" to the Las Vegas experience. I tended to be in the former camp since I was not a gambler and didn't fully appreciate the need to experience Las Vegas. Gambling just wasn't part of my DNA. Maybe it's just that I can be very cheap, but to me why would anyone make a series of bets when the odds are always in the house's favor? As a financial analyst I would never make an investment where I thought the odds were against me, so why in the world would I do so with my own money? In any case, this was a fascinating industry to study and to finance, and certainly the fantastic growth of this industry, both in and outside of Nevada, during the 1990's, proved that I was wrong and that millions were more than happy to "trade up" to the Las Vegas experience.

Another very attractive aspect of the gaming industry was that it was heavily regulated. Anyone wishing to obtain a gaming license and open a casino was subject to intense scrutiny by all state regulators. Prospects had to have impeccable records, legitimate sources of capital, and substantial casino operating expertise. Meshulam Riklis need not apply! Needless to say, these were the attributes of a solid investment that the high yield market craved. And, of course, these casinos produced ungodly amounts of free cash flow. Once you had a casino open (in just about any legal jurisdiction) you had a license to print money. Supply of casino space had simply not kept up with the insatiable public demand. In fact the construction of a new casino seemed to create its own new demand as publicity and media hype created a "must see" hysteria in the minds of the public. During the 1990's, gaming emerged from a rather seedy, back room activity to a broadly recognized and appreciated form of entertainment. All of this occurred, at least in part, because these casino companies had access to the high yield bond market. We were involved in the high yield issues of such companies as Circus Circus, Caesar's, Holiday Inns, Bally's Park Place, Tropicana Hotels, and others. Learning about this industry, why people gamble, what keeps people in a casino, what would be the impact of new jurisdictions, and how much growth this industry could absorb, were fascinating questions facing this industry then and still to this day.

The gaming industry was but one example of how high yield bonds were put to legitimate purposes during the 1990's. As the market finally began to recover, AGC was actively involved in the financing of hundreds of medium to large sized companies in entertainment, telecommunications, retail, medicine, manufacturing, textiles, auto parts, restaurants, utilities, food, energy, transportation, steel, hotels, consumer products, and the list goes on. The high yield market had come of age and it was a wonderful career during this period. We became allocators of somewhat risky long term debt to the high growth companies of that era. It was truly exciting to meet with company managements and to review their companies' prospects and risks and to make the critical decisions about purchasing bonds and at what price levels. Of course, I was still carrying the burden of Modelnetics/MEM around and spending lots of time writing investment committee memos, but I still loved my job.

Another example of one of the companies that we financed during this period was Harley-Davidson. I have been a life long motorcycle enthusiast and in late 1988 I purchased a new Harley-Davidson Sportster motorcycle after riding a friend's and reading many positive industry reports on the new Harley-Davidson product line. During the early 1980's, Harley had been on the verge of death's door because of intense industry competition from Japanese makers such as Honda, Kawasaki, Suzuki, and Yamaha. Harley successfully accused these firms of dumping their motorcycles on the U.S. market at prices below cost. Ultimately, the Reagan administration agreed with Harley and onerous new tariffs were placed on the larger Japanese motorcycles, effectively giving Harley a window of opportunity to become more competitive.

The truth was that while the Japanese were in fact dumping, Harley had other bigger internal problems. Their machines had horrible reputations for reliability. The bikes leaked oil, shook themselves to bits, and regularly stranded their owners. Harley had been owned by American Machine and Foundry (AMF) and had suffered from a severe lack of new capital investment and innovative new product development. Still to this day, no Harley purist would ever want to own an AMF Harley. But in 1981, the existing Harley management team, with the help of other investors, bought out AMF, recapitalized the company and began the necessary jobs of improving Harley's quality and manufacturing efficiencies. And it worked. The Harleys of the late 1980's were vastly superior to the earlier bikes and they began to sell extremely well.

My own experience with my Harley was also very positive so I decided to look more intensely at the company for a possible AGC investment. Harley had previously issued $100 mm of public high yield bonds with a coupon of 10% and, after extensive hours of credit research, I presented my Investment Committee Memorandum to Mr. Hook and the senior management of AGC recommending that AGC purchase up to $10 mm of these Harley-Davidson bonds in the secondary bond market. Now Mr. Hook was a very conservative guy. Dressed in his standard dark suit, Mr. Hook was known to be rather stern and formal. Remember, he liked things his way and he liked his Investment Committee meetings to be systematic, methodical, and predictable. He was uncomfortable with risk but he was also a reasonable man. But Harley-Davidson bonds? I am sure that in Mr. Hook's mind he had visions of Marlon Brando riding into town on a Harley terrorizing women and children. Harleys were the vehicle of choice for Hell's Angels and certainly did not represent the kind of company that AGC wanted to support. But sometimes you have to throw caution to the wind and do what you believe is right. I liked being a maverick and I liked the challenge of bringing different investment opportunities to AGC. As my presentation came up in the sequence, I could see Mr. Hook roll his eyes back in his head as though he was subtly telling me that "you've got to be kidding!" He made a few more caustic remarks and then I began. Harley was a classic turnaround story. Their products were selling at record levels and all of their financial metrics were very solid and continuing to improve. They had an exceptionally loyal customer base and an extremely successful brand. What wasn't to like?

Wouldn't you know it, Mr. Hook actually liked the deal and we got the go-ahead to purchase $10 mm par value of the Harley bonds. We were able to purchase the bonds at prices somewhat below par and we held the bonds for nearly three years until the bonds were called (bought in by the company) at a price of $106. So for this holding period our average annual return was about 13% (interest plus price appreciation) compared with 6-8% returns on investment grade bonds at the time. This was the kind of victory that I savored and the kind of experience that made my job so enjoyable. I had done my homework, challenged conventional thinking, and earned an extra return for my employer, all the while finding tremendous enjoyment in my work. And, of course, Harley-Davidson has gone on to become the world's foremost manufacturer of motorcycles with market shares now far exceeding all of the Japanese producers combined.

But just because the high yield market had stabilized and matured during the 1990', it was not without risk. These bonds had ratings below investment grade for a variety of reasons and it was the principal focus of my job to fully understand and assess these risks before investing. Once we felt we understood these risks we then had to make sure that we were being paid appropriately to take these risks. If it was quasi-equity that we were providing, we didn't want only a debt return (fixed interest rate).

One company that I thought provided an interesting investment opportunity was a company called Live Entertainment (Live). Live was based in Los Angeles and was engaged in the business of acquiring home video distribution rights to major and not-so-major Hollywood movies. Remember this was back in the early days of the VCR when home video was just in its infancy. Hollywood studios were still getting the lion's share of their revenues from the box office and some from cable, but home video was still small. Live would buy the home video distribution rights from the independent studios who lacked any expertise in this area. Live then marketed these videos into the rental market and made a very comfortable spread over their costs. Live's business was booming and they needed more long term capital to expand their purchases of these video rights. So Live's management with their investment bankers went on a nationwide "road show" to visit the large cities where high yield investors congregated. In each city, management would make their presentations to potential investors who were usually enjoying a "rubber chicken" lunch. Speaking for Live was its Chairman and CEO, Jose Menendez, an extremely engaging, eloquent, and knowledgeable gentleman of Cuban descent. Menendez was very impressive. He knew his industry thoroughly and appeared to have excellent contacts throughout the Hollywood studios. He was an excellent speaker and made it easy to understand an industry that most people were not familiar with. I continued to do my homework after the road show and went through the standard routine of completing my credit analysis and preparing my investment committee memo. After a few more rolled eyeballs from Mr. Hook, we got the OK.

We had originally thought that the bonds would be priced to yield in the 12-13% area, but because the industry was not well known the bonds actually came with a coupon of 14%. Wow! That was about 6.5% above treasury interest rates at the time and considered by me to be more than adequate compensation for the risks of investing in Live. So we bought $10 mm and once again my name was all over this company, at least in the minds of Julia Tucker and Harold Hook.

It was probably four or five months later that I got a phone call from Dave Atkinson. Dave was our salesman from Wertheim Schroeder, a medium sized investment bank with a modest high yield bond division. Wertheim Schroeder had actually been one of the firms that had sold the Live deal to us. Dave called all the time so I just expected to hear him pitching me his latest offering of bonds. But Dave had a very different tone, he just wasn't his usual perky self. Gordon, are you sitting down? Oh, shit! High yield bond people hate that question because it means bad news from somewhere in their portfolio. "Gordon, Jose Menendez has been murdered. He and his wife, Kitty, were gunned down in their Beverly Hills home while watching TV last night." It was almost like a Rick Chalet moment. Total anguish. How could this happen? Who could do such a thing? What did this mean for Live Entertainment? How was I going to explain this one to Mr. Hook and Julia Tucker? This whole experience was frightening from so many different perspectives.

Immediately these murders became a media event. Rumors circulated like wildfire. Was it just a random home break-in? Who had Menendez pissed off? Was anything stolen? Could it have been a mob hit? This guy was Cuban, could he have been involved with Castro? No one had any idea, but one thing was certain. Financial markets hate uncertainty. The price of the Live bonds immediately sank to $80 and if we tried to sell our $10 mm position the prices would have fallen well into the $70's. The rumor that seemed to be the most circulated was that the murders were related to organized crime. Any taint of organized crime within a company can spell disaster. Employees, vendors, investors, and customers will all flee and few companies can survive reports of actual organized crime involvement. Organized crime is precisely what all of the state gaming regulators are trying to prevent in their casinos. As days passed there was no evidence of any organized crime but it nonetheless began to negatively impact Live's ongoing business. Certainly the loss of Jose Menendez was bad enough but there was widespread suspicion throughout Hollywood which was devastating to the operations of Live Entertainment. So what do I do with my bonds? How do I assess this risk? The best I could hope for was that this was a random event and the organized crime theory would be proven false. But at what cost? We were confident that Live had some depth to their management, but could anyone do anything to save this company in light of all the rumors and innuendo?

Months passed with no news. Lots of rumors but no real answers. Live's bonds traded down into the $60's as there was no firm evidence to refute the organized crime theory. That is until news began to emanate from Beverly Hills that the police were now focusing on the Menendez's two sons, Lyle and Erik Menendez. Yeah, those guys!! Turns out that both had been acting very suspiciously, living the good life while spending lots of Daddy's money. Like a real jerk I was hoping it was the kids because my bonds would rally on that news. I was still cringing at the topic of Live Entertainment. I had single-handedly brought this mess to AGC and I had simply no way of explaining this outcome. "Who'd a thunk it." But soon there was more news out of Beverly Hills. Apparently, Erik, the younger brother, had been seeing a psychiatrist in Beverly Hills and rumors were circulating that he had confessed.

Well this event quickly became fertile ground for a lively legal debate. Erik's lawyer argued that any confession was inadmissible because of doctor/patient confidentiality. After weeks of legal wrangling the psychiatrist was required to testify and that was it for the Menendez brothers. In their murder trials they tried to allege that their parents had been abusing them for years and that murder was their only recourse. No credible evidence of abuse had ever been demonstrated and this proved to be only a last ditch effort by the boys to stay out of prison for life. It was widely believed that the Menendez boys acted out of an overwhelming sense of entitlement and greed. They simply wanted mom and dad's money without having to endure the usual disciplines that parents place on their children. Why get an education when murdering my parents will get me where I want to be that much sooner? This whole sad story was without a doubt the worst that I have ever seen in my career. Michael Milken, Meshulam Riklis, Ivan Boesky, and others demonstrated levels of greed and arrogance that I did not think could ever be surpassed. But the Menendez brothers who had grown up with lives of privilege and wealth, with loving and caring parents, acted in such an evil manner as to defy human understanding.

We eventually sold our Live Entertainment bonds at an average price of $60 and I had a lot of explaining to do back in Houston. Live went on to eventually file bankruptcy and, I believe, cease to exist. Live was certainly one of the many unintended victims of the Menendez brothers and their incredible disregard for the consequences of their own actions.

Another glaring example of the continuing risk in the high yield bond market was the story of HealthSouth. Certainly one of the most controversial figures I met in my career was Richard M. Scrushy, the former President and CEO of HealthSouth Corporation. Scrushy founded HealthSouth in 1984, as a provider of out-patient rehabilitation services. Later, in 1995, HealthSouth entered the out-patient surgery business and within less than ten years HealthSouth had nearly $4.4 billion in revenues, more than 50,000 employees, and 2000 medical facilities in the U.S. and five other countries. Scrushy was the visionary and the energy behind HealthSouth's meteoric growth. What he saw in the U.S. was a very expensive health care delivery system focused on the traditional, high cost, acute care, general hospital. The reality was that due to advances in medical technology and new treatments, many of the traditional patients of a general hospital could now be treated much more economically on an out-patient basis. Patients were happy, doctors were happy, insurance companies were happy, and Richard Scrushy became immensely wealthy.

HealthSouth's stock sold for about $10 per share on the date of its initial public offering in 1986 and the price reached a peak of $151 per share by April, 1998. During this period of time, HealthSouth offered several different issues of high yield bonds and I had the opportunity to meet Richard Scrushy during one of HealthSouth's investor roadshows. I can remember that Scrushy initially impressed me with his commanding presence and his apparent complete grasp of his company's financials and its business prospects. He came across as a natural leader and as someone who was very comfortable being at the center of attention. One bit of concern that I did have during this roadshow was that Scrushy clearly wanted to completely dominate the entire presentation to the investors. Very little time or opportunity was given to his other key managers to speak up. Clearly, Scrushy was the one in charge. Regardless, the company was very successful and appeared well managed, so we bought a large position in the bonds and held them for many years.

Over the years, Scrushy also became well known for his philanthropy, primarily in his native state of Alabama. He donated his time and great sums of money to numerous colleges, foundations, and other worthy causes. Buildings and highways were given his name in recognition of his generosity. Scrushy even found time to be the lead singer and guitarist in a local country and western band, *The Dallas County Line*. Undoubtedly well known for their big hit, "Honk if You Love to Honky Tonk." It was very evident that Scrushy enjoyed the spotlight.

One of the hazards of being in the medical services industry is that insurance companies, Medicare, and Medicaid are always trying to find ways to lower their collective payments to health care providers. HealthSouth's amazing growth and profitability became a glowing beacon to attract the medical cost-cutters of the world and by late 2002 HealthSouth was forced to report a large loss due in part to new government and insurance company policies restricting reimbursements for out-patient services. One of Scrushy's big mistakes was his selling of $75 million of his HealthSouth stock just before the company reported this large loss and the stock price plummeted. While Scrushy was never convicted of insider trading, his actions came to the attention of the Securities and Exchange Commission (SEC) and they began a full investigation into HealthSouth and its accounting. With the help of testimony from five former Chief Financial Officers (CFO) of HealthSouth, the SEC formally accused HealthSouth and Richard Scrushy of falsely inflating HealthSouth's earnings by $1.4 billion. By April 2003, HealthSouth's stock had fallen to 70 cents per share, the bonds were trading below $20, and the company was hovering on the brink of bankruptcy. Miraculously, HealthSouth did not file bankruptcy. The company struggled for many years under new management. Assets were sold. Debt was refinanced. Eventually HealthSouth regained its financial strength and the shares were re-listed on the New York Stock Exchange in 2006.

After Scrushy was accused by the SEC he was soon terminated by the HealthSouth Board. Immediately after the scandal broke, Scrushy converted to Christianity and joined a large, and mostly African-American, Birmingham, Alabama church (Scrushy is Caucasian). He became one of the church's featured speakers with his own TV show. Most felt that Scrushy's new-found religion was only a scheme to bias the potential jury pool towards him and against the prosecution. What so aggravated and bewildered the financial and legal worlds was that on June 28, 2005 the Birmingham jury acquitted Scrushy on all 36 charges against him, in spite of the testimonies of the last five Chief Financial Officers at HealthSouth, all of whom implicated Scrushy in the scandal.

This felt so wrong. I had met Scrushy on several occasions and I knew what kind of personality Scrushy had. He was always in charge. To believe that five different CFO's all under his command would all conspire independently to cook HealthSouth's books without

Scrushy's knowledge was completely preposterous. This felt like an O.J. Simpson verdict to me. The only plausible explanation was that Scrushy's foray into religion had worked even though it was nothing but a sham. It should also be noted that HealthSouth had very few African-American employees in positions of much responsibility.

But all was not lost! On October 26, 2005, just four months after being acquitted, Scrushy was indicted on new charges of bribery and mail fraud in connection with his attempt to obtain a seat on a state hospital regulatory board. Blissfully, Scrushy was convicted of these charges and on June 28, 2007, he began serving his 82 month prison sentence at a U.S. Penitentiary in Beaumont, Texas. Kind of like O.J. the second time around.

Scrushy was a man of immense talent and energy, but his ambition, greed, and arrogance all conspired to bring this man down. His ego was fed by his early successes and it grew out of control. He did not show confidence in his senior management team because, in his mind, none of them had his talents. He used his staff for his own gains and then abandoned them once all were accused of fraud. Scrushy wanted people around him simply so he could enjoy their adulation and praise. Richard Scrushy cared only about Richard Scrushy. Unfortunately for me, I would come to meet and work with several people of similar nature in the years to come.

In spite of sad stories such as Live Entertainment, Brookstone, and HealthSouth, our high yield performance overall at AGC was still very good. Our performance was consistently better than the major high yield bond indexes during most of the 1990's.

Although we had some defaults and did have to sell some bonds at losses, our performance was well supported by the attractive yields we were receiving and the frequent sales of bonds at gains. All of this put the high yield team in an excellent position to be recognized by the new management team about ready to arrive at AGC. This was a management team that actually wanted to showcase the abilities and the track record of my High Yield Bond Group at AGC.

Chapter 6: Changing of the Guard

It was in 1997 that Mr. Hook announced his complete retirement from AGC. I say complete retirement because unlike many of his corporate CEO peers, Mr. Hook did not wish to retain any board membership or other direct ties to AGC. Apparently, Mr. Hook had complete confidence in his management team and he was able to fully cede control to this new team without hesitation or regret. He felt they would do just fine without his involvement.

My reaction to Mr. Hook's retirement was mixed. He had been the architect that had created and built AGC into a prominent and successful financial services company, and he had done it in his own unique and methodical way. He was an ethical and honest CEO who had presided over AGC for 18 years, and he had left his own indelible mark on the culture of AGC. Unfortunately, this mark was heavily influenced by Mr. Hook's fervent belief in the MEM/Modelnetics management system that he had created and heavily sponsored at AGC. In my opinion, by 1997, MEM/Modelnetics had taken a stranglehold on AGC, creating huge burdens of paperwork, classes, and administrative bureaucracy. Most people felt that Mr. Hook's departure would inevitably mean some alleviation of this burden since none of his likely replacements seemed to fully embrace MEM/Modelnetics the way he did.

I also believed that I had a decent personal and professional relationship with Mr. Hook. Even after Brookstone, Live Entertainment, and a few other losses, Mr. Hook still understood the risk/return trade-off in high yield bonds. We had invested in many, many successful transactions and AGC had benefited from the additional interest income. I was confident that Mr. Hook had a reasonable degree of confidence in my recommendations and in some ways I felt as though I was losing a friend/father-figure. But I was also ready for change.

We soon learned that Robert Devlin would be the new Chairman and CEO of AGC. "Bob" Devlin was truly the antithesis of Harold Hook. "Hollywood Bob," as we occasionally and affectionately referred to him, had risen through the life insurance ranks over many years at AGC, and he was the consummate salesman. A bit Donald Trumpish, Bob Devlin was more a cheerleader than a thoughtful, introspective CEO. Impeccably dressed, with that perfect CEO/politician hair (so perfect you wonder if he would have gotten the job without it), Devlin certainly looked the CEO part. We used to jokingly do a post high yield bond road show evaluation of each CEO's hair. Too perfect and it became a genuine red flag for concerns about whether there was any real grey matter underneath. In any case, Bob Devlin paid great homage early on to the legacy of the management systems at AGC, but it was not difficult to read the handwriting on the walls. Perhaps, the days of MEM/Modelnetics were indeed numbered! What Devlin did bring to the table was an outward energy and enthusiasm for AGC that the more reserved and cerebral Mr. Hook had lacked. Devlin was a marketer and he excelled at the marketing of AGC to the financial community, both investors and investment bankers alike.

Another simultaneous management change involved the hiring of a new Chief Investment Officer (CIO) by the name of Richard Scott. Richard was about my age. He was bespectacled, bookish, and bald with thin wisps of his remaining blond hair curling about his ears and neck. Mr. Scott had been the CIO at Western National Insurance Company, which had recently become a 100% owned subsidiary of AGC. Prior to Western National, Mr. Scott had been a partner in the prestigious Houston law firm of Fulbright & Jaworski. No, not another lawyer, please!!!

It was my opinion at the time of Mr. Scott's hire that there were entirely too many lawyers in the top management of AGC and that too many were serving on the Investment Committee. The lawyers already on this committee seemed clueless as to the analysis of investment risks and they added zero value to the investment process, often broaching irrelevant legal issues which tended to gum-up the entire investment approval process. So now we had a new lawyer and this guy was the new CIO!! OK he had been the CIO at tiny Western National but nearly all of their investment asset management work was outsourced to third party asset managers. So what investment expertise did Richard Scott really bring to the table? It just seemed like too much of the same old investment bureaucracy and not enough, or any, new investment expertise or vision.

I could not have been more wrong about Richard Scott. Soon after his arrival at AGC, Richard asked me to lunch at his favorite swanky Houston restaurant, Cafe Annie, to discuss our high yield bond strategy. What I was expecting was a whole new set of rules, regulations, and limitations. Mr. Scott was pleasant and engaging at lunch but I came armed for battle and I was going to let him know, with clarity: 1) how inefficient and bureaucratic AGC's investment approval process had become, 2) how a high yield bond portfolio should be managed, and 3) how the Investment Department at AGC should be viewed as a profit center, not a cost center. As the pleasantries faded I launched into my strong feelings about how things should change at AGC and I noticed that Richard was actually listening attentively. He acknowledged my feelings, asked probing and insightful questions, and before I could come close to finishing my monologue I began to realize that he was agreeing with everything I was saying! How could this be? How could an outsider, an attorney no less, see things the same way I did? Did I ever have the wrong first impression of Richard Scott. By the end of our lunch Richard and I were in total agreement on the following important points:

- A high yield bond portfolio could not be effectively or efficiently managed through an Investment Committee type of approval process.
- The Investment Committee was an antiquated approval system of little real or tangible value.
- We needed, instead, to implement individual investment approval limits and report purchases and sales on a regular basis, after the fact.
- High yield bonds had been an attractive asset class for AGC and we needed to begin managing these assets for third parties (insurance companies, pension plans, endowments, etc.) in order to boost fee income to AGC.
- A growing fee income could be used to enhance compensation and reduce employee turnover within the Investment Department.

I was truly ecstatic! The gods smiled that day on me. These were exactly the changes we needed in the Investment Department at AGC. These changes would hopefully allow my High Yield Bond Group to be more responsive to market conditions and to allow us to better allocate our time to real credit/investment analysis, rather than the endless, bureaucratic approval process. We were also anxious to grow fee income and employee compensation in order to reduce the relatively high employee turnover, which had been a major thorn in my side for years.

After Mr. Hook's departure, Bob Devlin continued to chair the Investment Committee meetings, however, it became quickly obvious that "Hollywood Bob" just didn't have the background or stomach for reviewing and approving all of the weekly deals brought to his attention. Each weekly investment committee package was probably an inch thick with maybe 5-8 deals written up by various groups within the Investment Department. Even if he had read all the material, Devlin did not have the background for this part of the job and it was not long before he gladly accepted Richard Scott's proposal to abolish the Investment Committee. We were, of course, still held accountable for our investments and overall performance but I was given much more freedom to manage the portfolio as I deemed appropriate. Finally, after 21 years in the investment business, I had some real independence. I could not have asked for a better outcome. It was as though it was Christmas morning and I was five years old again. Things were really going my way. We were all ecstatic and with the help of my high yield bond trader, Mark Pauly, we created a faux tombstone/plaque to "sadly" commemorate the death of the Investment Committee ("Gone but not Forgotten"), which Richard proudly displayed prominently in his office for years to come.

My relationship with Richard also began to grow in several positive ways. Richard was extremely intelligent and he was a very quick study of investments. He was informal and engaging with me and others. We "clicked" in terms of how we approached investing and how we shared a low tolerance for excess bureaucracy and management inefficiencies. I gradually came to also believe that Richard was a friend who might engage with me in conversations of a more personal nature.

But things got even better! Bob Devlin announced around this time that MEM/Modelnetics would be "de-emphasized" at AGC. We weren't really sure what that meant, but it sure sounded great. In actuality, from that point on MEM/Modelnetics just seemed to fade away under Bob Devlin, and there were not that many mourners. MEM/Modelnetics seemed to go the way of an out-dated technology, and it was not replaced with any other management system of significance during the Devlin years.

Richard and I soon began the process of establishing AGC as a third party manager of high yield bonds for other investors. Since we already had an established credit research team of ten analysts, a high yield bond trader, and three portfolio managers; we could efficiently manage portfolios for other institutions at minimal additional costs, effectively boosting our profits. AGC did hire several institutional sales people to market our high yield and other investment management services. However, high yield asset management was truly the focus of their sales efforts for the following reasons:

- Management fees were higher than other types of bonds.
- High yield bonds had become an attractive asset class during the 1990's and many institutional investors were looking to start a high yield bond fund or to expand an existing fund.
- AGC had a strong track record in the management of its own high yield bonds.
- High yield bonds had become an important source of invest-ment diversification and yield for many institutions/investors especially as the overall level of interest rates fell.

Immediately I began marketing our high yield capabilities on a national basis. Our sales people would set up calls with pension funds, insurance companies, endowments, state funds, consultants, etc. and I would fly all over the country pitching our high yield capabilities. Being the new kid on the block wasn't easy as we were competing with much more established firms (such as PIMCO, Fidelity, Oaktree, etc.), which could present impressive lists of exist-ing clients, to our list of none.

In spite of our newcomer status, by 2000 we had grown our high yield bond third party assets to $1.425 billion, as summarized below:

- $500 million Texas state pension fund
- $100 million from three smaller insurance companies
- $25 million in mutual fund assets
- $800 million in Collateralized Bond Obligation (CBO) assets. (AGC sponsored three CBO's which were each sep-arate pools of high yield bonds financed by securities issued mostly to outside investors.)

Importantly, our fee income, which had been zero in 1997, had grown to an annual rate of almost $4.5 million by 2000, an accom-plishment that all of us on the high yield team were truly proud of. We were certainly pleased that Bob Devlin and Richard Scott were impressed by the early successes in the High-Yield Group, which had also turned in an excellent performance in the management of

AGC's own $3 billion of high-yield bond assets.

For my efforts, I was awarded a promotion to Executive Vice President of High-Yield at AGC. My base salary increased by a whopping 40%. I would now report directly to Richard Scott instead of Julia Tucker who was also an Executive Vice President. So, after more than 14 years of working directly for Julia Tucker I was now promoted to her peer or her equal, at least on the new organization chart. Sadly, during this transition period my relationship with Julia came under strain. Perhaps I had inadvertently made a comment or was insensitive to her loss of control, but I sensed an unwelcome change in our long term relationship. Without question, Julia had been my best boss during my career. We had been through so many highs and lows together and she always kept me smiling. I deeply regretted the apparent deterioration of this relationship. While we continued to work together to some degree going forward, we were now peers and things were not the same. This change still troubles me to this day. Nevertheless, with my new title, responsibilities, and independence, I was on top of the world. I loved my job and could now, hopefully, reach my and my team's full potential without the yoke of MEM/Modelnetics to pull. Things were going extremely well with Richard and our success with third party assets would hopefully mean higher compensation for my team and far less employee turnover. Things certainly could not have been better for me. I was exceptionally proud of my new promotion and of all we had done over the years to build the high-yield business and our superb track record. Sometimes I would actually stop and pinch myself to see if all of this was merely a dream. Everything I had always wanted in my career had come true and I was elated, at least for a while.

But just as financial markets can go in cycles, so can one's career. Everything was too perfect and I knew that perfection couldn't last for long. The problem is that we can never see the future well enough to anticipate those events which can change our lives irreversibly. For me this event was the acquisition of AGC in 2001.

During Bob Devlin's first year as the Chairman and CEO of AGC, he was granted AGC stock options worth an estimated $49 million (as valued by the well accepted Black-Scholes option valuation model). Yes $49 million! This was probably ten times his pre-CEO compensation. Add in his new salary, cash bonus, restricted stock and other perks and "Hollywood Bob" was probably earning around $60 million in his first year as CEO! I will never understand this extreme level of executive compensation. It was so unlike AGC and its Board to approve this level of pay to a brand new, unproven CEO. Would he have turned down the job for a mere $20 million? Of course not. In my opinion, no CEO of any corporation can ever claim to be this valuable. He or she may lead the team, but their ultimate success is totally dependent upon the entire corporation and all its employees who should be sharing more ratably in this success. This level of compensation was totally out of line with any contribution that Bob Devlin could ever expect to have made during his short tenure as AGC's CEO. His compensation package made absolutely no sense to me or anyone else at AGC, save perhaps AGC's Board of Directors.

In actuality, Devlin's options would only vest over a period of 3-4 years, unless AGC was acquired, in which case the options would vest immediately. So what do you suppose Devlin's motivations were? After all, he was not that long term, methodical corporate builder like Harold Hook. Devlin wanted to do a deal and he spent a lot of his time talking up AGC to investors and Wall Street alike. This was where Bob Devlin could shine, and shine he did. Under Bob Devlin, AGC's stock rose steadily.

Throughout 2000 and early 2001 there were almost constant rumors of potential suitors lurking about AGC. Our stock would occasionally "pop" in price on some juicy new takeover rumor. The first official announcement of an attempted takeover came in early 2001 when Prudential PLC (of Great Britain, not Newark, New Jersey) announced a friendly takeover of AGC at a price of $49.52 per share in Prudential PLC's stock, or a modest premium to the current market price of AGC's stock. This proposed merger was considered by the financial community to be a "merger of equals" in terms of size, and there didn't seem to be any great cost savings potential or operating synergies. There were also significant geographic as well as cultural barriers that would have had to be overcome.

Before too long the value of Prudential PLC's stock began to fall such that the takeover premium to the AGC shareholders disappeared, calling into question the willingness of the AGC shareholders to vote in favor of the merger. It was during this period of uncertainty in the spring of 2001, that American International Group (AIG) and its infamous Chairman and CEO, Hank Greenberg, placed a bid for AGC, and, unbeknownst to me, changed my life forever.

Chapter 7: Singing the Acquisition Blues

American General had been a predator. We had swallowed up some smaller fish in our time, one of the first insurance companies to grow successfully by doing so. Now it was our turn to be eaten. The only question was whose "acquisition target" we would become. In the weeks that followed our offices were abuzz with rumor, guesswork, calculation, and worry. Multiply all this disruption by the enormous surge in acquisitions in recent decades—many of which never deliver the results they set out to achieve—and you have an interesting challenge to American productivity. Meanwhile, we were mired in the day-to-day uncertainty such corporate shake-ups bestow upon the ranks of their employees: the confusion, blurred focus, tangled loyalties, and the countless hours wasted in fretting and speculation.

Prudential PLC had been our first suitor. Their share price drop allowed American juggernaut AIG to step in with an unsolicited bid that outweighed Prudential PLC's offer. Richard Scott, the closest of our group to the acquisition process, thought Prudential PLC would sweeten their bid rather than meekly back away from the contest with AIG. All of us were hoping for a bidding war and an escalating acquisition price. We had also heard rumors that Citicorp might emerge as a third suitor.

One day I received a call from a college friend who ran a commercial insurance brokerage firm in Northern California. His comment was succinct. "Pray to God it's not AIG," he said. "There is no one worse to deal with in the world of commercial insurance, than Hank Greenberg."

Great. "Thanks, pal."

Maurice Raymond Greenberg. One of the smartest, toughest, longest reigning CEOs of any major corporation in America. Born in 1925 to a candy store owner in the Lower East Side of Manhattan. He received the Bronze Star in World War II, where, as a U.S. Army Ranger, he participated in the brutal Normandy landing that Steven Spielberg immortalized in *Saving Private Ryan*. Law degree, 1950. He was the youngest vice president in the history of his first company before AIG founder C. V. Starr brought him aboard at AIG as a vice president at the age of 35.

Greenberg took his nickname from "Hammerin' Hank" Greenberg, star slugger for the Detroit Tigers, when young Maurice was a teenager. The younger Greenberg grew up to be equally hard hitting, swinging at fools rather than baseballs. His temper was legendary. Spurned by a rude employee in applying for his first job, he burst into the office of a company vice president and told him what a moron his personnel director was. The VP took him on as an underwriting trainee at $75 a week. Hank thought nothing of telling his colleagues what goddamn fools they were, or of belittling their grasp of the insurance business, which he almost always understood better than they did.

So we waited and watched the news services, followed every new release and struggled to decipher the latest rumors. Even without dictatorial CEOs, mergers can be traumatic: jobs lost, careers ended, families uprooted or even split. Many worried about their jobs, pondered the potential suitors and tried to calculate their different needs for American General personnel. Others were more optimistic. Many were excited at the prospect of having a new parent company. Our AGC stock options and restricted stock would vest immediately upon acquisition, and people mused aloud about what they could do with the money. Even those who feared for their jobs had some degree of comfort since AGC generously provided up to two years of severance pay for anyone who lost their job because of a merger. We were all too distracted to get much serious work done.

How would Prudential PLC respond to AIG's move? Their opening bid wasn't going to be their final offer, we assured each other. Who slaps their best offer on the table first and then walks away? By early March 2001, no other bidders had emerged. AIG's all-stock offer to purchase AGC was still the best on the table, and we resigned ourselves to the notion that soon we would all be working for Hank Greenberg. Perhaps Prudential PLC's senior management backed away from the idea of trying to outbid the deep-pocketed AIG. Some thought Greenberg might still sweeten *his* bid in order to assure a successful AGC shareholder vote. I could not imagine Greenberg topping his own bid, and I was right. On May 11, 2001, the merger agreement with AIG was signed and the agreement with Prudential PLC terminated. Though our marriage with Prudential was never consummated, the divorce cost us heavily, with AGC agreeing to pay its spurned suitor a "breakup fee" of $600 million.

The closing date was still months away and my college pal wasn't the only one predicting dire consequences of an AIG victory. In public, Hank Greenberg was urbane, charismatic, and reassuringly erudite about every aspect of the insurance business. But insiders warned of his dictatorial management style, his ruthless disposal of anyone who dared to challenge him, and his often confrontational responses to questions from Wall Street analysts on the company's quarterly conference calls.

Still, it was hard to argue with success. AIG was huge. They had over three hundred billion dollars in total assets and a Triple A bond rating from both Moody's and Standard & Poor's. They were a darling of Wall Street, their stock highly sought after. In 2000, the previous year, AIG's stock had traded at an average price-to-earnings ratio of 33.4 (the stock costing an average of $33.40 for every dollar it earned that year). This was well above any of its competitors in the insurance business. AIG was considered one of the most profitable of the property and casualty insurance companies, paying out much less in claims than its competitors. As for Hank Greenberg, we told ourselves, the guy was already over 75 years old! How much longer could the old geezer even stay awake?

Now that we knew who our new parent would be, we all had something new to worry about. Everyone at AGC focused on trying to determine exactly how we would fit professionally into a merged AIG/AGC—if at all. Those in investor relations, legal, treasury, and accounting seemed more vulnerable to layoffs. We in investments, on the other hand, felt relatively safe. AIG was a vast international company, yet its presence in the U.S. life insurance and annuity businesses was limited. Their investment staff was small and had a somewhat dubious reputation. This meant a good strategic fit with AGC and, we hoped, better job security for us.

Then we learned news that surprised and worried us. AIG's $7 billion of high-yield bonds were not managed by AIG's main investment department in lower Manhattan, but by Sun America's investment team in Los Angeles. AIG had acquired Sun America in 1998. The financial markets back then were enjoying one of their cyclical peaks, especially in high-yield bonds. Because of Sun America's perceived success in managing their high-yield bonds, AIG moved their own bonds to Los Angeles to be managed by Sun's group. The Los Angeles team managed more than twice the high-yield bonds that we did in Houston, and they apparently had a good reputation. Why then, would AIG not just send our Houston team packing?

We continued to fret about layoffs and to dream about those lucrative severance packages and immediate vesting of our stock options and restricted stock. My recent promotion to Executive Vice President had upped my severance package to three years, so I was feeling pretty safe and smug. Besides, the high-yield market was still reasonably strong and we had a solid track record. Our biggest concern was that we knew of very few other high-yield jobs in Houston. If we were laid off, we would likely have to uproot our families and move. My wife and I still had two boys in high school who had absolutely no interest in moving. Many other families were in similar positions.

In June of 2001, the senior management of AIG and Sun America descended upon our Houston offices to conduct their "due diligence" of American General's operations. We were asked to have ready detailed and extensive reports on all of our high-yield bond holdings, our historical track records, and our research and approval processes. Scott Richland and John Lapham represented the Sun America high-yield team, grilling me and my two high-yield portfolio managers, Jeff Gary and Tim Janszen. What percent of our high-yield portfolio was rated CCC? What percent was rated D? What was the total return on the AGC portfolio in 2000? How did that compare with the Lehman high-yield index? What was the total current market value of the portfolio as a percent of amortized cost? The questions went on and on.

Later, we heard that the AIG/Sun team had been impressed with the results of their investigations, with many positive things to say about our high-yield operation. This was good news and bad news. Maybe we'll keep our jobs, we thought. But we'll probably have to report to those Sun guys in L.A. This option had little appeal for me. I might be able to stay in Houston, but I would lose the management freedom that I had so recently gained, and keeping my job would not trigger my severance package. The psychological pendulum had swung again and all this uncertainty made me feel jittery and blue about my prospects.

Contributing to our uncertainty was our lack of hard data on the AIG/Sun high-yield bond portfolio. The "due diligence" process is supposed to go both ways in a stock-for-stock acquisition, the buyers providing all the requisite financial information to the company they propose to acquire. After all, both companies need to assess whether this merger is a good idea and both need to report to their shareholders. The process, however, was far from symmetrical. AIG was vast, its operations labyrinthine. We had no realistic possibility of vetting them in any comprehensive way. As its Triple-A rating showed, the company was clearly on solid financial footing, or so it seemed. And control of the whole acquisition process generally resides with the acquirer, not the acquiree. While we answered all of their questions about our portfolio and its historical performance, they at first shared little with us about theirs. "You'll get that opportunity at a later date," they said.

This made us curious, for we had growing reason to believe that the Sun high-yield portfolio was in less than stellar condition. We didn't yet have accurate and up-to-date financial data, but we had ways to start getting a general idea. AIG/Sun financial statements of prior years were a matter of public record and we could identify their high yield holdings. We also checked in with some of our Wall Street contacts and called a member of the Sun staff who used to work at AGC. Our initial impressions were that the Sun portfolio had real problems. But the full picture of the L.A. high-yield bond portfolio, including its historical track record and how the securities were then valued on AIG's books, strangely did not emerge until well after the acquisition closing date of August 29th.

The results were shocking. I can honestly say that never in my career had I seen an uglier high-yield bond portfolio than what AIG/Sun was holding. Their bonds had suffered massive unrealized market losses. They seemed to own every dog in the marketplace. The portfolio was poorly diversified, with too much risk. They'd made outsized bets on the riskiest companies in the high-yield universe. "What did these guys do," we joked, "corner the market on triple-C telco zeros?" That's shop talk for zero-coupon bonds—bonds that make no interest payments and are acquired for less than their par or face value— issued by fledgling telecommunications companies with no earnings and failing business plans. Suffice it to say that they're not the kind of holding you want to see too much of in a portfolio.

Apparently, Sun America had been a classic bull market shop. In the early and middle 1990s they had performed well, taking huge and risky bets on high-yield bonds that had paid off handsomely in a strong market. In 1998, Sun's CEO Eli Broad had sold Sun America to AIG for a princely sum. The price may have seemed fair at the time, but when the high-yield market softened, beginning in 2000, Sun's fortunes took a sudden reversal. Their exposures in telecommunications, internet, cable, and the dot-com companies resulted in massive losses. Well over a billion dollars of these losses were attributable to companies in bankruptcy, in default on interest payments, and with bonds worth only pennies on the dollar. AIG had no reason to hope that these investments would ever recover. By normal accounting standards, therefore, AIG should have already taken these losses as write-downs. They had not.

Why, we wondered, had we not learned this earlier from Scott Richland and John Lapham? To be fair, they had not been in their positions for very long. They did have prior investment experience, but not with Sun. Now they were primarily focused on Sun's purchases of syndicated bank loans, a complex class of assets that AGC did not deal in. But the main problem was that Sun's high-yield bond portfolio had become a corporate redheaded stepchild. It was so bad that no one wanted to claim it. In fact, we heard, its whopping unrealized losses had contributed to a massive rift between Sun's L.A. team and the New York offices of senior AIG investment management.

Suddenly, we realized that AIG needed our high-yield team a lot more than we needed AIG. Of course, we too had suffered some losses from the bursting of the high-tech bubble. But we had been relatively conservative investors, staying with the stronger internet and telecom companies and remaining underweighted in the industry. The percentage and magnitude of our losses were nowhere near those suffered by the AIG/Sun portfolio. Once we realized how adept our performance had been compared to theirs, we began to feel a lot more optimistic about our power when it came time to bargaining for salaries, bonus plans, and other perks with AIG.

Meanwhile, we waited. And we waited. We were told that AIG would be contacting us very soon about retention, responsibilities, and compensation for our high-yield team. Still, we waited. The closing date had been set for August 29, 2001. There did not seem to be any question that the Houston team would run the high-yield show going forward, but August was upon us. The closing date was drawing ever nearer and we wondered if AIG even knew what was happening. There was absolutely no communication from AIG in New York. The Houston team grew increasingly restless and irritated. Every day new résumés from my staff "hit the streets."

The streets responded. When news of this lengthy period of uncertainty filtered out, our high-yield team was contacted by CIGNA, a health care and financial services company based in Philadelphia and New York City. CIGNA's high-yield team had lost some key people. Their performance had suffered, they'd lost some important accounts, and they were anxious to rebuild and expand their high-yield business. They had heard about the quality and availability of the AGC team, and they proposed a possible "lift out" of up to ten members of our group.

This radical new option had a lot of appeal. CIGNA was all the things that AIG was not. They were motivated and persistent. They talked of generous compensation for their employees. After several weeks of interviews, meetings, and dinners, CIGNA put three very attractive offers on the table for myself, Jeff Gary, and Tim Janszen. The remaining offers would follow soon thereafter and would also prove generous. CIGNA was willing to set up our group at any Houston location we wanted. They offered New-York level compensation, a high degree of autonomy, and guaranteed bonuses for as long as three years. *Wow.* I never believed my compensation could approach this level. I wanted to accept on the spot, as did all of my other AGC associates, and CIGNA was putting huge pressure on me to do just that. I was the head of the group and it seemed as though everything hinged upon my decision.

I had two principal reservations. First, CIGNA's existing high-yield bond portfolio was worth only $1 billion and change. The collective compensation they were offering our group would be a heavy burden for such a relatively small portfolio. This meant that the gun was going to be at our heads to grow the portfolio quickly. The high-yield bond market was under growing stress, but if we didn't triple the size of the portfolio in two to three years we would all be on the streets, looking for work. Second, we still had not yet heard from AIG, who should logically have been more aggressive in trying to retain our team. Despite our frustration with AIG, we still wanted to hear their offers before accepting or declining the offers from CIGNA. Finally, after several more weeks of waiting, I went to

Richard Scott with an ultimatum: AIG had to put its offers on the table within a week, or we were all going with CIGNA. I did not tell Richard any of the specifics of the CIGNA offers.

Richard passed this information along to his superiors and finally, a few days shy of my deadline, they responded. I was invited to AIG's executive dining room at their New York City headquarters for a one-on-one lunch with Win Neuger, Richard's (post-merger new) boss. Mr. Neuger was the Chief Investment Officer at AIG, responsible for hundreds of billions of invested assets. He reported directly to Hank Greenberg and was, in corporate parlance, a very big cheese.

AIG's dining room had a distinctive Asian touch and was reputed to offer some of the finest food in New York City. The company's original waiters had been insurance employees brought over by AIG founder, C.V. Starr, when he fled the advance of the Communist army in China. Rumor had it that when the Chinese employees found themselves unable to work in the U.S. because of the language barrier, Starr made them kitchen staff and waiters, paid them like insurance executives, and gave them stock in the company. Hank Greenberg, a health nut, added his own slant to the nutritional offerings. No hot fudge sundaes for dessert, but you could have all the fresh fruit you wanted.

Win Neuger turned out to be a chubby and slightly disheveled man who gave the impression of carrying around far more facts than his absent-minded brain could handle. Our meal was indeed excellent. Halfway through our plates of perfectly cooked Chilean sea bass, keeping his voice low so as not to be heard by the adjacent tables, Mr. Neuger outlined AIG's proposal to me. He was offering me the position of Head of High-Yield at AIG. I would be managing one of the largest combined high-yield bond portfolios in the world. The size of my department would more than double, from twenty to forty-five employees. The assets under my management would triple, to roughly $10 billion. It was a huge promotion and a massive increase in my workload, including full responsibility for the hideous high-yield portfolio from Sun America.

For all this, Mr. Neuger offered me what was basically my existing AGC compensation package, with a few minor bells and whistles added. He had put in a lot of work, he said, to get this offer approved by Hank himself.

For a moment I was at a complete loss for words. What was Neuger thinking? His proposal was laughable. The compensation he proposed was less than half the going rate for people with my experience and the added responsibilities that I would assume. After all the delays, all the tension, all of the hype we had heard about AIG, it added insult to injury. Could AIG really be this clueless? For a moment I was so furious that I felt like flinging my Chilean sea bass into Neuger's portly face.

I excused myself and went in search of the restroom. I sprinkled a little water on my face to cool off, looked in the mirror, and vowed to remain calm. Returning to the table, I told Mr. Neuger that while I appreciated his confidence in me, the offer seemed inadequate under the circumstances. He countered by saying this was AIG's absolute maximum and final offer. Otherwise, they would be paying me more than my counterparts in New York, he said, and this they could not do. I remained courteous, thanked Mr. Neuger for his time and ended one of the more memorable lunches in my career in a state of utter disbelief.

I flew back to Houston thinking CIGNA was looking like a no-brainer. I had to assume that AIG's offers to members of my team would be equally inadequate. Richard called me into his office and asked me how it went, and I told him how disappointed I was with the AIG offer. Richard offered a half-hearted defense but promised to speak to Win. Several days passed with mounting pressure from my staff and no further communication from AIG. I became increasingly preoccupied, short with my associates, and snapped at my family at home. My kids told me I was scary when I was that mad. When I could stand it no longer, I entered Richard's office at the close of the day with a copy of my CIGNA offer. I intended to resign, I told him, along with many of my associates.

Richard's response was typical Richard. "Let me see what I can do."

I got up and stalked out, left the office, and headed for the employee parking lot, my jaw clenched and my brain aboil. Just as I was entering the parking lot, I ran into a welcome face. John Graf was one of my favorite people at AGC and considered perhaps the brightest young prospect within the company's senior management team. He was president of AGC's largest subsidiary, Variable Annuity Life Insurance Company (VALIC), and a close friend of Richard's. He knew of my ongoing compensation negotiations with AIG. John asked me how the negotiations were going.

"Badly," I growled, and I told him what I had just told Richard.

John was one of my biggest fans. VALIC was the largest holder of high-yield bonds within AGC and John greatly appreciated that extra yield my team had helped to deliver. He had also been identified by Hank Greenberg as a top future talent for AIG. His response to me was unhesitating.

"I'll talk to Hank."

The next day Richard asked to see all of the other CIGNA offer letters. Later that afternoon he called me back into his office. AIG was prepared to match all of the CIGNA offers, he said—on condition that we accept the AIG offers immediately. *So much for Neuger's New York salary caps*, I thought.

I quickly huddled with my team. The ensuing debate was vigorous: AIG or CIGNA? CIGNA was clearly the emotional favorite. All of us resented the initial indifference and lack of square dealing by AIG management. Nevertheless, AIG held almost ten times the high-yield assets that CIGNA did. In this case, size *did* matter. AIG would represent a much larger and better platform for us to grow the business, and to interact with Wall Street and the senior management teams of our portfolio companies.

Finally we agreed to accept the AIG offers, but our feelings in doing so were deeply conflicted. We all felt badly about declining the CIGNA offers. They were decent and honorable people who had negotiated in good faith with all of us. I was always open and honest with CIGNA about my concerns. They understood the risk that AIG could do exactly what it did. AIG had finally come through, but the way they had chosen to treat a team they badly needed to retain did not bode well for the future.

Strategically speaking, I felt I had played my cards well. I had used the CIGNA offer to leverage my own position, and it had paid off handsomely. I had a three-plus year guaranteed contract with AIG. My total compensation would almost triple. All of my stock options were fully vested and nicely in the money. My restricted stock vested and was converted into a large number of saleable AIG shares. It was a special time, a moment when I could savor, at least for a while, the accomplishments and successes that had accrued over my tumultuous sixteen-year career at AGC.

Financial prudence, however, dictated that I reduce some of my overwhelming exposure to AIG and its stock price, which accounted for over eighty percent of my personal net worth. In addition, I still felt uneasy about AIG and Hank Greenberg. This was a huge, diverse, and somewhat dysfunctional organization, and we had gotten off to a rocky start. AIG shares were valued at $79 each on the day of the merger and climbed to the mid-$80s within the following weeks. And so, in early September 2001, I sold half of my holdings of AIG stock. They fetched $85 a share, a price very close to the all-time high for AIG going forward.

Two days later Richard told me that Hank called. Hank was very angry, Richard said. "How could Massie sign that contract with us and then dump his stock?" This was troubling. Hank was not a man any AIG employee wanted as his enemy. Did I have to have all my assets in AIG stock for Hank to think I was loyal? He was a financial man. Didn't he understand diversification? (Apparently not then, or even much later in his career.)

At the ripe old age of fifty I was feeling financially comfortable, for the first time in my life. The sale of all that AIG stock had left the Massie family with a good deal of cash and we knew what to do with some of it. We had lived in the same house on a small lot for thirteen years. We had three energetic and very sociable kids and some grouchy neighbors who seemed to complain bitterly every time our kids splashed in our little backyard pool. It was time to trade up. We thought about remodeling, but the horror stories were too gruesome. So we did the math and decided to look into the higher-end market for homes near our neighborhood in The Woodlands, Texas.

Weeks went by, and we still hadn't found a house to our liking. Then Barbara got a call from a fellow member of the Woodlands Symphony Board. They were putting their Woodlands home on the market, the friend said, but she wanted Barbara to see it first. Maybe we could work out a deal. So off Barbara went.

My wife is not a woman who is easily impressed by houses. She can be very, very picky about buying a home. But she returned home after seeing this house gushing about how perfect it was. The house was newer than ours and about twice the size. Its lot—an entire acre, magnificently landscaped, with majestic oaks and a huge backyard pool and gazebo—would give us a great deal more privacy. Its three-car garage sounded good to me, loaded down as we were with my motorcycle collection—about ten bikes in all—not to mention my Jaguar and my wife's MG. Barbara loved the granite countertops, hardwood floors, elegant woodwork, and high ceilings. "I could move right in and not change a thing!" she said. "It is truly the most stunning home I have ever seen." I quickly agreed to go with her to see the property later that week.

"By the way," I asked during our short drive over there, "why are they selling?"

"Gee, I don't really know," Barbara said. She had never really thought to ask that question. She just loved this house! But now that I mentioned it, she thought perhaps the husband had worked for Enron.

Aha! My trader instincts lit up. Enron was collapsing at the time, and I smelled a deal. The house was every bit as beautiful as Barbara said it was, but I kept my cool. We waited several days, then offered an all-cash bid with few contingencies. Our bid was quickly accepted with no counteroffer. We had snagged ourselves a deal, I thought, though not without a qualm of conscience. Again I found myself in the business of using other people. First it was CIGNA, and now it was some guy who was probably about to lose his job and see a big decline in his net worth, thanks to Ken Lay, Jeff Skilling, Andy Fastow, and the other bright boys at Enron. In fact, now that we had "traded up," several of these Enron wizards turned out to be our new neighbors. Richard Causey, Enron's former chief accounting officer, lived just two doors down.

"Congratulations," one friend said caustically. "You just bought into a high-crime neighborhood."

Chapter 8: This Place Called AIG

It was September 2001, and I was now a full-fledged employee of AIG in Houston and I was now facing one of the steepest learning curves of my life. Remember that first day of college when you wandered around aimlessly trying to figure out your schedule and priorities? A day at AIG seemed to be forever like that first day of college. I had to get myself focused. My top priorities, as I approached my new responsibilities, were as follows:

- Let's understand exactly how AIG functions and how Hank Greenberg operates.
- We have to get "down and dirty" with the Sun portfolio and really figure out this mess we inherited.
- Integrate all of the new employees from around the country into the High-Yield Group.

In terms of the investment function at AIG, it was in some ways quite different than AGC. Basically, each asset class tended to be run independently without any investment committee or much in the way of direct oversight from Win Neuger, the Chief Investment Officer. Win's many direct reports managed their fiefdoms somewhat independently. Richard Scott had been promoted to the Head of

Fixed Income at AIG and was now working out of AIG's offices in lower Manhattan. Richard remained my direct boss and he reported directly to Win Neuger on the organization chart. In his new role, Richard pretty much ran Fixed Income as he saw fit, since Win was perpetually in Hank's office or traveling the globe for AIG. I was, of course, pleased that Richard gave us in high-yield a fair degree of autonomy, however, he did closely monitor our bond trades and our overall performance. The high-yield investment approval process at AIG was largely unchanged from the later days at AGC since the key personnel involved had not changed.

What was uniquely different about AIG was the presence of Hank Greenberg. Mr. Greenberg had an incredible grasp of all aspects of AIG's diverse operations in 131 countries. He worked long hours and weekends and readily expected people like Win Neuger and Richard Scott to be at his "beck and call," 24-hours a day, 7-days a week. Greenberg could strike fear into the hearts and minds of his subordinates. His total grasp of AIG related information was astonishing and he had minimal patience with those who did not share his brilliance. It was commonly known that Hank "did not suffer fools lightly," so you had better have your shit together in his presence. Hank was clearly in total control of all important, and not-so-important decisions made within AIG, perhaps with the slight exception of the investment decisions. He was an insurance man through and through and did not seem to meddle excessively in our activities.

The fact was that most decision-making of consequence at AIG relied upon Mr. Greenberg, which created ungodly bottlenecks. This was now a company with over $500 billion of total assets (after the AGC merger) and over 100,000 employees across 131 countries and yet Mr. Greenberg would not cede any significant control within his empire. Sure looked like a Tomato Plant problem to me! It was understood that Hank would completely dominate any meeting he attended. It was his agenda, always. He could be caustic, degrading, and rude to anyone that dared to speak or, heaven forbid, actually challenge his opinions or control. There was very little upside and loads of downside if you disagreed with Hank.

It was the summer of 2002 when I was asked to fly to New York and make a presentation to Hank and the senior management of AIG's Investment Department regarding our high-yield bond portfolio. The prospect of Hank being in the meeting was a bit daunting, but I felt confident that I could handle the task. So I spent days preparing my PowerPoint presentation and making sure all of my data and facts were current and accurate. As the days passed, I grew more nervous, especially since I was hearing a new Hank horror story hourly from my beloved associates. I began to feel that in spite of my fat contract, my job was going to be on the line. What if something I said rubbed him the wrong way? What if I drew a blank in response to one of his questions? What if he asked about my AIG stock sale? It happened to people all of the time. My stage fright and performance anxiety were getting out of control.

Finally, the day of my presentation arrived and cautiously and nervously I stepped into the hallowed halls of Hank's private conference room. Like many of these rooms, there was a distinctive Oriental decor, reflecting AIG's roots in China. There were about ten of us and we all took our assigned seats and waited patiently for his majesty, Mr. Greenberg. All the while I was fidgeting with my papers or aimlessly staring off into the room's elegant decor. Finally, Mr. Greenberg appeared and launched immediately into a monologue about some political issue of the day. At this point I had become so nervous I could not even tell you what his topic was. I was fully absorbed in my own mental preparation, for my own topic. A look at my watch showed that 20 of my allocated 45 minutes had already been used up and I hadn't said a word. High-yield bonds were among the riskiest of AIG's balance sheet assets and Ol' Hank seemed not to care. Another 10 minutes passed and Hank finally acknowledged my presence. I now had 15 minutes to rush through my presentation. At the end, no questions, no comments, no discussion, just thank you and good bye. Well, at least I didn't screw up. But it was as though Greenberg didn't want to discuss a topic if he wasn't the smartest guy in the room. He didn't want to cede control or appear vulnerable due to his limited knowledge of high-yield bonds. I was dumfounded! AIG/Sun had literally lost billions on high-yield bond investments and here Hank was hardly willing to acknowledge my presence. He would rather save face than gain genuine knowledge of a very risky asset class which represented about 7% of AIG's total invested assets. Very, very strange, but that was Hank and he was always in charge.

This is purely my opinion and it is probably unfair to many senior executives at AIG, but because of Hank's strong and caustic personality, I believe he tended to surround himself with "yes" men. Strong willed, independent thinkers were not generally welcome in Hank's inner circle. Hank wanted complicity, loyalty, and obedience. Talented people like John Graf saw what life was like firsthand under Hank and soon parted company. Even Hank's two sons, Evan and Jeffrey Greenberg, who at times were considered possible successors to their father, left AIG rather than deal with dad. In my four years with AIG, I just wasn't impressed with senior management. They just seemed to me to be entirely too willing to defer to Hank on all matters of consequence. Sadly, a very bad omen for the future.

Another problem with the New York staff of AIG was low compensation and high employee turnover. AIG tended to be among the lowest payers in the New York community of financial institutions. Investment banks, hedge funds, investment managers, private equity funds, and mutual funds all offered more generous compensation packages than AIG and our fellow insurance competitors. Now again this is just my opinion, but at least in the investment business, AIG was either a training ground for those with precious little experience or a permanent home for those who could not find higher paying jobs elsewhere on Wall Street. It was pretty simple to me. Why work at AIG for say, $200,000 in total compensation as a financial analyst when you can go a few blocks away and, if you're good, double your compensation? If you have to tolerate the high cost of living in New York City you have to maximize your income. So why stay at AIG in New York?

As you can imagine, high employee turnover created a whole host of operational nightmares. Judy Terry was my administrative assistant in Houston and she had an absolute heart of gold. She had been with AGC for over 30 years and she was extremely efficient, hard working, dedicated, knowledgeable and kind. I used to call her St. Jude. However, my St. Jude turned into "Ivan the Terrible" when she had to deal with the inefficiencies of the AIG bureaucracy in New York. "Everything is a struggle, nothing is simple or easy," she used to holler. People seemed to often be new in their jobs with no idea as to how to get things done. Communications were poor, responsibilities were vague, departments overlapped, and it seemed that many staffers were rude, indifferent, or just plain incompetent. I found myself the giver of regular pep talks of encouragement to my beloved St. Jude.

The last issue with AIG in New York was that it completely lacked any type of cohesive management system. Now I was not suggesting the return of MEM/Modelnetics, but we needed some sense of rules and order for navigating the complex and bewildering bureaucracy that was AIG. Rules and regulations tended to be based on oral history and were just passed verbally from one employee to the next. And, of course, everyone had a different interpretation of that oral history. At times it was like trying to drive the length of Manhattan without street lights or traffic laws. Pure chaos! At AIG there were always lots of opinions but very few hard and fast rules unless, of course, Mr. Greenberg spoke.

My second challenge was getting my arms around the Sun high-yield bond portfolio. I can't say it enough. Sun's portfolio was God-awful!! Where can I start? A typical position was a $50 million par value holding of the unsecured, subordinated debt in a bankrupt telecommunications start-up company. This was the norm not the exception. What were these people thinking? Did they just buy this stuff because it had a big coupon? Where was the credit analysis? Where was the risk analysis? Where was the management supervision? Huge concentrations in internet, telecommunications, dot com, and other failed enterprises littered the portfolio.

My first order of business was to separate the Sun portfolio into what we called the "Good Bank" and the "Bad Bank." The Good Bank represented high-yield bonds of companies we wanted to continue to hold and to possibly increase our holdings. The Bad Bank represented high-yield bonds of very distressed companies that we wished to liquidate as soon as possible. Either on a par value basis, or a company/issuer basis the ratio of Bad Bank holdings to Good Bank holdings was an astonishing 8 to 1. Yes, it was that bad, and Sun had almost 100 separate holdings of various companies' bonds. As an example, take a holding of $50 million par value of PSI Net, a bankrupt internet company with bonds trading at $5 (remember 5% of par value). Then try to make a decision if you should sell at the $5 price or maybe hold out for $6 but also risk getting $0 in the future. It was, very simply, a no-win situation and our prevailing attitude toward the Bad Bank was to just dump (sell) everything ASAP.

The principal obstacle to this "sell all" approach was that AIG did not want to take (realize) the losses. Let me bore you with a hopefully brief insurance company accounting lesson. If an insurance company sells a bond at a loss, they record that loss through the income statement as an Investment Loss. If, instead, they continue to hold that bond, which is trading below their cost, they do not have to report any investment loss on their income statement, unless the bond is considered to be "permanently impaired" or never to recover full value in the future. Permanent impairment is one of those bits of accounting terminology that is subject to endless debate. Certainly for a company that is in bankruptcy, has no hope of paying off its debts, and has bonds trading at $5; it is clear that their bonds are permanently impaired. In that case, the bonds will be subject to a permanent impairment write-down (usually to the current market value) and that write-down or loss will flow through the holder's income statement even though the bonds have not been sold. The real permanent impairment debate occurs when a company gets into some level of financial distress but one can still argue that the company can ultimately survive and that one day the bonds will be worth par value, so a permanent impairment write-down is not necessary. Investment professionals and independent auditors should spend many days each quarter debating these potential write-downs. Clearly, if a company is too lenient on these write-downs they are effectively overstating their current income at the expense of future losses (when the write-downs or losses ultimately have to be taken). Enough accounting for now but this stuff is critical as we go forward.

But AIG did not want to show (realize) these losses, which in most cases, in my opinion, should have been taken well before the AGC acquisition. AIG wanted to manage or smooth out its earnings and was determined to take these losses at their own pace in the future when they could be better hidden and absorbed by future gains. So what about the accountants? Well AIG had somehow managed to convince these astute CPA's that AIG's imbedded, unrealized losses in its high-yield bond portfolio were "not material" given the overall size of AIG. It was my opinion that these losses deemed "not material" by Price Waterhouse could have easily exceeded $1.5 billion. Not material? The price-earnings ratio of AIG's stock at this time was around 33, so it could be argued that $1 billion of losses ($1.5 billion after-tax) equated to a reduction of $33 billion in market equity value. That was more than the total acquisition price of American General! Wasn't that material? Could Hank have had compromising photos of the Price Waterhouse partner assigned to the AIG account? This is just another example of how big companies can easily bully their "independent" auditors into submission. The reality was that AIG's stock was trading at a huge P/E ratio (more than double that of most other insurance companies at the time) because the market was anticipating stellar future growth from AIG and certainly no negative earnings surprises (losses). Had AIG come clean about its unrealized losses at the time not only would its earnings have fallen but, in all likelihood, AIG's growth prospects would have come into question leading to a probable decline in its lofty P/E ratio and a further decline in the stock price.

Another explanation given to me as to why these write-downs need not be taken was that AIG had substantial gains elsewhere in its common stock, private equity, and hedge fund portfolios which had not yet been realized (gains taken through the income statement). My reaction was "well that's fine except those are not the accounting rules." Private equity, hedge fund, and common stock gains are subject to their own specific accounting rules which are totally independent of the accounting rules applicable to bond losses. AIG can't just arbitrarily decide the accounting rules it wants to use.

So why did I care? What was the big deal? THIS WAS ACCOUNTING FRAUD! AIG's stock price was arguably being fraudulently supported and this stock had been used as the "currency" to purchase AGC in a stock-for-stock acquisition. AIG was significantly overstating its income and asset values. My entire career was based, at least in part, on my credit judgments which were based on (hopefully) accurate financial statements of borrowing companies. And here my own employer was misrepresenting its earnings and financial strength. Furthermore, we were precluded from effectively managing the Bad Bank portfolio because if we sold anything we created an unwanted, ill-timed, and unapproved loss.

Members of the high-yield team and I had numerous conversations with Richard Scott about this situation. We strongly felt that continuing to hold Bad Bank bonds (with substantial losses not yet subject to permanent impairment write-downs) was utterly stupid because the losses were only going to continue to increase as the market values fell, and ultimately, larger losses would have to be taken in the future. In other words, we were risking future losses in order to perpetuate an accounting fraud. In spite of our pleas to Richard Scott, AIG allowed us to take only relatively small losses from the Bad Bank portfolio each quarter after we took over management of the portfolio. In my opinion, AIG had been clearly overstating its current income, and presumably, fraudulently supporting its stock price.

But how hard could I push this? We were the new kids on the block. We had reported the situation to Richard Scott. Richard had discussed the situation numerous times with Win Nueger and AIG's Chief Financial Officer, Howard Smith. We had heard AIG's explanations. Price Waterhouse was aware of the situation. My choice was to basically "Take it or Leave it." So we lived with the decision of senior management, dutifully following orders and taking our corporate approved losses each and every quarter, thereafter. But none of us from American General were at all happy about this situation.

Finally, the integration of my new staff into the High-Yield Group was a major new challenge at AIG. The L.A. staff was divided into a Bank Loan Group and a High-Yield Bond Group, the latter reporting to me in Houston. Also, Sun America maintained a small high-yield group in New York to manage Sun's high-yield mutual funds, and these folks now reported to me in Houston. There were also some new hires in Houston, as well as a couple of transfer employees from other departments within AGC. All told, I had 20 analysts, three traders, four portfolio managers and lots of administrative people reporting to me from three cities. Just a few personnel integration issues! Everyone was jockeying for their position and there were inevitably loads of power struggles and bruised egos. Sometimes I felt like a coach on the first day of team practice, trying as best I could to identify my talent and build a team, all the while watching a $10 billion portfolio. My clear challenge was to build a cohesive team while keeping my staff fully utilized and focused on the new combined portfolio. We started by creating an organization chart and working directly with each employee on establishing their positions and responsibilities. This one-on-one contact with each employee was essential to me. I wanted to hear from each person exactly what role they wanted in the Group and everything within reason was done to accommodate each staff member. Following these initial meetings, I asked all to meet in Houston for the purpose of meeting their co-workers and gaining an understanding of our high-yield strategies and investment processes. It was imperative to me that all felt included, appreciated, and part of an important effort. I had always believed that people often left their jobs because they did not feel appreciated as part of a larger group. Building this cohesive group, in my mind, was the key to reducing employee turnover.

It was also imperative to me that everyone on the high-yield team have a clear understanding of what my beliefs and tenets were. What did I stand for? What did I expect of them? Recall that under Mr. Hook we had MEM/Modelnetics. I wasn't ready to go there but I still felt that at least in the High-Yield Group there ought to be certain concepts of management that were advocated by me and understood by all. We certainly did not need 150 models, but everyone needed to understand what was expected of them in terms of how they performed on their jobs. So, I boiled all my thoughts down to the following ten basic concepts and circulated these concepts to all in the High-Yield Department:

1) Create a positive, supportive work environment where all can do their work with minimal bureaucracy, ample resources, above market compensation, and a clear vision of management's expectations.
2) Give AIG your full commitment. Do your work with energy, passion, and enthusiasm.
3) Pay for performance. No exceptions. No entitlements.
4) Investing is a team sport. Share your knowledge freely. Cheer and be cheered.
5) Respect the talents and uniqueness of your co-workers. Age, race, personal lifestyle, rank, or religion are totally irrelevant. Care only about the quality of one's work and the content of his or her character.
6) Open and lively debate is vital to our success. Have a well researched opinion and defend it. Do not be meek or timid.
7) Respect your customers, vendors, investors, and Wall Street relationships. Arrogance to anyone is completely unacceptable.
8) Good, honest communication is essential. Praise openly, criticize privately, discuss your differences. Keep your doors open.
9) Have fun. Learn to laugh at yourself...you'll live longer and better.
10) Take immense pride in yourself, your career, and AIG. Focus on solutions, not flaws. We can become the world's best high-yield shop.

So there you have it. My management philosophy in a nutshell. No classes, no unnecessary bureaucracy, no models, no three ring binders, no brainwashing, just an honest simple expression of what was important to me. And it was all received by nothing more than a big, collective yawn by the whole group! Talk about a blow to my ego. Common responses were, "What is this a mission statement?"; "You're not starting Modelnetics again, are you?" "Well isn't that sweet, but can't you just pay me more and I'll be happy?" In spite of this less than enthusiastic initial response, I found that over the years, these principles and concepts became fundamental to our group and were incorporated either directly or indirectly into day-to-day management as well as into important departmental decisions.

It sounds trite, but the people in our group were all that mattered to our success. In the investment business people are your only real asset. Without a competent staff our results would suffer and our asset base would dwindle. Keeping my staff happy and focused was essential to keeping turnover low and our results above expectations. Investment department turnover had plagued AGC primarily due to its management systems and low compensation. While compensation at AIG had improved for many, one of the biggest challenges was making sure that all were paid appropriately and that everyone felt useful, challenged, appreciated, and part of our team. This would prove to be a huge challenge for me at AIG.

In spite of all these obstacles and challenges at AIG, my first 30 months were relatively successful. Our "Good Bank" bonds combined with AGC's portfolio performed very well against the various high-yield bonds indexes. We steadily reduced the size of the Bad Bank. Our mutual funds grew in size and received steadily improving rankings from the various mutual fund rating firms. The performance in our third party funds was excellent, which led to steady growth in this area. We also had extremely positive results in our Emerging Market Debt portfolio and in our Distressed Debt portfolio. Also, our high-yield team had initiated and organized a Fixed Income department wide program of meeting directly and regularly with our major Wall Street trading partners as a cohesive Fixed Income group. We stressed the overall size and trading strength of AIG in order to improve and maintain these essential relationships.

All of this occurred in spite of the fact that employee turnover in my group remained excessively high. Yes, even with my efforts to keep people happy and involved our turnover was averaging about 35% per year, which was a great source of frustration to me. The major reasons for this turnover were as follows:

1) Many of the Sun high-yield people felt displaced by the merger and found other positions in L.A. or New York.
2) Mutual funds, investment banks, insurance companies, hedge funds, and asset managers were all competing aggressively for high-yield people.
3) Compensation was always an issue.
4) AIG was simply not an employee sensitive/friendly organization.

As to this last point, I would like to share a perfect example of AIG's insensitivity to employees. Every non-administrative person in my group had a base salary and a target bonus. The target bonus was expressed as a percentage of the base salary, ranging from 10% to 100%. For every one of these employees target performance objectives were established at the beginning of each calendar year (usually based on the performance of the bonds we owned in the industries they covered). If an employee had a base salary of $100,000 and a 60% target bonus, he would receive a $60,000 cash bonus if he met his target objectives. If he exceeded his objectives he could receive up to twice his target, or in this case, a $120,000 cash bonus. In theory, the target bonus percentages were reviewed annually and tended to increase every few years for an employee if his or her performance warranted an increase. In the above example, an employee's maximum cash compensation was $220,000 ($100,000 + 2 X $60,000). If that employee's target was raised to 80% the maximum cash compensation would rise from $220,000 to $260,000 ($100,000 + 2 X $80,000), nearly a 20% increase. Thus, an increase in an employee's target could be much more significant than a salary increase which was typically less than 5% per year.

It was early 2004 and I had just given out fairly modest salary increases to my grumbling staff, but with the promise that target bonuses were being reviewed for all and they would soon be adjusted as we deemed appropriate. Now recall that we were already experiencing high employee turnover and target bonus increases were an important method of reducing this turnover, if only I could get AIG in New York to approve my recommendations. The first quarter of 2004 ended with no ruling on my target bonus recommendations for the current year and there was plenty of moaning and griping. The second quarter of 2004 ended with no ruling and I had just lost three valued employees. The third quarter of 2004 ended with no ruling and I had lost two more key employees. Finally, in October (yes, October) all of my target bonus recommendations were approved by Hank Greenberg.

In the highly paid, big ego world of investment management you simply cannot ask anyone to work ten months of the year without knowing what their compensation package will be. By October, my entire team was livid. It wasn't just their own personal uncertainty, but it was the message that AIG really didn't give a damn about timeliness on this topic. This in my mind was a sure-fire way to antagonize everyone, especially your top performers who lacked patience and had plenty of job options. Why is this taking so long, I asked repeatedly? Why do we have to needlessly piss everyone off? The answer was very simple, Mr. Greenberg did not have time!!! Back to that old control issue again. The fact was that Mr. Greenberg had to approve the compensation for all employees making over $100,000 per year and apparently he just had not gotten around to it. I was seething. I was doing everything humanly possible to keep this team together and yet New York seemed largely indifferent to the employee reactions to this ridiculous delay. Another one of my moments of sheer anger and frustration. What are these bozos thinking? Employee morale was simply not a priority at AIG and yet top performance was routinely expected. I did not care for this formula at all. We were constantly dealing with employee turnover and relying on younger, less experienced analysts to achieve our consistently rising performance objectives. A potentially very lethal combination. Regardless of my many frustrations with AIG, I was determined to move forward in as positive a way as possible with AIG. We could not have much of an impact on AIG New York but we could build a high-yield team and our own culture in Houston. My ten basic concepts of investment management were to be the foundation of our own culture, and I personally did everything possible to communicate regularly (one-on-one and in groups) with my employees. I always wanted them to know where they stood (both good and bad) and I always wanted them to feel that they were an integral part of our team. I couldn't do as much as I wanted about compensation or attitudes in New York, but I could still be the builder of a positive, supportive culture. To this end, we had annual dinners with spouses to commemorate each year's performance. We had several large family picnics at my home, complete with pool events, inflatable jumping gyms, clowns, and catered meals that I subsidized. I wanted to bring closeness to the members of our team, and perhaps these events with spouses and/or kids could help build some sense of cohesiveness. In fact, I even prepared a list of "25 Positive Attributes of AIG" which I circulated to all my staff. I was growing weary of all the grousing and complaining so I composed and circulated this list to all including Win Neuger and Richard Scott. Again, this was part of my effort to create a positive culture and work environment, at least within our group at AIG.

I suppose that in part due to these efforts and the excellent performance of our high-yield team, in 2003 I was promoted to the Head of Leveraged Finance at AIG and took over the added responsibilities for AIG's Bank Loan Group in Los Angeles and its Bond Workout Team in New York, bringing another 25 people and $5 billion of assets under my management. Well, in spite of my frustrations with AIG, at least I felt recognized and I was again very proud of this promotion. Maybe these guys weren't so clueless after all.

Chapter 9: $400 Million of Enron Bonds!

The Los Angeles Bank Loan Group was the last vestige of the ill-fated Sun America Investment Department. Virtually all of these people were relatively new to the AIG organization and they had had little to do with the disastrous losses suffered by Sun in the high-yield bond market in the 2000-2002 period. Nevertheless, this group was tainted by their affiliation with Sun and I believe they saw themselves as being on the wrong side of the rift between L.A. and the senior management of AIG's Investment Department. The head of this group, Scott Richland, had recently left the company and I was asked to assume responsibility for the supervision of this group. Richard Scott and I flew to L.A. (he in first class and me in coach) to visit the offices and help in the management transition. During the flight I had time to ponder my new responsibilities. As so often happens in large corporate cultures there can be severe misconceptions about different divisions or groups of people, especially those we know little about and have not worked with directly. My misconception about the folks in L.A. was that their credit or analytical skills were weak, they had precious little loyalty to AIG, and if they had any talent they would have long ago left the company. I felt as though I was taking on a potential babysitting role with very little upside, a lot like the Bad Bank bonds we inherited earlier from Sun. Richard stayed only a half day in L.A. solely for the purpose of announcing my new management role. I stayed for the next two days and used that time to meet one-on-one with every non-administrative employee.

Once again, my preconceived notions about people were quickly dashed! This group in L.A. was loaded with talent. You could read that on their résumés, hear it as they talked about their business, and see the fire in their eyes. These were skilled and knowledgeable professionals who wanted to be recognized for their current and planned contributions to AIG. But they felt horribly disenfranchised while part of AIG. Not only were they 3000 miles away from the mother ship in New York, but they felt "unloved" because of their affiliation with Sun. Senior management from AIG rarely visited the Bank Loan Group and they all felt as though they were toiling away in obscurity on a relatively small base of assets. After two days in L.A., I was thrilled at the prospect of taking over this group. They didn't need hand holding or baby sitting or close supervision, they needed someone to give them direction and a vision, along with a heavy dose of sponsorship with AIG senior management.

During the next 18 months, I visited L.A. for at least two days a month, every month, and I had a blast every time. I became their cheerleader and not their school teacher. I was the Bob Devlin of Los Angeles, without the CEO hair. I encouraged them to grow their asset base, to add analytical and administrative staff, to market directly to Wall Street to enhance their deal flow, and to build directly their relationships with the New York senior management. And it was all so easy and fun. Together we developed a vision and a strategic plan, and they executed beautifully. I was simply on the sidelines cheering and they ran all the plays. It was like watching someone hit full stride and flourish after years of shyness. During this period the bank loan group grew their assets by almost $2 billion, or 40%, and similarly increased their fee income. Because of this success I was able to dramatically increase levels of compensation for most of the L.A. staff, and they were delighted. L.A. was just a wonderful success story for all involved and this still represents to me one of my most joyous and fulfilling of professional experiences.

By sharp contrast, the other group that I gained responsibility for was the Workout Group which was based in New York City. These folks were the undertakers of the corporate bond world. They would come in typically after a company had filed bankruptcy and were there to salvage whatever value might possibly remain for the bondholders. Corporate bankruptcies can take years to resolve and these people were there to represent AIG's interests throughout these protracted legal proceedings. It can be dismal, confrontational work and it takes a special type of personality to persevere in this world. Still, I inherited three very capable people who toiled away diligently on multiple bankruptcies with very few complaints, and my role was to generally supervise their work in these various bankruptcies. I had done bankruptcy work at AGC, so I knew what I was getting into, but this wasn't anywhere near as much fun as cheerleading in L.A.

One of the largest workouts that this group had been assigned involved AIG's $400 million position in the bonds of Enron Corp (then trading at $20-$30). Yes, $400 million! Enron bonds which had been rated investment grade up until a few weeks before its ultimate collapse in late 2001. We high-yield people never really studied Enron because it was only rated below investment grade for a brief period. It was interesting to note that while AIG had $400 million in Enron bonds when it blew up, AGC had had no exposure to Enron for the several years prior to its demise. Corey Kilpack was the energy analyst for AGC during this period and he had steadfastly refused to own any position in Enron bonds. When asked why he hated Enron so much, Corey's answer was eloquently simple, "I can't understand their financial statements." Turns out that Corey's reaction to Enron's financial statements was identical to my reaction to those of Rapid American. There were too many red flags, too many complex structures, and too much in the way of insider dealing. Corey was simply not going to recommend a company that he did not have confidence in, regardless of the strong bond ratings and attractive yields at the time. Corey was a sharp analyst, he did his homework, and he saved AGC potentially hundreds of millions in losses.

Enron to me represented the corporate poster child for arrogance, greed, and accounting fraud, and it really hit home when I saw first hand the huge, negative impact on AIG. And all the while I was living only two doors down from Richard Causey, the former Chief Accounting Officer of Enron.

I had the opportunity during 2002 to "bump into" one of these fallen financial wizards from Enron, Andrew Fastow, their infamous Chief Financial Officer. "Andy" had actually interviewed for a job at AGC during the 1990's, potentially working for Julia in Private Placements. During this period, Andy and his wife were re-locating to Houston, which was her hometown. I did not meet Andy during his visit to AGC but everyone who did described him as the most cocky and arrogant person they had ever met. Apparently those dubious qualities were all that was needed for him, instead, to fit in beautifully at Enron. Regardless, everybody who read the financial press knew what Fastow looked like because his mug shot was a daily front page feature during Enron's collapse. Recall that the Houston Astros ballpark was named Enron Field during this period and Enron executives regularly occupied the best seats in the park. I had taken a friend and my two sons to a game one evening and we were seated in the lower field boxes but nowhere near the front row seats of the Enron elite. Between innings I rose and climbed the steps to purchase a couple of overpriced beers for myself and my friend. As you can imagine, the concession stand was very crowded, with everyone elbow to elbow, jockeying for position in front of the next available beerman. I finally placed my order, picked up my two beers, and slowly and carefully turned around so that I might exit through this maddening crowd. As I performed my about-face, I found myself looking directly into the hollow eyes of one Andrew Fastow, who was next in line behind me. So I was staring at public enemy number one (at the time in Houston) with two very full mega-cups of expensive ballpark beer in my hands and, at least for one brief shining moment, I contemplated the idea of depositing my very expensive beer "accidentally" all over Mr. Fastow's evening attire. It would have been so perfect and I'm sure I would have received a round of applause from my fellow beer patrons. But I hesitated. Wouldn't that be very cruel? Besides, this was $14 worth of beer! And as the crowd moved I missed my window of opportunity. But I am glad to report that Mr. Fastow is currently serving 7+ years at a Federal Penitentiary in Louisiana and, undoubtedly, consuming very little ballpark beer.

In sharp contrast to Andy, my career at AIG was sailing along reasonably well in 2004. By the end of the third quarter our results were again indicating a very good year in terms of overall performance. Our own AIG balance sheet high-yield bonds were performing very well against the benchmark high-yield bond indexes, assets under management were growing, our mutual funds had top performances versus their high-yield competitors, and our specialized Emerging Market and Distressed Debt portfolios were generating spectacular results. I previously mentioned the success of our Bank Loan group and even the Workout group was seeing several successful bankruptcy resolutions. In terms of the overall performance of my Leveraged Finance Group, I was delighted. But my frustrations with AIG in New York continued unabated. All the inefficiencies, all the bottlenecks created by Hank Greenberg, all the bureaucracy, all the insanities created by a truly dysfunctional behemoth known as AIG, drove me to the limits of my patience. We were generating excellent results and doing everything that we were asked and the folks in New York seemed too dazed and confused about their world to even care about what the Leveraged Finance Group was up to.

Here is another example of dysfunction at AIG. AIG had fixed income (bond) analysts all over the world in places like China, Japan, Germany, Great Britain, and the USA. This type of size and market presence should have worked to our competitive advantage, but it did not. It did not because the fixed income analysts in these different locations never talked to one another. They didn't even know that the other groups existed! Now imagine if you are an automobile industry analyst in New York with AIG and you follow the domestic auto industry. Would it not make sense to know your counterparts in Japan who follow the Japanese auto industry, and your counterparts in Berlin who follow the German auto industry and so on? It just did not work that way.

AIG was so large, geographically diverse, and so dysfunctional that people rarely knew what was going on in the company. Putting all of these auto industry analysts together in the same room would have been a great accomplishment since they might just learn to communicate with one another and the result for AIG might be a well thought out, consistent, and complete world view of the auto industry, rather than totally independent, regional views which could have been in conflict with each other. Made sense to me.

Rather than sit on my hands and complain about this situation, in late September of 2004, I initiated and organized the First Annual AIG Fixed income Credit Conference, to be held in early November 2004, at the Woodlands Conference Center, just north of Houston. The idea was simple. Bring all of these geographically diverse corporate bond analysts together for a few days. Have them meet each other and collectively develop comprehensive and consistent views of their industries, which could be shared with the rest of the group. Win Neuger and Richard Scott thought the idea had merit, so we had their blessing and a budget to get started. We invited analytical teams from London, Geneva, Berlin, Tokyo, Beijing, New York, Los Angeles, and Houston. To our surprise and delight, they all showed up. There were about 100 people in attendance for this three day conference and all seemed to think it was a huge success. People talked to each other and you could quickly see the barriers fall as people shared a common interest in the industries they covered. Ideas were exchanged, relationships were begun, and people who had formerly been strangers were sharing e-mail addresses and phone numbers. For the final evening event all were invited to my home in the Woodlands community for a catered meal of Tex-Mex (the Texas version of Mexican food), great conversation, poker, beer and wine, and national election night viewing on four prominently placed televisions. I looked around my home and I was very proud of what I had done to create this conference. There were people in my home from all over the world and they were smiling, laughing, and engaged . . . a true rarity at AIG. I felt that I was doing the right thing, trying to build connections throughout this diverse organization. AIG could be much stronger as a unified group of people rather than a series of independent fiefdoms that never shared their ideas with one another. At the conclusion of this conference, I was personally commended by both Win Neuger and Richard Scott for having the vision and the energy to make this conference happen.

As 2004 drew to a close, I was feeling very proud of my contributions at AIG. The Leveraged Finance Group was performing above all expectations and I was taking the right steps to connect with other groups within AIG. We had miles to go to overcome the embedded dysfunctional aspects of AIG, but at least things were moving in the right direction. I also had a keen interest in how all of these successes would effect my upcoming compensation package. My initial contract with AIG expired at the end of 2004, and I was expecting to be recognized for my contributions during the prior 3+ year period. Along these lines, in late 2004, Richard Scott told me that my performance had warranted an invitation to participate in the ownership of AIG stock via one of two private partnerships, C.V. Starr and Starr Investment Co. (SICO). These two private partnerships were formed at the time AIG became a public company in 1969. AIG's founder, C.V. Starr, had donated a large number of his now publicly traded shares to these partnerships for the purpose of future compensation of key individuals within AIG. I was told that being asked to participate was a high honor bestowed upon very few at AIG.

Initially, I was pleased at being offered the chance to participate in these partnerships since the stock grants were often very generous. Richard explained that participation in these partnerships precluded me from any participation in AIG's more traditional restricted stock program, but not to worry since the private partnerships were far more generous. So I asked Richard to see the documentation for participants in the private partnerships. And nothing came. After several more requests Richard sheepishly told me that there was no documentation available to the participants in these partnerships! I would receive a simple letter at year-end telling me the number of shares set aside for me and that was it. I was incredulous. No documentation. How can this be? We were talking about potentially tens of thousands of AIG shares set aside in my name and I had no documentation whatsoever! Only at AIG could this happen. Richard did explain to me that shares began vesting in about nine years and I could only become fully vested once I turned 65. By contrast the plain old restricted stock vested fully over four years. So let me get this straight. I was allotted this pile of AIG stock but I had to stay at AIG another 12 years and be ready for Medicare before I could ever get my hands on any of the shares? Yes, and I had no documentation, whatsoever, to even substantiate my rights under these partnerships.

My response to Richard, after about two nanoseconds of consideration, was "thanks, but no thanks. I'll stay with the regular restricted stock plan." Richard was aghast. No one had ever turned this offer down. This was a high honor and I was not being a team player. In my mind this had nothing to do with being a team player. This was about my personal net worth and my retirement assets and the logic of signing on with one of these absurd partnerships totally escaped me. Regardless, from that point on I seemed to be a marked man at AIG, and my compensation issues were just about to begin.

It was the end of 2004, and I was anxiously awaiting the unveiling of my new compensation package. After all, the High-Yield Group had had great performance, I had taken on broader responsibilities with the Bank Loan and Workout Groups and they were thriving. I had taken a number of extra initiatives within AIG, and I had had no raise in more than three years. On top of all of this, the overall level of market compensation for investment professionals had risen markedly during the last three years. To my utter disbelief, after all was said and done, AIG rewarded me with a 1% salary increase effective January 1, 2005. This felt like a repeat of my infamous lunch with Win Neuger, except I had no Chilean Sea Bass to fling at Richard. This whole thing was just so AIG, so completely absurd. By then I had become numb. What more could I have possibly done to demonstrate my abilities and commitment to AIG? In a conversation with Richard I was told that I was already overpaid and they did not want to overpay me by any more. All of this occurred during a period of very high investment department turnover. I had felt like I was beginning to thrive within this dysfunctional beast known as AIG and in the space of a few seconds, all of my hopes were dashed. Of course, I complained to Win Neuger and Richard Scott, but this was all that Hank would approve and, after all, Hank knew best. I was totally crushed and deflated. What more could I have done to perform for these bozos?

Richard knew that I was very upset by my miniscule salary increase and I think the truth was that he had been "asleep at the switch" when making his salary increase recommendation for me. There wasn't anything he could do to rectify the salary adjustment, but he did have the ability to adjust my bonus and, to placate me, he promised to "do what he could" when the March bonuses were paid. Having heard this sort of language from Richard many times, I was not optimistic about any change in my bonus since it was largely formula driven and capped at no more than 200% of my salary. But this time I was wrong about Richard. In March of 2005, I received my bonus for 2004, and it amounted to 213% of my base salary, or 13% above the formula maximum. Well OK, maybe I didn't get much of a salary increase, but I got it in a bonus. And so my roller coaster ride of emotional highs and lows with AIG continued on. Even though Richard had been "asleep at the switch" he came through and, at least to some degree, my opinion of AIG was partially restored. Was I too critical of AIG? Was I expecting too much from this company? I don't think so. I had worked for four other large corporations in the past and I had never experienced anywhere near the level of frustration that I did at AIG. It was huge, it was diverse, it was bureaucratic, it was dysfunctional, and it was a strange place to work. As St Jude would always say, "nothing is ever easy at AIG."

Something at AIG that was easy was enjoying a business environment filled with all the perks and pleasures related to my position as Head of Leveraged Finance. Certainly at American General we enjoyed the occasional dinner or ball game with one of our Wall Street brokers, but at AIG it was a whole new experience. At AIG our assets under management had more than tripled and we managed one of the largest high-yield bond and bank loan portfolios in the world. It was like being called up to the major leagues after years in the minors. Now we were on the "must visit" list of all our brokers. Broadway shows, golf outings, box seats to any game, playoff tickets, five star restaurants, limousines, music concerts, fishing trips, and the best hotels were only some of the ways that Wall Street would woo our massive account. In fact, when I traveled to New York I regularly had to keep my travel plans secretive because our brokers would be upset if they did not have the opportunity to "wine and dine" me or members of my team. Just as an example, in February 2004, the Super Bowl was played at the brand new Reliant Stadium in Houston. There was so much Wall St. interest in "smooshing" with us during the game and all of the related pre-game events that we had to collectively allocate all the group's time and carefully inform our brokers exactly what events and sumptuous dinners they could sponsor for our group.

But even within AIG, fancy meals and lavish entertainment were considered the norm. In spite of generally low employee compensation, AIG seemed to spare no expense when it came to client entertainment. During my tenure we had client conferences in Whistler, British Columbia; Prague in the Czech Republic; and Beijing, China. No expense was spared. We stayed in five star hotels, ate at the finest restaurants, and traveled first class. Hopping on one of AIG's private jets that regularly flew between Houston and New York and London was not out of the question. Playing a round of golf at AIG's private golf course and resort, Morefar, near Brewster, New York, was relatively common at my position in the company. Even when no clients were involved, if you were traveling with senior management the sky was the limit. The best meals, the best wine, and the best tables, all while personal limousines waited for hours outside these restaurants to escort each of us to our elegant evening accommodations.

Richard Scott, of course, loved this opulent lifestyle. He often told me that he loved to travel because he could live like a king. I would be lying if I told you that I didn't enjoy this lavish style of living, at least for a while. Actually, I'm more of a beer and burger guy and these six-course, four-hour dinners began to wear on me, and my waistline. I remember once at a very fancy New York eatery Richard told me that I should definitely have the *foie gras* appetizer. "It was the best in the city," he explained. Being something of a commoner, I had no idea what this was. Seeing the item on the menu, I thoroughly embarrassed myself by asking "what is fooey grass?" Richard was clearly astounded by my ignorance.

Richard seemed to relish all of the status but for me it wasn't real. This was all happening because we controlled loads of money and had absolutely nothing to do with who I was as an individual. To me it was a showy, opulent lifestyle that lacked real substance. It was the "Lifestyles of the Rich and Famous" but that was a group of people that I never aspired to join. Sure it was fun and exciting for a while but I often found myself wishing that I could just get back to my hotel room and watch TV. For some unknown reason, during my entire tenure with AIG, there was this voice in my head which always said the same thing, "this cannot last."

Chapter 10: Rocking the Boat

Rule #1 for relationships with most bosses: Don't rock their boat. Don't make waves. My relationship with Richard Scott, Head of AIG's Fixed Income Department, seemed like smooth sailing at first, got increasingly tippy as time went on, and finally became completely unseaworthy. There was a real, tangible boat, too, though it was only about a foot long.

Richard owned a summer cabin near the coast of Maine. He loved telling us about the wondrous summer days he'd spend with his family up there, hobnobbing with the New York elite. He was an avid sailor, and he owned a classic wooden sailboat that he kept stored along the Maine shoreline. Once he confided to me that if he ever found a wooden model boat similar to his full-sized one, he would love to build it and display it in his office.

As luck would have it, a good friend of mine had spent his boyhood on the coast of Florida, where he had spent many a happy hour messing around in an old wooden sailboat. By the time I knew him in Houston, Keith had become an avid builder and collector of scale-model wooden boats. He had since moved out to Colorado, but the next time we spoke I mentioned Richard's keen interest in that particular model. Less than a week later Keith called me. He had found exactly the model Richard was looking for. Eighty bucks on eBay.

He went ahead and bought it, although I'd never instructed him to do so, and he sent it to me in Houston. Sure enough, the model kit arrived, a package the size of a long shoebox. So I waited several months until Richard's birthday and gave it to him the next time I went up to the New York offices. I felt a little awkward. Was I crossing some invisible corporate line? Would Richard see the gift as kissing ass? But what else could I do with the damn thing? I told him I'd found it on eBay at a steal. Couldn't resist, I said.

Richard seemed pleasantly surprised by the gift. He said he was going to take it right home and build it. For now he would just put it right over here, on this pile of papers behind his desk.

And there, in plain sight, it sat. At first I thought Richard might just need encouragement. That boat sure will look nice once it's built, I remarked. To no avail. Days turned into weeks, weeks into months. Richard's next two birthdays came and went. There on that pile of old documents the model boat box lay becalmed. In the afternoon the Manhattan sunshine would beam in Richard's window and slide slowly across it. The ink on the kit started to fade, and every month it got a little dustier. The thing that got me was, why didn't Richard just take it home? Had he simply forgotten my gesture? Or did he think the gift had been inappropriate, and that I needed a constant reminder not to cross that line again?

I was a big boy; if Richard didn't want the boat, that was okay. Still, Richard's indifference—or being put in my place like that; I never could tell which—hurt. It was a constant reminder of that treacherous no-man's-land that lies, in the workplace, between status and self-interest, on the one hand, and any real sense of camaraderie on the other. At one time, especially back at AGC, I had believed that Richard and I might have a friendship of sorts. Richard could be engaging, informal, and supportive, at least on the surface. He and I would travel on business together, and I always hoped that we might go play a round of golf, or do a little sightseeing together, or that our professional conversations would blossom into more personal ones. We were both family men: I had three children, Richard had six, three with his first wife and three with his second. Our wives had met at several conferences and seemed to hit it off well.

Richard was a well-educated and intelligent man, a very quick study of investments, and he and I "clicked" in our approaches to the challenges of high-yield investing. We also shared a low tolerance for excess bureaucracy and inefficient management. Richard had a sarcastic wit and a very caustic view of Modelnetics and MEM, and we used to joke about it all the time. Like everyone else on a management track, he had been required to take Modelnetics when he joined American General, a level of indignity that he refused to submit to. He simply didn't show up, and we all had a lot of laughs about that. Richard's vocabulary was well above and beyond the common man, a fact he took great delight in. He was always throwing ten-dollar words around that nobody else could understand. He liked living high on the hog, too. He was the kind of guy who would go to a business dinner in a Manhattan restaurant and buy a $400 bottle of wine, or have a limo waiting for him the whole time at the curb, all at company expense. We'd tease him about his high-living habits, and he seemed to enjoy the attention.

But Richard was also ambitious—very ambitious. Not long after AIG acquired American General, Richard told me in no uncertain terms that he wanted to take Hank Greenberg's place, and that he felt he "had the horsepower to do it." He respected Greenberg's intelligence and talent, but felt he'd surrounded himself with "yes men," men that Richard thought were not of his caliber. Greenberg was getting older, but he still ran the show with an iron hand. It was evident that Hank would be selecting his own successor, and Richard felt that he had maybe five-plus years to get on that inside track. Win Neuger, Richard's boss and the layer between Richard and Hank, was not strong competition in most people's minds. Richard was sure he could outshine Neuger. So Richard was very sensitive about how he appeared in the minds of senior management. He wanted to look as perfect in Hank's eyes as possible. Anything—anything at all—that might tarnish his reputation or call into question his loyalty and competentcy was totally unacceptable.

The model wooden boat became something of a symbol for me.

The musical *Guys and Dolls* has a song whose chorus is a frantic "Sit down, sit down, sit down, sit down, sit down, you're rocking the boat!" This might have been written for Richard. As long as I was productive and non-confrontational we got along reasonably well. But rock the boat, even a little, or do anything that might tarnish his image with Greenberg and the top AIG brass, and I was risking his wrath. It was business with Richard, first, last, and always, and I came to believe that any real friendship between us was impossible. We might have some laughs along the way, but he seemed to erect some sort of wall around himself, with frequent signposts: KEEP YOUR DISTANCE.

Richard and I were also very different in our readiness to go to bat with management for the employees we supervised. I was persistent in advocating for adequate compensation for my staff. This was just common sense. The larger the salary gap between us and Wall Street, the more capable and well-trained employees we would lose. By Richard's reckoning, agitating for higher salaries was worth neither the risk nor the effort. I came to believe that Richard had done very little to urge AIG's senior management to do whatever was necessary to keep us from going with CIGNA, for example. It was John Graf, I believe, who fought for us with Hank Greenberg and won. Richard's interest would have been to downplay the problem, impressing our new bosses with his ability to manage his people and keep their compensation low. In advocating to pay our people better over subsequent years, I was getting in his way.

Throughout 2004, I felt my relationship with Richard becoming increasingly less productive and more edgy. One area of considerable conflict was the growing turf wars between two groups that Richard supervised: the Investment Grade Bond Group, managed by Rich Mercante in New York and my High-Yield Group in Houston. One of Richard Scott's favorite managerial aphorisms was that he liked to hire "people who can play well in the sandbox together." In fact our two groups played in very different sorts of sand. As long as the economy was strong, all was peaceful at the playground. As the economy began to soften, however, our different ways of operating began to lead to tensions.

The turf wars were fought over bonds that were currently considered investment grade, but that were in danger of being downgraded by Moody's and Standard & Poor's to below investment grade. All investment-grade corporate bonds were managed by Rich Mercante's group in New York. Any rating below the lower medium-grade category put a bond into the speculative grade categories. These bonds were—or became, if we inherited them from the Mercante group—the province of my Leveraged Finance Group.

For the first couple of years, our two groups didn't cross paths that much, and we had few problems when we did. Rich Mercante had come down to Houston for the conference I had organized in November, 2004, with the idea of improving the spirit of cooperation across the company. Rich looked a little like a barroom bouncer, a short, stocky, tough-talking New Yorker. But we managed our portfolios in parallel universes, with relatively few bond positions crossing the line between us. Gradually, however, economic conditions began to deteriorate, and industries like airlines, telephone companies, and auto companies started feeling the pressure. A flurry of downgrades began, and we started to inherit Rich's riskier positions, and the potential for conflict started to grow.

During the winter months of 2005, General Motors (GM) became the subject of considerable debate. GM's bonds were still rated in the lower medium grade category (Baa2/BBB) and were managed by the Mercante group. But GM was running at a net operating loss. If their bonds were downgraded to speculative status they would become the responsibility of my High-Yield Group. So we would watch such situations from afar, keeping an eye on those companies while rarely involving ourselves directly.

The size of our GM position, though, was sobering. For bonds in the lower investment grade category, Rich Mercante's group could purchase up to a $500 million position in any one company, and he was holding about $400 million in GM bonds. Because of the riskier nature of bonds that we managed, my group was limited to a $150 million maximum exposure to any one issuing company. If GM bonds were downgraded, we in the high-yield group would inherit

$400 million of Rich Mercante's GM bonds, a gigantic position that scared us high-yield people half to death.

I spoke to Damian Geistekemper, our high-yield analyst for the automobile industry, and asked him to do a quiet analysis of his own, without letting on to the people in New York at first. I wanted to understand Rich's position. "We need to figure out why they're not only comfortable holding $400 million of GM bonds but are buying more," I told Damian. "What is it that they see that we don't see?"

Damien did his analysis, and he came back with a very negative evaluation. GM had been losing money and market share for years. Most of their cars were dated, of little interest to the younger, more affluent buyers. The company also suffered from enormous retiree health and pension costs. The United Auto Workers kept union wages high, putting GM at an additional cost disadvantage to its non-union competitors. GM's cars were therefore $1,500 more expensive to produce, on average, than foreign cars. The only GM cars that seemed to make money were their large trucks and SUVs, gas-guzzlers that were especially vulnerable to any increase in gas prices. To us in high-yield, therefore, GM was a slow-moving disaster.

Rich Mercante and his team disagreed. Rich was not worried about potential bond downgrades. He thought GM had a bright future. To the investment-grade guys, GM bonds were a bargain. Triple-B bonds were still investment grade, but they were cheaper than most and therefore carried a higher than normal market yield. Besides, Rich argued, *They've got ten billion dollars in cash.* Sure, that doesn't guarantee anything about their long-term viability, but they've got plenty of liquidity, could withstand any cyclical downturn in the auto industry, and were in no danger of defaulting on their bonds in the foreseeable future. So the Mercante group smelled a bargain. They weren't selling. In fact, they intended to buy more.

I got on the phone with Mercante in New York. We in High-Yield were concerned, I said. We felt a further downgrade in GM's bond rating was imminent. And a $400 million position in GM bonds, if we inherited it, would be more than twice our largest position in any other bond. That would take us back into having to manage a huge position with vast embedded losses. By acting now, on the other hand, Rich's investment-grade team could still sell the bonds around par, without taking any great loss. I knew I was encroaching on Rich's territory, so I tried to be courteous and respectful, but Rich was a proud man, and I could tell that he deeply resented my intrusion. Rich was not inclined to take the High-Yield Group's fears into account. He intended to keep on buying. "Don't tell me how to do my job," he said. "This doesn't involve you, and we can manage this without your input."

The problem lay not only in our perception of GM itself, but in the way the two teams viewed each other. To Rich, we high-yield guys were like Chicken Little, always seeing the worst in everything, running around as if the sky were falling. He was partially right, of course. Having seen what happens as companies weakened financially, we did tend to sound the voice of caution when it came to positions with a potential for a downgrade. Richard's group dealt with huge portfolios of investment-grade bonds issued by large, well-established companies. Good rating? Good price? Good yield? He was a buyer. His investment grade group didn't examine their holdings the way we did. They mostly relied on the ratings and didn't lie awake at night worrying.

We in high-yield saw our jobs very differently. We did our own independent research. We cultivated the art of credit analysis because our job required it. We regarded the rating agencies as fallible. We knew how they worked. They had no special talents or crystal balls. They didn't re-audit the company and scour their books. They just took the company's public financial statements, added in other information from the public domain, ran it through their system and came up with a rating. Moreover, they were short-staffed and subject to rapid turnover, just like everybody else.

"Why is this bond rated double B?" we'd ask them. "We think it should be investment grade."

"Oh, yes," they'd say. "We haven't really looked at that recently. We don't have the staff." Or: "So-and-so was responsible for that, but he left the company."

The result was that their ratings were always playing catch-up, lagging behind the rapidly changing events on Wall Street. So our view of the ratings was that they represented only one opinion, and not necessarily a very reliable one. (Our wariness has since been borne out. The rating agencies were subject to severe criticism for slapping triple-A ratings on subprime mortgage securities. Anyone who did their homework and looked at the composition of these securities closely would have realized they were nowhere near triple-A.) Rich's complacency was all very well when skies were blue, we thought, but if you had a company that was starting to falter and could fall to below investment grade—like GM—you needed to roll up your sleeves and dig in.

This was potentially a more serious issue for AIG than your average in-house turf squabbling. If $400 million in GM bonds were to drop ten percent in price, that's a $40 million hit to a portfolio's total return. The larger a chunk of your portfolio those bonds represent, the harder the hit and the worse your performance will be when measured up against your competition and the market indices. Nor will your portfolio be the only one to take a loss. A part of AIG's business was managing third-party money—portfolios of other insurance companies, mutual funds, pension funds, and endowments, which we managed for a fee. Any poor performance would be reflected in those third-party portfolios as well. When we tried to woo third-party investors, trying to convince them to place their portfolios with us under management, they naturally wanted to know how we were doing with our current investments. Thus, losses also endangered new third-party business.

Potential losses of this magnitude were clearly not in the best interests of AIG, and I did not feel that I could let this matter rest. I therefore turned to Richard Scott, to whom both Rich Mercante and I reported. I'm worried about this, I told him. I feel pretty strongly that far from adding to our GM exposure, AIG should be reducing it.

Richard wasn't particularly interested in the underlying fundamental analysis for or against General Motors. To him, this was a political question—a sandbox question. *How am I going to stop these boys from fighting?* Richard's biggest concern, it seemed, was that this squabbling would make his department look dysfunctional in the eyes of his bosses. He was as uncomfortable with conflict as he was with being a friend. Like Hank Greenberg himself, he wanted the people who worked for him to be passive and compliant, yet very successful at the same time, something that in any ongoing real-world situation was almost a contradiction.

Richard reluctantly agreed to referee the conflict. In a short three-way conference call with Rich Mercante and me, he split the situation down the middle. Mercante could keep his existing GM position but not buy any more. From a strictly political point of view this approach seemed reasonable enough. But I still felt strongly that AIG was risking significant shareholder and third-party assets with the magnitude of its GM exposure, something I felt Richard Scott would have seen had he based his decision on a GM credit analysis rather than office politics.

This was a purely professional argument. A disagreement about the best position for AIG to take vis-à-vis GM should not have left a personal residue. But it did. My distance from the other two men— me in Houston, them in New York—worked to my disadvantage. Rich Mercante and Richard Scott worked side by side. They saw each other constantly and had lunch frequently. After this disagreement, I felt that Rich began to use their closeness to undermine my position with Richard Scott. In one of those subtle office shifts that is hard to put your finger on, I had become the antagonist and Rich Mercante the aggrieved. "You shouldn't have been so critical of Rich," Richard Scott would say later. "You should have been more sensitive to his pride. You shouldn't have jumped on him like that." Somehow the whole situation turned into a power struggle, rather than a question of making the right call on a $400 million investment. It did not improve my relationship with either man.

In predicting possible losses, of course, one hopes to be wrong. Unfortunately, that's not the way things panned out. GM bonds were downgraded later that year to below investment grade, and their bonds, which had traded near par, fell in price to the low 90s. At that point AIG started reducing its position, but such a large holding can't be just dumped without causing major disruption to the rest of the market. From 2005 to 2009, GM bonds fell slowly but steadily. In 2008, the company lost $31 billion dollars, $9 billion in the final quarter alone. As of this writing, late summer 2009, GM is dependent on government bailouts, deep in the bankruptcy process, their bonds trading in the teens. The losses AIG suffered on their GM position alone must have been enormous. But politics and power struggles had trumped common sense, and shareholders had suffered the consequences. Meanwhile, as I was later to learn, I had made a powerful enemy in Rich Mercante.

Chapter 11: Attacks from Without

How do the mighty weaken?

When the external attacks on AIG began, they found a target fractured by poor management and falling morale, at least among the people I dealt with at AIG. Senior management didn't see it that way. In their own eyes, they were the leanest, toughest guys in the business. "The AIG culture is entrepreneurial to the *n*th degree, and puts profitable growth above all else," wrote Ron Shelp in *Fallen Giant: The Amazing Story of Hank Greenberg and the History of AIG.* "The standard AIG executives were held to when I was at the company was 15 percent growth in revenue, 15 percent growth in profit, and 15 percent return on equity year in and year out. It still is."

True—but that magical 15 percent applied to the whole corporation. The demands placed upon the investment group were even more relentless. Since our campaign to grow third-party assets and fee income, at the behest of Win Neuger, had begun from a relatively small base, we were expected to grow more quickly. We did in fact rack up some very lofty growth percentages. It made no difference. The top brass still raised the bar on us every year, their goals based less on any kind of market reality than on the need to satisfy Hank Greenberg. The hurdles, in real terms, became bigger and bigger. We'd have a very nice year-over-year increase, but the budget goals set for us for the following year would seem almost unachievable. It became another version of the Wal-Mart problem. If you want to double your income, you have to double your stores—every year. We'd have meetings: *These are the results for '03. This is what we have to achieve for '04. How on earth are we gonna make those numbers?*

Furthermore, as is so often the case, AIG was a lot clearer in their demands placed upon us than in the need to support the employees tasked with fulfilling those demands. The management of "yes men" that Greenberg surrounded himself with, the sloppy bureaucracy and senseless turf wars, the frustrating wait until well into the year to find out what our target bonuses would be—these and other factors led to high employee discontent and turnover. We were forever replacing seasoned senior people with junior ones, which made achieving our goals that much harder.

Meanwhile, the regulatory climate had become much more purposeful and unforgiving in the aftermath of Enron. Investors expected the regulatory agencies—the Securities and Exchange Commission (SEC), the Department of Justice, and others—to regulate much more aggressively now. Congress was watchful, too, and didn't hesitate to raise a ruckus if they thought the public's investments were in danger.[1]

AIG had come to the notice of the SEC as early as 2000, when regulators began investigating AIG's role in what eventually became the Brightpoint case. Brightpoint, a cell phone distributor in Plainfield, Indiana, needed to hide about $12 million in losses. AIG suggested a way to provide retroactive insurance for those losses. "In fact," accused an SEC document, "the 'retroactive coverage' should not have been accounted for as insurance. It was merely a 'round-trip' of cash—a mechanism for Brightpoint to deposit money with AIG, in the form of monthly 'premiums,' which AIG was then to refund to Brightpoint as purported 'insurance claim payments.'"[2] AIG paid a $20 million fine to the SEC to settle this case—a fine that had been doubled due to AIG's failure to co-operate with the SEC investigation. But AIG admitted no wrongdoing.

Similar features came up in the case of the PNC Financial Services Group, a bank holding company. This time AIG was investigated by both the SEC and the United States Department of Justice for facilitating an accounting fraud with PNC. AIG, they determined, had set up a special-purpose, off-balance-sheet entity to hold $762 million of PNC's distressed assets. The intent, again, was to allow PNC to falsely report higher earnings. AIG at first agreed to settle with the regulators, but at the last minute Hank Greenberg backed out, vowed to fight the case, and took the disagreement public. After months of wrangling, AIG eventually agreed to a settlement. It was assessed a fine of $126 million. Greenberg's truculence earned us a fine $20 million higher than the original settlement offer from the SEC.[3]

Then Greenberg's eventual nemesis, New York Attorney General Eliot Spitzer, launched his own investigation. His target was an alleged scheme orchestrated by Marsh & McLennan (MMC), the world's largest insurance broker, in collusion with various insurance companies, including AIG. The basic charge was bid-rigging. A circle of favored insurance companies would submit falsely high bids to MMC, which was seeking insurance coverage for their clients. Another insurance company would submit a lower (but still very profitable) bid and win the business. All of this bidding was prearranged. The higher-bidding insurance companies, who had lost the bid on this round, would be selected in turn to be the winning bidders for future clients. This scheme gave the impression that the participating insurance companies were legitimately bidding for insurance coverage when in fact they were colluding to raise prices, their winning "lowball" bids still well above legitimate market prices.[4]

On October 14, 2004, Spitzer brought a civil action against MMC. Ultimately, the case was settled out of court. Seventeen insurance industry executives pled guilty to criminal charges in connection to the scheme, including four from AIG. Fortunately for Hank Greenberg, AIG's actions took place far enough down the organizational totem pole that he and his senior team were not implicated. However, the CEO of MMC, who was forced to resign, was Jeffrey W. Greenberg—Hank Greenberg's son.

The attacks reached a crescendo in early 2005, when AIG was accused of improperly inflating AIG's insurance reserves—an overstatement of some $500 million—through a complex series of transactions with General Re Corporation, an international reinsurance giant owned by Warren Buffet's massive Berkshire Hathaway holding company. The transactions had taken place in late 2000 and early 2001. Unlike the MMC case, where any demonstrable AIG malfeasance was well below top management level, the Gen Re accusations alleged direct involvement by Hank Greenberg.

How did all this look from the inside? How did it affect the rank and file who worked at AIG?

The effects of the regulatory scandals on us as AIG employees were complex and far-reaching. Normally employees would rally around their chairman in such a situation— and we did. When Greenberg was indicted, we reacted defensively. "Spitzer must have an ulterior motive," we scoffed. "This must be his road to the governorship." We felt that AIG was being singled out in a drama that was less legal than political. These are not matters of great consequence, we felt. Why is our company being targeted so publicly, with so devastating an effect on our credibility and fortunes? We wanted to believe that all these charges were trumped up and immaterial. After all, our jobs, retirement, and professional reputations were all bound up in AIG.

Furthermore, establishing guilt or innocence in these matters is not easy. Accounting rules, like any other rule system, have their gray areas. The indictment alleged that our accounting was fraudulent. Surely, we felt, this just came down to our view of the accounting rules versus someone else's view. Even if AIG had acted improperly, the magnitude of the wrongdoing was far from clear to us. Hank Greenberg, in a conference call announcing AIG's latest earnings, had famously dismissed Spitzer's investigations as blown way out of proportion. Greenberg, a tennis player, had used a tennis-court metaphor to denote a minor transgression. "When you begin to look at foot faults and make them into a murder charge," he said, "then you have gone too far."[5]

Still, I had my doubts. I had seen what AIG could do with their accounting. I worried that we had taken similarly illegal measures in other areas. Perhaps AIG *was* being singled out for behavior that had been tacitly accepted in the industry all along. But the accounting and managerial shenanigans that we had witnessed planted seeds of doubt. What if the regulators were right? What else could be lurking beneath the surface?

In truth, our speculations, even as employees of the company, were based on woefully imperfect knowledge. An organization as big as AIG employed hundreds of thousands of people around the world. When something like this became public, the vast majority of those employees were totally in the dark. The accusations often related to arcane aspects of the insurance business that were completely opaque to us. Yes, we had a general sense of what was going on. With the Gen Re case, for instance, we knew that AIG, like all other insurance companies, had reserves to guard against future losses. In prior quarters, AIG had been criticized for not having sufficient reserves, so we understood the motive for propping them up. The details of the allegations, on the other hand, went deep into reserve accounting and insurance lingo. It was highly esoteric stuff, and very few of us were in a position to fully understand it.

Whatever our uncertainty as to the allegations themselves, what quickly became clear was the effect of the investigations on our day-to-day work performance. Our group was busily trying to market our investment management services to third parties. In normal circumstances, AIG was enough of a heavyweight that many clients would automatically consider us serious contenders for their business. But the mudslinging between Hank Greenberg and Eliot Spitzer was in full force, grist for endless gossip in and outside the world of high finance. When stories of your company's possible accounting fraud are in the *Wall Street Journal* every day, you don't make that final cut. Long before the regulators' investigations drew any conclusions, Wall Street was wondering: *What else is there?*

What so enraged and embarrassed me about all of these external attacks was not only that AIG turned out to be guilty as charged. It was the problem of explaining this to our existing and potential customers. The integrity of the financial industry's publicly reported financial statements was fundamental to my successful performance on the job. And yet here was AIG spreading the mantra of fraudulent accounting to the world, offering "financial products"—scams—to other companies for the sole purpose of helping them falsify their income statements.

Despite everything I could do, my group was not only failing to gain new clients but losing established ones as well. Blue Cross Blue Shield of California had placed $50 million dollars of high-yield bonds with us to manage. This was a plum account to have won, and we promptly started using it to market our services to "Blues" in other states. When AIG's recent shenanigans became public, however, BCBS California pulled their account with us. That hurt! And that was just one example. The boards of trustees that supervise pension plans, both public and private, tend to be highly conservative. Our public feuds with the New York State Attorney General did not go over well. "We think this is going to be a distraction for you," prospective clients would say politely. Or, "Our board is concerned about our liability in the event of a decline in your performance." Our credibility on Wall Street was under enormous pressure.

So was AIG stock. By the end of April 2005, AIG's share price had fallen to $50 a share from the $70 a share they had fetched before Spitzer and the SEC had filed their subpoenas. Because AIG had compensated me and much of my staff with restricted stock and stock options, this decline in AIG's share price represented a discouraging decline in our net worths. Virtually everyone's stock options were now "out of the money," meaning that the current market price had fallen well below the price at which the stock option had been granted. This made employees less attached to AIG and more interested in exploring other employment opportunities, further aggravating our ongoing turnover problems.

Another difficulty was the continuing presence of a swarm of regulators. In addition to the New York Attorney General, the SEC, and the U. S. Department of Justice, we had the New York State

Insurance Commission, Price Waterhouse, and who knows who else, all continuing to investigate AIG and its dubious accounting practices. Most of the investigations were conducted at the New York offices, but the repercussions would be felt company-wide. These guys, we realized, were not going to go away any time soon. What more might they find? Who else could be implicated? How would they affect our ongoing business operations? We worried that AIG would become much more defensive in its business strategy, diminishing our appetite for risk and the cash available for our group to invest. We worried that more control by regulators would result in a bureaucratic drag that—for those who remembered our days at American General—would be like going back to MEM and Modelnetics.

Morale, among members of my sixty-person staff, was hitting an all-time low. As employees, we felt highly vulnerable to the outcome of the investigations, in any number of ways. As time went on, we became more and more resigned to the idea that there was some legitimacy to these attacks. This feeling was borne out by events.

AIG responded to Spitzer's subpoenas by agreeing to cooperate with the regulators and to launch its own full-scale internal investigation of these allegations. Since his name was all over the improper transaction with Berkshire Hathaway, Greenberg was clearly painted by the financial press as the villain. But unlike Harold Hook of AGC, who retired voluntarily and gracefully on his own when he turned 65, Hank was not going peacefully. He fought desperately to keep his job. Ultimately, however, the Gen Re affair led to Greenberg stepping down, first as CEO, on March 14, 2005, and then, two weeks later, as chairman of AIG.

The mighty had fallen, with a crash that continued to echo. As a result of its own internal investigation, AIG was soon to report that "certain former members of senior management were finding ways around internal controls," and that numerous accounting irregularities had been uncovered. The reference to such senior management figures as Hank Greenberg and Chief Financial Officer Howard Smith, who was fired on March 22, was clear. The company warned that an adverse opinion on these controls would be expressed by its auditors, Price Waterhouse, in their upcoming financial report. Such an "adverse opinion" would be a huge red flag to anyone thinking about doing business with AIG or investing in AIG's securities. AIG further announced that it was restating its financial reports for the period from 2000 through the third quarter of 2004, reducing the company's net worth by $2.7 billion.

The report confirmed for all to see what I had learned in 2001 about AIG's accounting practices. Maybe Eliot Spitzer had been politically motivated. Maybe the accounting laws were less than crystal clear. But you didn't reduce your declared income by $2.7 billion dollars over a gray area. Or a foot fault.

Notes to Chapter 11

1. http://www.businessweek.com/magazine/content/ 04_42/b3904039_mz011.htm.

2. See http://www.sec.gov/litigation/complaints/comp18340.htm.

3. http://www.crocodyl.org/wiki/american_international_group_aig (which has a wealth of info about AIG's troubles) says AIG agreed to pay this fine on November 30, 2004.

4. See http://www.businessweek.com/bwdaily/dnflash/oct2004/ nf20041015_7888_db016.htm.

5. See http://www.businessmirror.com.ph/home/perspective/4113-1998-2005-aig-a-the-anatomy-of-the-crash.html.

Chapter 12: Whistleblower

In April 2005, the regulatory agencies were circling the company like wolves. Hoping to at least partially placate them, AIG created a new and improved Employee Code of Conduct.[1] Entitled *Delivering On Our Commitments*, it was a twenty six–page booklet with photos on the cover picturing AIG customers and employees from around the world—business types and families alike. They all looked happy, smart, and wholesome. This new Code of Conduct was to change my life.

We had seen early drafts of the Code. The fellows from Legal who were involved in drafting it were one floor below us in Houston, and we spoke with them regularly. Given the regulatory climate, the attorneys involved thought we'd appreciate a heads-up. *If you guys do have any of these accounting issues, this is what will be coming your way.* The Code had the usual stuff about honesty, integrity, and not trading on inside information. But it also emphasized the need for company employees to come forward if they were aware of any accounting irregularities that may have occurred, or be ongoing, within the various departments within AIG. Anyone who knew of any accounting fraud, past or present, must speak to the appropriate individuals. AIG no doubt believed that enactment of the Code would assure all these regulators that any remaining accounting fraud would be rooted out by diligent employees fingering the wrong-doers. Right!

As I read through the early drafts I realized that I had to face up to AIG's failure to properly write down so much of the AIG/Sun high-yield bond portfolio before buying American General. Just as the transaction with Berkshire Hathaway had inflated AIG's insurance reserves, the delayed write-downs of bad bonds had inflated the value of AIG's investment portfolio. Recall that AIG had used its stock as the currency to purchase AGC. Accounting violations such as these had arguably overvalued AIG's stock before the merger—and it was people and institutions like the former AGC stockholders that were paying the price. Yes, AIG had eventually taken the write-downs on the high-yield bonds from Sun, but not until well after AIG used its inflated stock to buy AGC. Now that this and other fraudulent accounting practices had come to light, AIG shares had lost about a third of their value, falling from $79 a share at the time of the merger to a then current value of $50/share.

All this made me very nervous. The Code was clear about what I was supposed to do. As the Corporate Compliance Group's web site would say, "If you see something you believe violates the law or the AIG Code of Conduct, speak up." The only problem was that speaking up meant taking direct aim at the highest levels of management, including Win Neuger. When we proposed the initial write-downs in 2001, Neuger and CFO Howard Smith were the ones who controlled how much we could write down and when. Ratting on Win Neuger, my boss's boss, I suspected, was not going to be good for my career. I was already in the doghouse over the General Motors controversy. Speaking up, I feared, would demote me from doghouse to dungeon.

At the same time, I was tired of all the accounting crap at AIG. Wasn't this the right thing to do? How was the AIG ship ever going to right itself unless people like me came forward? How could I just remain silent? Besides, the Code was clear that whistleblowers would be safe from harm. *AIG prohibits retaliation against any employee for making a good faith report of actual or suspected violations of this Code, laws, regulations or AIG policy.*

As I agonized over this decision, one person's experience came consistently to mind. Richard Causey lived two doors down from the house Barbara and I bought in The Woodlands after the AIG/AGC merger. Causey had been the Executive Vice President and Chief Accounting Officer at Enron. Even before we'd moved, I had known about him from my close friends, Brady and Kelly Hull, who lived across the street from the Causeys. When Causey made the papers as part of the Enron scandal, I was curious. *What kind of guy is he?* I'd ask Brady. *Did you have any idea he was involved?*

We first met Richard Causey and his wife, Elizabeth, at a neighborhood get-together in The Woodlands, back in 2002. The Spence family, who lived in a luxurious ten-thousand-square-foot house between the Causeys and ourselves, threw a Christmas bash every year. Their house was a mansion, with rich furnishings, Roman columns and an elaborate pool, and their elegant Christmas parties were the neighborhood event of the year, catered by the town's finest restaurant, with the best champagne and wine, valet parking, and a gift—a little silver tray or the like—for each couple who attended. Brady had told me that "Rick" was going to be there, and I spent several days before the event trying to figure out exactly how I would approach this fallen financial wizard.

Causey represented everything I hated in the world of accounting fraud. All the press about Enron portrayed him as a sinister figure, the mastermind accountant who was able to sell the wild schemes of Jeff Skilling and Andy Fastow to Enron's auditors through a maze of Byzantine accounting techniques. The accounting at Enron was legendary for its gross distortions and ingenious obfuscation of Enron's true financial condition. Their books were a house of cards, fraught with fraudulent accounts and fictitious revenues—all this, the media informed us, at the behest of Richard Causey.

How was I going to interact with this guy? He was, to me, a disgrace to our profession. One accountant like him can besmirch the reputations of ten thousand who are honest and take pride in their work. I detested the man before I even met him. I wanted to give him a heavy dose of what I thought of his work. I had fleeting fantasies about humiliating him, making him feel ashamed for even being alive. But then I thought of Rick Chalet, who had committed suicide after I'd derided his performance at Brookstone. I had better restrain myself, I thought. After all, Causey had recently been fired from Enron as a result of the SEC investigation and was facing probable indictments for fraud and insider trading. He was going through enough pain. And a Christmas party at Dan Spence's house was hardly the right place to take a stand. Better to keep my mouth shut, I decided.

When we reached the party, Brady and Kelly steered us over. "Gordon, Barbara—this is Rick and Bitsy Causey."

"Oh, yes! You live two doors down." We exchanged the usual pleasantries, talked about our families and interests, kept it light. We quickly mapped out some lines of connection. Rick and Bitsy had met at the business school at the University of Texas at Austin, which they had both attended. Really? Our oldest son was there now. Our younger son, Hunter, played on the same golf team as their son Chris at The Woodlands High School. Soon enough, Barbara and Bitsy split off into their own conversation. Rick and I discovered a shared passion for college football. In spite of all my pre-conceived notions, I found myself enjoying Rick's company. He was smart, funny, and engaging, a committed family man and regular church-goer, as unpretentious a guy as you would ever wanted to meet.

By the end of the evening, my anger and resentment toward Rick were gone. In its place was an unexpected empathy and a deep sense of sadness for this very likable family man. Rick Causey seemed the kind of man that anyone would be proud to call a friend. Yet if the federal prosecutor's suspicions about his role at Enron were substantiated, he would in all likelihood go to prison. As I came to know Rick over the years, and as I found myself in potentially compromising ethical positions, I strove to understand his story. In retrospect it seems like the story of our entire industry in microcosm.

Could a friendly, community-minded, family man like Rick Causey possibly have played such a pivotal role in perpetrating accounting fraud? How can someone who appears to have such down-to-earth integrity be implicated in all of this graft and corruption? What happens to our moral compass in such situations? How might we lose the ability to see the error of our company's ways and distance ourselves from them? I never had the heart to ask Rick these questions directly, but I asked them of myself many times. As the years went by and the story recounted here unfurled, I felt that my own experience in the corporate world had given me more than a little understanding of where Rick was coming from.

Rick Causey was an integral part of the team at Enron, rewarded for his accomplishments both financially and professionally. Like so many of the rest of us who gave their best waking hours to their workplaces, he became imbued with the Enron culture and wanted to be part of its growth and success. He bought into the promises of Ken Lay and Jeff Skilling and willingly took on their assignments. Did he not realize that they were asking him to commit fraud? If so, how much choice did he feel he had? If he refused to participate he would be canned in a heartbeat. He had a family to support. And all he would be doing was what his bosses ordered him to do. A person in that position, with weighty responsibilities and demanding superiors to oblige, can easily turn into a "people pleaser," anxious to be perceived as a can-do guy. One of the boys. Part of the team. Maybe he just couldn't see the larger impact of what he did. Maybe he could somehow rationalize his actions as being "immaterial" in the big picture. Maybe he himself did nothing wrong, as he still claims. But did he simply ignore the wrongs of others when he could have stopped them? Is turning a blind eye to fraud doing nothing wrong?

All this, of course, is my own speculation, but the sad unfolding of Rick's case is a matter of public record. When the music stopped, Rick was caught without a chair, and his legal troubles began. In January 2004, he would be charged with a six-count indictment for securities fraud and conspiracy.[2] He pleaded not guilty at first, but almost two years later, on December 28, 2005, changed his plea to guilty and agreed to testify. On November 15, 2006, in a Federal court room in Houston, he was sentenced to five and a half years in prison. And on January 2, 2007, my neighbor and friend reported to the Bastrop Federal Correctional Institution, about 30 miles south-

east of Austin, Texas, to begin his five-plus years in a Federal penitentiary. Rick was just a week shy of his 47th birthday. His wife and
brother-in-law were with him when he drove up to the prison. His
three children were not.

Five years. Five years of his own life, his aging parents' lives, his
wife and children's lives. Rick's son Chris was a top-five golfer on
his high school team. That year, 2007, The Woodlands High School
won the state golf championship, with Chris posting some of the
team's best scores. Rick was unable to witness his son's triumph.
When the news of Chris's victory came in, I thought of Rick again,
as I had so many times before. I could only begin to imagine the
pain and isolation he felt.

All this was in the future when I first met Richard Causey, but
his road to prison and public disgrace had already begun. His example had a profound personal impact on me. Had he blown the whistle on Enron, Rick would have had his picture next to his associate,
Sherron Watkins, on the cover of *TIME* as a corporate hero. Instead
he was facing years in prison, not only for his alleged actions but for
his silence. If I remained silent on these delayed write-downs could
it not be inferred that I was somehow complicit? Sure, I had protest-
ed verbally at the time, but I had no written evidence whatsoever to
support my position. Was it better to hold off and do nothing, hoping this army of regulators never uncovered the problem? Or should
I speak up, explain my original position, and risk the consequences
to my career at AIG? Many sleepless nights. I couldn't stop thinking of Rick and his family—or about how I myself would handle
even a single day in prison. But most of all I thought about my parents, the way they brought me up, and my father's loving words to
me just before he died. "I think we raised you right."

Then I had an idea. Ed Holmes was a friend of mine and
Associate General Counsel in AIG's Legal Department in Houston.
I had worked with Ed for a number of years, and I trusted his judg-
ment and honesty. I gave Ed a call.

"I need to pick your brain, Ed," I told him. "I'll buy you lunch
for your time."

We met for lunch the next day, and I told Ed the whole story. "What do you advise?" I said. "What should I do?"

Ed was a down-to-earth, straight-shooter kind of guy, and his answer was blunt. "You have no choice. Based upon what you've told me, either you come forward—or I'll have to."

My God, I thought. What had I gotten myself into? I *had* to blow the whistle now. I no longer had any choice in the matter. By confiding in Ed, I realized, I had just burned a major bridge behind me. If I didn't blow the whistle now, I would fail to fulfill the Employee Code of Conduct—and the regulators would hear the whole story anyway from Ed. I had to move forward.

So I did. I called Richard Scott first. I've read the new Code, I told him, and I'm concerned about Sun's failure to write down these high-yield bond assets back in '01. I just want to go on record as objecting to the accounting treatment at the time. Richard didn't seem bothered by the idea.

Then, in an internal memo dated April, 4, 2005, I wrote a memo relating the massive delayed accounting write-downs in the AIG/Sun high-yield bond portfolio. The memo was only a page and a half long and couched in the undramatic language of our trade. The subject line was "Historical Permanent Impairment Write-downs." I described "large disparities between the book values and the market values of both the Sun and AIG portfolios" when the AGC team began its review of these portfolios in September, 2001, after the merger of our companies. I expressed my belief that "a comprehensive investigation into the timing of these write-downs is warranted." I included all the specific details and all the supporting accounting evidence. Writing the memo took me only an hour or two. I gave a rough draft to Judy, asked her to prepare it, read it over a couple of times, asked Judy to run it by Ed, and off it went. The memo was sent internally, addressed to Richard Scott, Ed Holmes, and others inside and outside of AIG, as recommended by company protocol.

Then I waited.

The day after the memo was sent, I received an irate phone call from Richard Scott. He did not disagree with anything in my memo, Richard said, but he strongly objected to my tone. He was very angry. That memo, Richard promised darkly, will have negative consequences for you.

My tone? I went back and read the memo again. I had done everything I could to ensure that my tone was entirely factual. Richard's response surprised me. For one thing, I had checked the idea with him beforehand. For another, I genuinely thought Richard would want to get this matter off his chest as much as I did. Both of us, after all, came from American General. He had been just as new at AIG as I was. Richard had nothing to do with creating the Sun losses, and he probably had no more control over AIG's write-down decisions than I did. I didn't see Richard as being culpable at all. But Richard was my boss. His main worry, it appeared, was how my memo would reflect on him. To Win Neuger, Howard Smith, and Hank Greenberg, it was Richard's department that was causing the problem. It was Richard's man who had written a whistleblowing memo that was—though I had named no names, simply describing the behavior—implicating *them*. So Richard was very angry with me, and I was going to have to deal with the consequences. It wasn't the content that bothered him, I thought. It wasn't the tone, either. It was—well, the fact that such a thing had to be written at all. The correctness of my action was indisputable, both in the eyes of the law and according to the AIG Code of Conduct. So all Richard could seize on was *how* it was written.

Over the next few weeks I received several phone calls from different accountants asking for more details. When were these write-downs eventually taken? When do you feel that the write-downs *should* have been taken? What was their market value at the time? What process are you following in taking write-downs going forward? Questions about specific securities: Were these secured? Were these subordinated? I dutifully supplied all the information they asked for.

Once the dust had a chance to settle, Richard calmed down and seemed somewhat more civil. I began to believe that maybe the storm had passed without too much damage and that things were getting back to normal. Besides, as a whistleblower, I was protected against any form of corporate retaliation. From a legal point of view, I was Teflon. With all of these regulators lurking about in the halls and the ink barely dry on our new Code of Conduct, surely AIG would want to avoid any further conflict with me.

I was wrong.

Notes to Chapter 12

1. At the time of this writing, a copy of this Code is freely available here: http://media.corporate-ir.net/media_files/irol/76/76115/AIGcoconduct.pdf.

2. See http://findarticles.com/p/articles/mi_pjus/is_200401/ai_4091922231/

Chapter 13: Sandwiched

It was now early May 2005, about a month since I wrote my internal memo. April had been a tumultuous month at AIG. Hank Greenberg had fallen, as had our stock and our reputation. The regulators had AIG under their microscopes, and in-house rumors were circulating that the company would soon announce a long list of additional accounting problems and other misdeeds. All this was actually something of a relief to me. Greenberg was a driven and powerful man, with an unmatched knowledge of his business, an army of friends in high places, and an unquenchable thirst for building AIG into an ever bigger colossus. He was also one of the industry's most feared and hated figures. Greenberg grated on many, and had a caustic opinion about everything. He knew better than the analysts, better than the regulators, better than the people under his command. Better, I thought, to have him gone.

Second, my antennae were still up, watching for any managerial attempt to even the score after my memo. Now that the scale of AIG fraud was public knowledge, I began to feel less vulnerable. With so many accounting sins surfacing on so many different fronts, surely AIG would realize that I was just a small player in this. Maybe they would even see my memo as the kind of vigilance that we department heads should have been displaying all along.

AIG's recent $2.7 billion write-down and other accounting misdeeds had cost us some credibility, I knew, but I was hopeful, even optimistic. Yes, I thought, we're undergoing major trauma here. We're removing this managerial cancer we've been suffering from. But with Greenberg gone, we could hope for more rational and responsible management. Our groups in Houston and Los Angeles could get on with what we did well, which was managing assets responsibly and growing our clients' wealth. AIG's stock had fallen, but the financial markets were reasonably strong, and our own group had been firing on all cylinders, delivering consistently strong returns. Our employees were understandably demoralized, but my own outlook was reassuring and upbeat. Let's not overreact. Let's try to find the best in this situation. To paraphrase Julia Tucker, this is still "the land of opportunity."

In Houston, so far from the storm clouds of New York, everything seemed to be marching steadily along. Richard Scott was scheduled to fly into Houston later that week in May for one of his routine visits as Head of Fixed Income. These meetings were generally routine. He'd sit down at the head of the large conference room table, and my senior analysts, traders, and portfolio managers would present which bonds we'd bought recently and how they affected our exposure to different industries. Richard would fire questions at them, which they generally had no trouble answering. He was an admirably hands-off guy as a manager, smart enough to project the sense that he knew what was going on but very rarely second-guessing our decisions. He loved the informality of our Houston office after the suit-and-tie dress code on Wall Street, so he'd come in wearing threadbare khakis and slip off his loafers as soon as he sat down, running the meeting in his socks.

Richard could also be relied upon for a great meal at company expense, usually in a private room at his favorite Houston haunt, Café Annie. In the zoning anarchy that is Houston, Annie's had located itself in a low-slung strip of drab buildings near the much higher-rent Galleria shopping center. The restaurant's neo-Southwestern creations won top awards for their chef and a place on every must-see list for Houston visitors. Sure enough, Richard had invited several of the more senior Houston staff to have dinner with him on Wednesday evening, including myself, Tim Janszen, and Sam Tillinghast, the new Head of Private Placements following Julia Tucker's retirement.

Then, a day or two before Richard's visit, I got a phone message from Rich Mercante. He would be coming down to Houston with Richard, he said. Could he and I meet one-on-one on Thursday morning? Oh, and he'd be joining us for dinner the previous night.

That's strange, I thought. For one thing, why was he coming down? None of Mercante's Investment Grade group was based in Houston. Second, Rich and I did not speak often. The battle of General Motors was still fresh in both our minds. Mercante was coarse and aggressive, not the kind of guy who was likely to offer me an olive branch. I wondered what he wanted to see me about.

Wednesday evening rolled around, Rich and Richard drove in from the airport, and Houston's senior investment people gathered for dinner with them. We weren't at Café Annie's after all—their private rooms were often snatched up well in advance—but in the darkened "Wine Cellar" room of McCormick & Schmick's, a nondescript suburban seafood chain. The meal and the wine had been pleasant enough, with the usual Wall Street chat about the financial markets. Richard Scott seemed his normal sociable self, but I was in a less than chatty mood. Something just didn't feel right. *Mercante didn't know anything about high-yield bonds. Why was he here?*

After our dirty dishes had been whisked away, Richard asked if anyone wanted coffee or dessert. Just as our waiter returned with variations of caffeine and sugar, Richard cleared his throat, tapped his knife gently against his wine glass, and asked for everyone's undivided attention.

"I have two important announcements this evening, which I am very excited to share with all of you here. First, Rich Mercante is being promoted to the new Head of Fixed Income at AIG. Secondly, Tim Janszen is being promoted to the new Head of High-Yield Bonds."

Richard continued. "It has become readily apparent both to Win Neuger and myself that I have entirely too many managers reporting directly to me. Gordon, you and Sam will now be reporting direct-ly to Rich, and he will report directly to me. This will give me more time and availability to take on additional work from Win. We also want to acknowledge the significant contribution that Tim Janszen has made to our high-yield bond effort over the past several years."

"Are you being promoted as well, Richard?" Sam Tillinghast asked.

"Not officially at this time," Richard responded. "But I will be taking on added responsibilities."

There was a dutiful murmur of congratulatory voices around the table, but you could almost hear the Houston gears grinding as we tried to parse out what this really meant. The corporate world can be a strange place. The buttered tones in which such seismic shifts are usually announced reveal little about the motivations behind them. This was the kind of reshuffle we'd expect if Win Neuger had been promoted and Richard Scott had taken his job. But Richard's title wasn't changing — yet he seemed to be promoting Mercante into his own position. *Do we have two heads of Fixed Income now?*

I stared into my coffee cup, stirring, stirring. I was happy for Tim Janszen. He had been effectively running the High-Yield Group of late, and I'd recommended his promotion months before. Having managed the group for well over a decade, I had branched out con-siderably in recent years. As Head of Leveraged Finance, I now man-aged not only the Houston team, but the Workout Group in New York and the Bank Loan Group in Los Angeles as well. My respon-sibilities included not only maximizing all three groups' direct con-tributions to the company's bottom line but supervising the atten-dant administrative burdens as well: hiring and firing, compensation, compliance with SEC guidelines, interaction with other AIG depart-ments, attending interminable meetings in New York, and the care and feeding of young hotshots with outsized egos.

Nor had my work been limited to AIG's own balance sheet investments. The task of growing our investments and third-party fees, so dear to the heart of Win Neuger, had meant a great deal more travel in the United States and Europe, pitching our portfolio management prowess to insurance companies, pension funds, state funds—shops with portfolios of high-yield bonds or bank loans to manage and little or no in-house expertise. Soon we would be expanding these efforts to Asia. Being able to rely on Tim Janszen as I did allowed me to broaden my own contributions, and his promotion was, if anything, overdue.

Being sandwiched between Tim and Rich, though, was another matter. *Rich Mercante, Head of Fixed Income?* That meant I'd be reporting to him, instead of to Richard. Was I supposed to smile and act happy for this guy, like I was the runner-up at a beauty pageant? With another layer of management sliding in above me, I had just effectively been demoted. I had been Rich's peer, and now I would be his subordinate.

Why was this happening? What did it mean? If Mercante was AIG's new Head of Fixed Income, then, in any normal organizational chart, Tim Janszen of High-Yield, John Lapham of the LA Bank Loan Group, and Sam Tillinghast of Private Placements—all groups of comparable size and importance—should now all report directly to Mercante. If this logic was followed, the reshuffle would leave me with almost a non-job, swinging in the wind like a useless appendage. What then would my role be?

Houston financial people tended to get to work early, trickling in between 7:00 and 8:00 in the morning; you wanted to be at your desk when Wall Street was at theirs, and we were an hour behind New York. First thing the next morning, before my scheduled meeting with Rich Mercante at 9 a.m., I went in to see Richard Scott in the spare office he used on the thirty-sixth floor. "You've got to give me a better explanation as to what's really going on," I told him. "I need more details here." Richard knew I didn't like Rich Mercante. He knew as well as I did that in the corporate world, being sandwiched in the way that I had been marked you as someone who was on his way out. But Richard swore up and down that he was taking on broader responsibilities for Win Neuger and that he had to reduce the number of direct reports. Rich was the logical choice, Richard said. He's based in New York. And he's "an excellent manager of people. The folks on his team up here in New York love him."

"I have instructed Rich to oversee the High-Yield Group pretty much the same way I've been overseeing it," Richard told me. "This is a long overdue reorganization, Gordon. You have no reason whatsoever to be concerned."

But I *was* concerned, and I wanted Richard to know it. Yes, I had written that memo. I had called a foul on the top management of the Investment Department—chiefly Win Neuger, whom I saw as primarily responsible and for whom I had little respect. I could see how Win might want me ejected from the game. But by law, and by the AIG Code of Conduct, I was untouchable. There was no way they could retaliate against me and get away with it. Regulators were everywhere. Richard had been a lawyer. He knew the score. Just in case, though, I wanted to make sure Richard knew that I would be on the lookout for any forms of retaliation, subtle or not so subtle. I kept my tone casual as I got up to go. "It just feels to me like this might be related to my recent memo regarding the delayed write-downs," I said.

"Gordon," Richard said firmly, "this is not retaliatory in any way."

When you've worked with somebody for a while, you know that tone. *Don't argue with me on this. I'm not going to change my mind.*

And the truth was, I badly wanted to believe him. Richard *did* have too many managers reporting to him—as many as ten different departments, from all over the world. Getting his ear was becoming harder and harder. Richard worked hard and was smart and politically savvy. Senior management thought he was doing a great job, so they kept giving him more and more assignments. We all knew that Win Neuger was overworked and overwhelmed and needed any help he could get. Believing Richard meant that this re-organization had nothing to do with my memo—that I was just overreacting and that I really didn't have anything to get upset about. Other than that humiliating slip down the organizational chart, nothing had really changed. I was still responsible for the Leveraged Finance Group, wasn't I? Tim Janszen was still reporting to me, and we'd be working closely together on steering our high-yield portfolio and growing our business. The Bank Loan and Workout groups were still part of my domain. Richard had always overseen my Leveraged Finance Group with a great deal of latitude. If Rich Mercante was not going to change anything, I just needed to settle down, stop worrying, and get back to work. True, I was dubious about Rich's people-management skills. I had not seen them in evidence during my conflict with him over AIG's massive General Motors position. But who knows? I told myself. The people in New York who worked for Rich seemed to get along with him okay. I wanted to believe Richard, but I just didn't know what to think. These two quick promotions had effectively boxed me in, and everyone knew it.

My meeting with Richard over, I strolled casually out into the trading room, thoughts swirling madly in my head. It was not yet 9 a.m., but news of promotions travels fast. Last night's announcement was already common knowledge. Tom Reeg, a senior portfolio manager, and Mark Pauly, our head trader, both came over to me.

"Gordon," they chorused, almost in unison. "You just got screwed."

Everyone else was quiet, staring at their computer screens.

Chapter 14: Here Comes the New Boss

At 9 a.m. I went into my meeting with my new boss. Rich Mercante's tone was cold, condescending, and almost militarily businesslike. If I was hoping that an "excellent manager of people" might put aside past differences enough to greet his new subordinate with at least surface-level pleasantries, I was disappointed. He wanted reports on all of our portfolios, customers, performance data, Wall Street contacts, and on and on, and he wanted them on his desk in New York by Monday morning. The requests were reasonable, but the way Rich conveyed them was humiliating. I was the group's most senior manager, but Rich made me feel like his assistant clerk.

I went back to my office and sat down at my desk. The desk had once been Bob Devlin's. Promoted to become American General's CEO after Harold Hook retired, Devlin was reportedly among Houston's highest paid executives, earning over $40 million a year. After the merger with AIG, Devlin had largely moved his operations to New York, and I had inherited his furniture: a beautiful mahogany desk with a credenza supplying plenty of drawer space; a conference table, also mahogany, with four plush padded chairs; and a stately bookcase to match—a far cry from the rumpus room castoffs of a middle-class boy. I had a corner office on the thirty-seventh floor with a spectacular view of the Houston skyline. I managed billions of dollars of assets for one of the top five holders of high-yield bonds and bank loans in the world. We were on everybody's radar screen. I had the power and the institutional authority to change people's lives. Conversations among my staff stopped when I walked into the room.

AIG had lately reaffirmed my contributions to the company in the most convincing language the marketplace had at its disposal. I had specifically delayed the release of my whistleblower memo until several weeks after the bonuses for the year 2004 were paid, seeking to confirm my worth to AIG and to add an extra layer of protection against becoming the target for any retaliation. My cash bonus, awarded by Richard, had been $850,000—fifty thousand dollars over the maximum possible bonus payable to me by AIG's usually rigid formula. Adding in the values of my salary, restricted stock and option grants, my total compensation for that year was over two million dollars. "They just paid me fifty thousand dollars more than they had to," I thought. "Surely they couldn't have changed their minds so quickly."

Suddenly, though, I felt vulnerable. My value to the organization had, with a few smooth sentences from Richard, been questioned for all to see. Tom Reeg and Mark Pauly knew it. My whole staff must be talking. *Gordon's fall from grace.*

I walked out of my office. People's reaction to me seemed subtly changed. Once friendly faces now averted their gaze, seemingly preoccupied with other things. I felt as if I could see my humiliation reflected in their eyes. Other than "You got screwed" and a small, quiet comment or two from those who felt I was mistreated, I heard few words of encouragement or support. Most kept their distance. I felt like damaged goods. I had never quite realized how heavily my self-esteem was invested in my job and in my power base, which right now looked as wobbly as jello. My entire thirty-year career seemed at stake, and I felt the cold vise of dread. My own weakness surprised me. *Why was I not being tougher about this? Can't I fight back and win against an idiot like Mercante? What kind of man was I, anyway?* Maybe I was still living in a "Leave It to Beaver" world. My rumpus room fort was under siege, and I wasn't sure these patchy old pillows could survive the onslaught.

I had to be patient and see how this would play out. The moves that continued to undermine my confidence and position were small and cumulative. Rich would call Tim Janszen to discuss the strategy and tactics of the High-Yield Group going forward, conversations I was not privy to. My name was left off of Rich's emails. At first I thought it was just an innocent omission. "Hey, don't forget to include me on those emails."

"Oh yeah, yeah, my mistake."

But it happened again. And again. Meetings and conference calls would take place that I should have been informed about. I started thinking that this was no innocent mistake. Rich was bypassing me every chance he had. One day, less than a week after Rich's promotion, Tim Janszen told me that Rich had given one of our senior high-yield bond traders a raise. From Rich's point of view, this might have sounded like a simple thing. True, the employee was three rungs below him on the organizational chart, but hey, he liked the guy, he thought he was doing a good job, so he decided to give him a raise. From my point of view, though, Rich was not thinking like the stellar manager of people Richard claimed he was. First, the staff's compensation packages had just been finalized in April. If you started awarding off-cycle salary increases, you're likely to ruffle some feathers. We had two senior high-yield bond traders. Since they performed the same function and were about equally good, they were paid on par. If you awarded the first one a raise, how was the second one going to feel when he heard about it—as he will, sooner or later?

Second, if you wanted to give a high-yield staffer a raise, you should inform the Head of Leveraged Finance, rather than making him look like he didn't know what's going on in his own department. I certainly had no objection to anyone in the group making more money—I'd been the one who was advocating so consistently for pay raises all along. Rich had tossed out this largesse without informing or consulting me, without even having the time to identify the most valuable and deserving members of the team. Rich's new fiefdom included other fixed-income departments as well, but our High-Yield Group was the only province to receive such favor.

I couldn't help suspecting that Rich's raises—which Richard Scott had approved—seemed designed to portray Mercante as the new benevolent source of power, at the same time demonstrating how ineffective and politically inept all my efforts had been. *Gordon doesn't matter now. It's Mercante who counts.*

But was I sure? No, I wasn't sure. I wasn't sure of anything at that point.

I asked Richard Scott about Rich's maneuvers. Richard seemed surprised. He would talk to Rich, he said. He may have, but Rich's behavior didn't change. Rich operated out of New York, as Richard had, coming down for occasional on-site visits, but his management style was nothing like Richard's. Richard was strictly hands off. He conducted his due diligence, but he knew our track record. We clearly knew what we were doing. Rich, on the other hand, didn't hesitate to give buy/sell orders, re-weighting portfolios this way and that. His instructions often seemed capricious and impulsive to me. I wasn't sure Rich had ever cracked a financial statement on any of these companies he was trading. Yet Richard backed him up. "I'm very pleased with the long overdue changes Rich has initiated."

You seemed very pleased before Rich got here, too, I thought. *First time I'm hearing about long overdue changes.*

Slowly I started coming to terms with the fact that the High-Yield Group was being taken out of my hands. Tim had taken on supervision of the group's day-to-day tactical maneuvers. He was still going to report to me on the department's strategic direction, according to Richard's original announcement, but Mercante simply pushed me aside. As his underling, and absent any redirection from Richard, I was powerless to stop him. My involvement in the Los Angeles and New York groups was only part time. Both teams were very competent, their managers running them without a lot of day-to-day involvement from me. Our sales presentations and marketing activities had dropped considerably. With all of AIG's bad PR, we simply weren't making the final cut. Industry consultants read the *Wall Street Journal* articles about AIG's accounting issues and steered their asset management clients away from us. No longer was I traveling the United States and to Europe and landing the much-sought-after new accounts. Not only had I been demoted, pushed down a layer in the organization. I was rapidly becoming just an empty box in the organization chart.

My mind began playing tricks on me. *Whatever happened to the Teflon man?* They've planned this all along, I thought. How far up the ladder did this go? Did Win Neuger sign on to this? Might he even have orchestrated it? I had no way of knowing. In the past I wouldn't even have been surprised if these moves had the tacit agreement of Hank Greenberg, given his response when I'd dared to sell some AIG stock. But Hank had been gone for almost two months. The only level of management that I knew must be in on this was Richard Scott, who I strongly suspected as the source of these decisions. Nothing explicit, perhaps. Just a wink and a nod to Mercante. *You know, Gordon's been a thorn in my side. Why don't you deal with him.* After the battle of General Motors this would have been music to Rich's ears. *I would love to run this guy over. He's a pain in my ass, too.* I imagined him and Richard sniggering together behind closed doors, laying bets on how long I would last at AIG.

How could I shore up my position? I cast my mind about for allies. John Graf, my highly placed colleague who had gone around Richard Scott to intercede directly with Hank Greenberg on my behalf, might have headed off moves against me. But Graf and Greenberg were both gone. As for my staff, they seemed to keep their distance now. Phone calls were not returned as promptly as they once were. People just seemed unavailable. They might feel I got screwed, but this was the American work place. Nobody was going to pound the table and shout *foul*. What if I threatened to leave AIG and take all my accounts with me? Wouldn't losing a man who accomplished so much, and losing him at such an unstable time for AIG, strike a blow they'd be reluctant to sustain? *They didn't care*, I realized, with a sinking feeling. They knew our high-level clients wouldn't follow a one-man band. They didn't care what I had accomplished. They didn't care about my history with this company, my track record, the example they'd be setting for other loyal, hardworking employees by getting rid of me. That didn't matter to them. They just wanted me out. The assets I thought I had, the things I'd worked for that I thought they wanted to retain, weren't there! I felt lonely, abandoned. What happened to all that goodwill I tried to build? I thought. How could my power base erode so fast? I had no support, no allies, no political power. I was at the mercy of whatever Rich and Richard wanted to do to me. I was totally expendable.

The only thing I did at that point was to draw up an organization chart and my position on it before and after Richard's dinner announcement. As my feeling that something fishy was happening grew, I started jotting down entries on a sheet of paper as a way to jog my memory, just in case that should become necessary in the future.

Corporate reorg, see attached chart.

Left out of Wednesday staff meeting—no email from RM.

Raise given to senior trader w/o my knowledge

I noted the date and as much hard information as I could ascertain about each entry, which wasn't much. I could never be sure, in those early days, whether actions that felt so suspicious were somehow directed at me, or whether I was just imagining things. All I could do was write them down. I didn't need to note the emotions that went with them.

I had been used to stress. Life below investment grade was tricky. You had to think quickly, act fast, stay ahead of the game. High-yield was one side of the coin; high risk was the other. You can win big and lose big. Mistakes could cost tens of millions of dollars. But these were risks I could get a handle on. The moves were clear: buy, sell, hold. We took risks every day, but they were prudent risks. We were well diversified, did our homework, had a good team of analysts and an excellent track record. We were professionals. Certainly we made our mistakes, and those hurt. But we always had lots of positives to offset the negatives. I never doubted that we were doing the right thing.

This was a very different flavor of stress, an anxiety shot through with dread. My career was being ripped to shreds in a matter of weeks. I no longer felt I had any control over what was happening to my world. Every day became another endurance test of subtle personal jabs and public humiliation. My anxiety began to manifest itself physically. I couldn't relax. My head hurt, my stomach ached, and for the first time in my life I was sleeping poorly, waking up tired after nights of fitful unease.

I considered my options, more seriously this time. Should I quit? I had been with AGC and AIG for almost twenty years. I had recently turned 54. One more year and I'd be able to take early retirement. If I quit before then, I couldn't touch my pension until I was 65. Leaving AIG would cost me hundreds of thousands of dollars in unvested stock options, restricted stock and retirement benefits. And I wasn't ready to throw in the towel, dammit! I had built the Leveraged Finance Group into a well managed and highly successful investment team, one that consistently beat our benchmark index and was rapidly growing the size and number of the third-party portfolios we managed. We had hand-picked analysts, traders, and portfolio managers working together like a well-oiled machine. Mercante knew nothing about high-yield bonds, bank loans, workouts, emerging market debt, or distressed debt. Why should I walk away without a struggle? But what else could I do?

I shared all my worries with my wife, Barbara, who listened thoughtfully and had some wise advice of her own. "Maybe you've been working in Houston too long," she said. "You need some new co-workers and new challenges." From the time American General was acquired by AIG, she reminded me that Richard Scott had wanted me to follow him to New York. He knew he could rely on me to get things done. I would be a valuable asset in Richard's own ambitious plans. He had been complaining for years about the lack of management talent at AIG's Investment Department in New York.

But I had never wanted to make the move. Thanks to early successes, I found myself well compensated. Holding the position I did at a firm the size of AIG, I was near the top of the heap in Houston. Jumping ship to the financial world of Wall Street would mean relocating my family from The Woodlands to a place like Westchester County and commuting into lower Manhattan every day. I didn't see that as a value trade-off. The pace in New York had never appealed to me. But now our two oldest children had flown the nest for college and graduate school, and only our youngest, Hunter, was left at home. He would be heading off to college in two years and was pretty much self-sufficient. Barbara, who had never been one to leave our kids to come with me on my business trips, had begun to accompany me more often, with Hunter staying in Houston with friends. We had a wonderful trip together to Prague for an AIG conference there, and she liked the idea of a little more travel in our lives.

It was time, Barbara suggested, to consider relocating my work life to New York. I needed a change of scenery in my career and the company headquarters at 70 Pine Street might be just the place. I was a generation older than most of my Houston staff. We were like a major league ball club, a bunch of young hotshots and a grizzled old coach. The mid-level people, well trained and underpaid at AIG, were typically picked off by other companies, who preyed aggressively on our staff. In New York I would be working with older and more experienced people and could work my way up through the senior ranks at AIG.

Barbara originally hailed from Valhalla, New York, near White Plains, and her sister lived in upstate New York. She liked the idea of being up there more often. "We'll be fine," Barbara said. "You can come home on the weekend, or I can come up to New York. You and I can have some great little trips."

So I offered up an olive branch to Richard Scott and Rich Mercante. Recognizing that the scope of my work in Houston was now limited, I offered to work out of AIG's lower Manhattan offices. I would retain my position as the Head of the Leveraged Finance group (albeit in a reduced capacity, given Rich's bypassing tactics). I could also take on some additional responsibilities in New York, handling some of Richard's excess work load. I would agree to be in New York five days a week, and I asked that AIG fly me home on weekends. I outlined my ideas in a written proposal to both Richard and Rich. It seemed like a sensible solution to me. I figured I would stick it out until February 2006, when I turned 55. Who knew? Maybe it would even work out well, and I would agree to re-locate to New York permanently.

Both Richard and Rich responded very positively to my proposal. Rich called and told me it was a "breath of fresh air." Richard read the memo and asked that I fly up to New York the next day to discuss with him over lunch exactly how this assignment would work and what my added responsibilities would entail. So off to the airport I went. During the entire flight I sat silently absorbed in my thoughts about AIG and my career. Things had definitely changed for the worse. But I felt that the situation could be salvaged. I was ready to take on new responsibilities. I found myself looking forward to my lunch with Richard.

My cab from La Guardia brought me directly to Delmonico's, a swanky New York eatery a few blocks off Wall Street. Richard was pleasant and cordial, and a quiet alcove made for easier conversation. He seemed genuinely enthusiastic about my relocation proposal, and talk quickly turned to a list of specific assignments he had for me. AIG was then considering the purchase of a large commercial bank in China, Richard said. He wouldn't name the bank yet, but he would need their loan portfolio scrutinized. Richard also wanted the overall controls on the purchase of corporate debt by AIG to be reviewed and evaluated. Since group compensation had always been an issue with me, Richard wanted me to take a comprehensive look at AIG's competitiveness in the marketplace for investment talent. Richard also mentioned the success I had had with the Wall Street marketing initiatives. Yes, I would continue my involvement in this area. He again commented on the success of the credit conference I had organized, and asked that I take the lead for a similar conference upcoming in the fall. We touched on things I might do to improve the overall quality and consistency of the credit analysis work throughout all of AIG. We even talked about office space. He hoped an office would soon be available near his, Richard said, since we would be working closely together.

The lunch went as well as I had hoped. Richard even ordered wine as a celebratory gesture. Looking around at the rich mahogany décor, plush red carpet, and tables packed with the Wall Street power brokers and deal-doers, I could envision being part of this world of wealth and privilege. It all seemed to be coming together. Though no real fan of New York City, I was intrigued by the excitement and challenges of working here, and it really did seem like the next logical move upward in my career. Perhaps Barbara was right, as she usually was. I had been working out of Houston for thirty years and I was ready for a change. Richard's warm reception suggested that maybe I had overreacted to the recent organizational changes and that I would be genuinely welcomed in New York. Or did they just want me out of Houston, away from what was left of my power base? This was the main question that I pondered as I left the restaurant. Was Richard leveling with me? Could I trust him and Rich Mercante to let bygones be bygones and throw ourselves into the work that needed to be done? I wasn't a hundred percent sure. But I *wanted* to believe them. I could feel my mental pendulum swinging from despair and fear toward a new sense of enthusiasm and opportunity.

The meeting with Richard was so positive that I stayed on to look for an apartment in Manhattan. Conventional wisdom suggested heading uptown. I opted to head south instead, and after a couple of days I found a furnished one-bedroom "luxury suite" at the Liberty View apartments, near the southern tip of Manhattan. I was just off the esplanade and the green-lawned stretches of Battery Park. The streets were peaceful after hours and lined with trees. The rent for this tiny kingdom was $6,000 a month. The cost didn't trouble me too much, as AIG was picking up the tab. What with my rent, weekly airfares, limo rides to and from the airport, and living expenses, I figured AIG would be shelling out almost $10,000 extra per month just to have me in New York. The tight-fisted folks in Human Resources granted all of my initial reimbursement requests swiftly and without a hitch. A good sign, I thought. They had to want me, right? Why would any organization agree to spend almost $10,000 more a month—$120,000 a year—on an employee they no longer valued?

During that New York visit I also asked Richard's assistant, Ursula, to see if a meeting with Win Neuger was possible. I wanted a direct sense. How did Win feel about my move to New York? Did I have any reason to suspect a further undermining of my position?

Win made time available for me, and he, too, was engaging and cordial. He was enthusiastic about this new assignment, he said, and welcomed me to New York.

Richard and Win's reception gave me a surge of confidence. I felt that I had made the best of a bad situation. Even if things turned out differently than planned, I was still sure I could last the nine months until my 55th birthday. Barbara, who had never fully embraced Houston as her home, was excited about the possibility of moving to New York permanently. I was even cautiously optimistic about the future of AIG. Now that Hank Greenberg was gone, no one really knew what future lay in store for us. Hank's successor, Martin Sullivan, seemed well regarded. Maybe he could provide the kind of leadership and vision that AIG so badly needed. Maybe we could change our culture for the better. We could adopt some real organizational controls and put all these accounting issues behind us. We wouldn't need to be the biggest and slowest—or the sneakiest—kid on the playground any more. Maybe this behemoth could nurture and retain some real talent at the highest management levels. I even imagined, in my dreamland future, that there might be a significant senior management role for me.

I was to start in New York on June 1. On Sunday afternoon, May 31, 2005, I boarded a Continental flight to La Guardia airport. Taking the solitary limo drive to my new and rather sterile little place in Battery Park, I needed to convince myself one more time that I had made the right decision. I was already missing Barbara and the family. But I had a job to do, and I was going to report to work first thing tomorrow morning with a bright and positive attitude. I was determined to make this assignment work for me and AIG.

Chapter 15: "You Pissed Off the Wrong People"

"Beware of all enterprises that require new clothes," Thoreau wrote, "and not rather a new wearer of clothes." I was determined to bring new enterprise and enthusiasm to my AIG situation, but Barbara thought I needed to beef up my wardrobe first. Our Houston office had gone casual right after Harold Hook retired from American General in 1997. The former Sun America team in Los Angeles was similarly laid back. I always considered this a no-cost employee benefit. People just seemed to loosen up when you went from suits to casual attire, and I saw no evidence that they took their work a whit less seriously. But AIG in New York required business suits every day, had done so for decades, and I had to comply. Barbara was excited. She had always liked a man in a suit and was delighted to take me shopping for a couple of new ones in the days leading up to my new assignment. She was excited by my new opportunity in New York and wanted me looking my best. I tolerated the fittings but felt ill at ease. I thought I had enough suits for now. I felt uncomfortable about buying more until I knew I was really welcome in New York. If I wasn't, all these new clothes would mean nothing. How did I know I wasn't spending all this money for what might turn out to be a burial suit?

By contrast, being able to walk to work in New York, after my daily seventy-mile round trip in Houston, was a true pleasure. The walk from Battery Park to AIG's offices at 70 Pine St. was a real slice of New York City reality, and I immediately began the practice of taking a different route every day. I could walk along the Hudson River, past parks and museums, along narrow, bending, lower-Manhattan streets, past cafés and ancient churches, and onward through the canyons of Wall Street. Here was an opportunity to see the true variety of life in lower Manhattan, to experience some of life's daily joys away from the office and the stressful daily pressures of the financial world.

As I walked in that first morning, wearing one of the new suits I'd bought with Barbara, I thought back to many other first days on the job. I remembered how excited Julia Tucker had been to welcome me to American General, twenty years ago now, in 1985. My new AGC co-workers had treated me to lunch. Eighteen years before that, even the con man, Billy Knox, had spent an hour or so showing me the ropes around the Chevron station. As the new kid back then, of course, I had to be prepared to endure a little hazing. "Guess who gets to clean the restrooms now?" Billy joked. After all these years, and as well as I knew AIG's New York offices, I still felt nervous and uncertain at the prospect of a first day on the job. But I'd always been welcomed warmly before, and my meetings with Richard and Win had given me reason to hope I'd get a similar reception today.

I quickly found out how wrong I was. When Ursula, Richard's assistant, ushered me to my new office, my heart sank. I had expected my New York digs to be smaller and more basic than my Houston domain, but I wasn't quite prepared for what I found. The office was tiny, a cubicle with walls. Its rudimentary metal furnishings seemed especially cold and cheerless after the warm and elegant mahogany of Houston. A single-paned window looked over an alley, where I would watch the grimy garbage trucks trudging along in the morning, picking up yesterday's piles of waste. Across the alley, a drab, gray stone building seemed to reflect back to me my newly shaken self-esteem. "Sorry about this," Ursula said, and left without further explanation.

I said nothing and moved in. My first office would be temporary, Richard had assured me during our recent lunch. He never did say another word about my office. Nor did he ever wander down the corridors to find me.

Or perhaps he got lost trying. I was on the same floor as the Investment Department but quite remote from the center of activity, especially the offices of Richard Scott and Rich Mercante. Most of the offices around me were empty. Nobody walked me around and introduced me to my co-workers. Nobody asked me to lunch. It was as though I had somehow snuck onto the premises, and no one knew I was here. It was not difficult to read the expressions of the very few people who eventually found their way to my corner of the world. I was in no man's land.

For the first week at AIG I had one telephone line and no computer. My office supplies consisted of what the prior tenant had so kindly left behind. I inquired about receiving my own daily copy of the *Wall Street Journal*, like almost everyone else in the Investment Department in New York. Richard would have to approve my request, Ursula told me, but that approval never materialized. For the first week my employee passcard to the men's room door worked only sporadically. Why not wait for another male employee to go in or out? Ursula suggested. So I often found myself lurking about the men's room door, sometimes doing the bathroom dance, waiting for someone else's nature to call.

I felt so small, so insignificant, so humiliated during that first week. I considered raising a fuss, but I already felt uneasy enough. Angry, too. *I am not going to give in to their childish behavior*, I thought grimly. *Okay, they want to humiliate me. I can take it.* I was, I knew, alone in this fight. But I was determined to contribute to this organization, regardless of the size of my work space. I had my Houston and Los Angeles work to keep me busy until Richard could involve me in his new assignments. I refused to compromise my positive mental attitude over this disturbing introduction to AIG New York.

Life that first week was solitary indeed. In the evenings I would wend my way home, taking a different route each time. I was in no hurry to return to my lonely apartment. From my tiny terrace on the seventeenth floor I would gaze out over Manhattan's busy West Side Highway, listening to the twenty-four-hour bustle of this massive city. It was so much noisier than I was used to in the quiet Woodlands at home, but comforting, too, to a lonely man—comforting or occasionally disturbing, when late-night sirens screamed in the distance.

In the evenings I would call Barbara and tell her how lonely and isolated I felt. Barbara urged me not to be discouraged. "You're the new guy, you've just moved in, but you're a senior person now," she reminded me. "It's not like when you first came down to Houston for Texas Commerce Bank, where a bunch of you were in that credit training group. You were all young, just starting out. Everyone was looking to meet new people, and you all had fun. Now everybody's got their life and their little niche. Everybody's set in their positions. Maybe it's just going to take a while. Folks in New York are not as friendly as they are down here, at first."

She was right. One compelling advantage to being in New York was being able to meet and speak face-to-face with so many people from AIG that I had only spoken to on the phone or met briefly in the past. Everyone was right here at 70 Pine Street in lower Manhattan. And if they would not take the initiative with me, I could still take the initiative with them.

I thought of my father. Dad was one of the most gregarious men I ever knew. He had a real estate business, and the secret to his success was how comfortable he was with people. He was president of the Rotary Club, played a lot of tennis, was active in the country club. He knew everyone, and everyone knew him, and when people needed to sell their house, who did they think of? Why, they thought of Stan Massie. I was very shy as a child, but my father always used to impress upon me the importance of meeting and socializing and conversing with people. "Give 'em a good handshake, look 'em in the eye. *Engage* them. Don't just yammer on about yourself. Ask them about themselves." He'd say this all the time. "If they have a Rotary pin on their lapel, ask them about their rotary pin. If you know they went to a particular university, ask them about their football team that year." Dad never knew a stranger. As I grew older, a little more sure of myself, more outgoing with people, I modeled myself after him.

So I started smiling and dialing. During the next couple of months I took numerous people to lunch. My Roledex files were full of human resource people, legal staff, marketing professionals, investment-grade credit analysts, treasury people, members of the Workout Group, Sun America mutual-fund staff, mortgage-backed securities guys, people I had known from American General in Houston, and loads of Wall Street contacts. I reached out to them all. I did not know what they knew about my whistleblowing memo, but I was going to sit down with them one-on-one and let them get to know me for themselves. I was going to demonstrate to AIG that in spite of our differences I could rise above these humiliations and build relationships within the organization.

Few within the company ever reciprocated. Were New Yorkers just a tough group to get to know? Was I tainted goods? Were they afraid to associate with me? Could Richard be powerful enough to declare me off limits? Or was I just expecting too much? I had no way of knowing.

After three weeks I had heard nothing from Richard about the myriad of new responsibilities we had previously discussed. I contacted his assistant, Ursula, and explained that I wanted to discuss these new assignments. Richard has a window available in two days, Ursula told me. She'd set up an appointment for me to see him then. Two days? I was taken aback. Whenever Richard had come to Houston, or during my frequent visits to New York, I had always been able to see him on a moment's notice. Now I had to wait two days?

When my appointment with Richard came around he did not seem to know what I was doing in his office. "So, Gordon, tell me again why you wanted to schedule this meeting," he said brusquely. "As you can see, I am very busy." This, too, was strange. In the past Richard was typically well prepared for any topic I wished to discuss.

I dutifully went down the list of previously discussed assignments. "Look, I only have a few minutes," Richard cut in impatiently. "If you want to get involved, take a look at this." He plucked a file from the chaos atop his back credenza and handed it to me. I flipped through it quickly. The file was in complete disarray. After a minute Richard stood up and acted as though he was about to leave. His eyes refused to meet mine. I took the hint and the messy file and returned to my office.

The file consisted of a random set of documents pertaining to what appeared to be early discussions between AIG and the unnamed state bank in China. There were some scattered financial statements and a few bits of correspondence. Nothing to really study and opine on. Two days later I saw Richard in the hallway and mentioned the file. "Forget about it," Richard said abruptly. "I have John Chu working on it now."

That was the last conversation I had with Richard about my new assignments. When I broached the subject on several subsequent occasions, Richard would scowl as if I had said something inappropriate, then change the subject. Despite our friendly and substantive conversation when I first proposed coming to New York, it was now becoming obvious to me that the authority I had lost would never be replaced, and that Richard had no intention of involving me in any new projects. I felt disgusted with myself. How could I have been so gullible?

Yet I was still uncertain. How could compliance with a code of ethics warrant this kind of response, and on such a high level? Could they have actually sat down and planned this? I tried to reconstruct the conversation that might have taken place. The suggestion that I come to New York was mine. They jumped on it, made it sound like a great idea, came up with a list of solid reasons for me to move my operations up here ... and then, nothing. What might they have been thinking? *This is interesting. Getting Gordon out of Houston could work to our advantage. He's too independent down there, got too much of a power base. Let's have him come to New York. That way we'll have more control. Let's see how this plays out.*

If Richard simply ignored me, Rich Mercante was much more businesslike. His assistant called me and said Rich wanted to see me in his office in twenty minutes. Our first meeting turned out to be an opportunity to watch a power play in action. When I appeared at Rich's door twenty minutes later, he told me to wait outside his office. Ten minutes later his assistant called me in, and I seated myself across from Rich's mahogany desk. Again, Rich wasted no time on pleasantries. He had only one question, which he delivered in icy tones. "I want to know why the Workout Group should continue to report to you and remain part of the Leveraged Finance Group."

I understood Rich's sudden question all too clearly. *Tell me why I shouldn't take this group away from you.* Startled as I was, though, the reasons were not hard to come up with.

Imagine that we in high-yield were holding a significant position in a company that had gotten itself deeper and deeper into financial trouble and finally filed for bankruptcy. Our holdings were hardly risk-free, after all; about two or three percent of them, on average, would default every year. One of our analysts would, of course, have been following the case all along, but the fall in the company's fortunes would now put that investment into the hands of the Workout team. Bankruptcy dragged a host of activity in its wake: committees, meetings, endless legal haggling back and forth. We always had the option to sell that bond position. The question was when. Sell now, and recover only pennies on the dollar? Or wait and see whether the company will recover, risking an even greater loss if it doesn't? The three people on the workout team would be tracking ten or fifteen such companies through the bankruptcy process at any given time. The decision to sell would still be in the hands of the high-yield analyst, so the workout guy would keep him closely posted. "This is going to go on forever," the workout guy might say. "I don't see any value here. We might get two or three cents on dollar, but it will take us five years. If we unloaded this position now, though, we'd get eight cents on dollar, so maybe we should go ahead and sell." Despite the handoff from high-yield to workout, then, the two teams still needed to work closely together until the situation was resolved. Moving the Workout Group into another department made no sense.

That wasn't good enough for Rich. He knew my status at AIG was gravely weakened and seemed hell-bent on reducing it further if he could. Until that happened, though, he could have a little fun at my expense. I want you to write me a memo, he said, that fully documents all the reasons the Workout Group should continue to report to you—and all the reasons that it shouldn't. The very suggestion was infuriating. Richard Scott had brought the Workout Group under my command only a year and a half earlier. Given how closely we worked together, it had been a wise decision, and there was no logical reason to change it. I had little choice in the matter, though, and I delivered a three-page document to Rich two days later. This wasn't good enough, Rich said. You haven't given a fair hearing to both sides of the issue. You'll need to rewrite it. Rich was treating me like a first-year college student who couldn't write a proper essay to meet his lofty standards. But again, I had no choice but to comply.

In the meantime, Mercante was taking every opportunity to bypass me as Head of Leveraged Finance and deal directly with my subordinates, and he apparently allowed those dealings to stray beyond the strict confines of business. Not long after I arrived in New York, Tim Janszen called me. He was concerned. "Rich has been walking all over you, Gordon," he said. "He's made some pretty nasty remarks. He said you really pissed off the wrong people." Tim didn't needed to specify *how* I pissed those people off; I had told him about my memo. He hated to say it, Tim said, but I might want to think about freshening up my résumé and getting it out there. Even if I stuck around at AIG, he said, it didn't look like I had much of a career left.

After all the uncertainty I'd been feeling, this was a harsh dose of reality. I'd been expecting it, but it really hurt me badly. I liked Tim and trusted him. I had never felt any reason to doubt his word. But his call confirmed to me that my job was evaporating before my eyes. I wasn't ready to lose this fight, though. I had done nothing wrong, and I wasn't going to crater this easily. Caving in to AIG was tantamount to an admission of guilt or defeat, and I wasn't going to lose at their game. They were going to have to fire me. This retaliation was another AIG crime on top of the original AIG crime of accounting fraud. I refused to be another victim.

My life up here in the City, on my own, increasingly became one of anger, frustration, and loneliness. Even occasional visits by friends and family couldn't cheer me up for long. I met close friends from Houston in Little Italy one evening for dinner, but I couldn't shake my dark mood or muster up anything positive to say about my work here. Barbara flew up for a weekend in June with our two sons and a friend. We all stayed together, crammed into my little apartment, the youngsters tiptoeing through our bedroom at night to get to the bathroom. We took in a show and walked around lower Manhattan. At some point we found ourselves on Pine Street. "There's my building," I said.

"Let's go up!" Barbara said at once.

"Nooo, you don't want to see my office," I said. "It's nothing. Really."

"We do!" they chorused. "We really want to see it." Visiting Dad's office had been a part of my kids' childhood. I had always been proud to take my family up to where I worked. I'd walk them all over the building, introduce them to everybody, take them to the storeroom and let them pick out pencils and pens for themselves. But this time I refused. Their visit meant more to me than I could express, but I did not want them to see how far I had fallen.

Sometimes, after weekends at home, I would stay on to work out of the Houston office, fulfilling my responsibilities to the High-Yield Group. One standard reason to be there were the visits from Richard and now Rich, every six weeks or so, to review all of our recently purchased high-yield bonds. (The presence of both men was a bit of a mystery. The changes in the organization chart that Richard announced suggested that Rich would head up these reviews himself. In fact, Richard made no discernible changes in his work patterns, and continued to show up when it was time for our reviews.) On this particular visit, their usual entourage included Don McHugh, the Head of Credit Analysis for Rich's Investment Grade team.

The review took two or three hours, with ten or so of us seated around the table in the large glassed-in conference room. When the review was over, Richard asked everyone to stay in the room for an important announcement. "I am pleased to report that all members of the Workout Team will now be reporting directly to Don McHugh."

I actually felt this announcement physically. A sharp pain shot through my gut. Unlike Richard's first such announcement, the implications of which took some time to sort out, this time my public humiliation was too obvious to ignore. I was being stripped of more responsibilities right in front of my Houston staff, like a disgraced officer having his insignia ripped off in front of the entire company. I had not been informed ahead of time. I had heard no further discussion of the memo I had written and rewritten for Rich. A line like "Gordon will be taking on other responsibilities," as untrue as it was, could have eased my shame, but clearly these boys didn't play that way. I looked over at Richard and Rich and could imagine the glint in their eyes. *We got you now.* I felt like the skinny kid on the playground the bullies abused just for the fun of it.

On the playground, of course, a friend might stand up for you. Doing the right thing was simpler then; you might earn a bloody nose, but you didn't yet have a job to lose. By the time we reach the working world, things have changed. We're reduced to just watching such things happen, paralyzed by fear, praying we can stay out of the fray. Everyone in the room knew how stupid this reassignment was. Don McHugh had been an investment-grade guy his entire working life. He knew nothing about bankruptcies, for the simple reason that investment-grade companies rarely went bankrupt without falling into the below-investment-grade category first. The high-yield and workout teams therefore interacted closely on almost all bankruptcies. In the corporate world, needless to say, no one was going to point out how ridiculous this re-organization was. We were not on the playground any more.

I understood this. In here, you can be humiliated in a way that would be unthinkable in the street right outside the building, but no one will come to your aid. What upset me was how few people came to me quietly, in private, to express some kind of regret at the way I was being treated. This was my team. I had done so much to hire them, train them, promote them, fight for their compensation, befriend them. I knew all the reasonable explanations for their silence, but—almost five years later now—it still hurts me to think about it.

The following Monday back in New York I asked Ursula for another one-on-one meeting with Richard. This time I got in to see him right away. I asked Richard to explain the logic of this recent move, and he was ready with his answer. He told me in no uncertain terms that I was no longer adding any value to AIG. I was "too far removed from the marketplace," he said. I just was no longer on top of the minute-by-minute changes in the financial markets that I covered, the buy-and-sell decisions that make the difference between an average portfolio and an outstanding one.

This cut me to the core. Richard and I had had conversations about just this point, and he knew it. As my responsibilities expanded well beyond the High-Yield Group, I had checked in with him to make sure I had my priorities right.

"Richard, you realize that if you want me to come to New York for five days for a conference, that's five days I'm away from the marketplace. If you want me to go marketing in Europe for a week, that's a week away from the marketplace. I can't be up-to-the-minute on the high-yield market if I'm discussing bank loans in L.A."

His response was always decisive. "I fully understand. This is part of your job. This is part of your maturation as a senior manager of AIG." He made it very clear that I had his understanding and endorsement of the growing range of my responsibilities. For him to then turn around and say, "You're too far from the marketplace" was therefore especially cruel.

Richard added another charge. I was entirely too confrontational with him and with others, he said. Here, too—especially given all my efforts to reach out to the staff of AIG New York—I was at a loss as to what confrontations Richard was referring to, other than the one with Rich Mercante about General Motors. Certainly I'd always been persistent in advocating for adequate compensation for my staff, but that had never risen to the level of confrontation since AIG bought American General four years before. Once that issue was resolved it never came up again.

I thought I knew what was really bothering Richard. *Gordon's in New York, but he's not playing the game like we want him to. He's still not our boy yet. He's still agitating about compensation, still chafing at what Rich is doing to him. Let's make him unhappy. Let's just see if we can get him to storm out voluntarily."*

As troubling as all this was, I thought the facts, and my record, were on my side. I reminded Richard of the long list of things he had previously commended me for: the excellent results since I had taken over the combined AIG/American General high-yield bond portfolio, the success of the bank loan group, the growth in third-party assets, the credit conference, the Wall Street marketing initiatives, my promotions, my raises, my bonuses, the invitation to participate in AIG's exclusive Starr International (SICO) partnership. Richard dismissed them all.

"None of that matters now if we have serious concerns about your confrontational style going forward," he said. "Oh, and with regard to the next Credit Conference, Don McHugh will be running the conference next Fall. You can help if you want, but it's Don's show."

For the next few months the retaliation continued unabated. After a while it seemed like AIG was paying me a sizable amount of compensation and $120,000 extra a year to keep me in New York just so they could publicly humiliate me. *Talk about a waste of shareholder assets*, I thought. Richard seemed to enjoy such "Oh, by the way" comments as a way of stripping me of another area of responsibility. Oh, by the way, he told me in a subsequent meeting, I was no longer going to be involved in any Wall Street marketing activities. This brought to an end another important and challenging chunk of my work for AIG.

August 8, 2005, two months after I moved up to New York, was my twentieth anniversary with the company. I had been sixteen years with American General, four with AIG, but they always looked at the total. Since there was such high turnover at AIG, very few people made it as far as their fifth year, and a twentieth anniversary was an extremely rare event. Any significant milestone like that was celebrated like a birthday. The employee could select a gift from a catalogue, and a cake was brought in with a candle for each year. The employee was publicly recognized for their service, their gift presented by their supervisor, and the cake was shared by all. Given recent events, I knew better than to expect anything, and that was what I got. My anniversary wasn't even noted in the company newsletter. A crystal lamp that Barbara had selected from the catalogue was forwarded to my home in Houston. As far as any public recognition for twenty years of service was concerned, the day came and went without a whisper.

What did all this mean? What was AIG really communicating to me but also to my fellow associates? The message was clear. Don't mess with entrenched power. It really didn't matter what you contributed unless you paid proper homage to the powers that be. AIG was spending hundreds of thousands of dollars solely to humiliate me, and this was fully endorsed by top management. All expenditures of this amount had to be approved by top management. I believed I was the example for everyone thinking about being a whistleblower in the future. Don't do it or you will end up like Gordon. Socially and professionally ostracized, publicly humiliated, and left stripped of all responsibilities and dignity. Although I tried to maintain my innocence and self worth, four months of retaliation had truly taken its toll. I had never really experienced profound anxiety until now. I was clinically depressed (I would later learn) and I was suffering from an array of negative feelings including shame, guilt, remorse and deep sadness. In spite of my defenses, I was breaking down and starting to believe that I must have truly done something wrong. Otherwise how could anyone explain this treatment of me. I had once been a proud and productive employee and now I was reduced to shambles. I couldn't face my friends, my family, or my co-workers without a deep sense of shame and loss.

But what could I do? What were all these laws protecting whistleblowers? Did I really have a case for retaliation? I knew it was retaliation but how could I prove it? AIG was certainly not the kind of organization that would admit to anything like retaliation. I had a huge case to prove and a very formidable opponent. The crux of the problem in being a whistleblower was that any company which sought retaliation can so easily mask any act of retaliation. There were always going to be other plausible reasons given by a company for what may have appeared as retaliation. As Richard told me, "This is just a long overdue corporate reorganization." How do I disprove that? Does a tiny office and no lunchmates rise to the level of retaliation? Does being moved from one assignment to another constitute retaliation? Hopefully, you can see the problem here. All of these subtle and not so subtle forms of retaliation can be glibly explained away as simply an over active imagination on the part of the claimant. I can hear AIG saying in a court of law, "We simply treat people differently in New York than in Houston and we apparently hurt Mr. Massie's feelings." How can I prove this retaliation? How can I gain the confidence to file a case for retaliation since I was clearly burning any bridge of returning to AIG if I failed. And even if one can prove that bad things were done, a company like AIG can easily attribute these acts to some type of offenses committed by the employee. Did I incorrectly submit some bill on an expense account? Did I pull up a personal web site on company time? Was I really a "perennial malcontent" as Richard had alleged? Or there is also the frequently used "reduction in staff" excuse for terminations. If you blow the whistle, especially in today's economy, don't you think that you have just moved yourself to the top of the next list of those to be laid off? "We are not retaliating against you, we are just downsizing."

Corporate America needs whistleblowers to police the inner world of corruption. We can't rely on the SEC or the Justice Department or any other regulator to accurately monitor what goes on behind closed office doors in corporate America. That's an impossible job for any regulators. Insiders are our best source of information about true corporate fraud and corruption and yet these insiders are the most vulnerable to retaliation. Most people are scared to death to come forward and it is nearly impossible to remain anonymous. Rick Causey is not an evil human being but he found himself in very evil circumstances. I thought I was doing the right thing and I was naive enough to actually believe that I was safe. AIG threw me to the wolves like a sacrificial lamb and there was no organization on earth that needed whistleblowers more than AIG. It was my opinion that AIG was corrupt to its core because all of this retaliation required the full endorsement of top management. AIG's actions in my opinion were clear violations of the law and no one cared. What other laws was top management so willing to easily violate? In my opinion, anything they could get away with. Entrenched management at AIG wanted absolute and unquestioned power. Doing the right thing for shareholders was not part of their vocabulary. In spite of my twenty years of loyalty and successes, I was destroyed because I questioned this power.

Filing a claim of retaliation with the Department of Labor was a possible avenue for me to pursue. But again this was a one way street. I had to have a strong case to win because if I lost that would be the end of my career at AIG and possibly in the industry. And who were these bureaucrats at the Department of Labor? I may have thought I had a great case but would the DOL pursue it? Were they already overloaded? Were they in AIG's pocket? I knew in my heart what was going on, but I still did not have the confidence of knowing I had a solid case. I really did not see anyway out of this mess, short of simply enduring the ongoing humiliation until I was ultimately fired for some trumped up reason. Yes, I could go public with my allegations. Since AIG was still prominent in the news, an announcement that one of their long term, senior investment people had filed a grievance with the DOL alleging retaliation by AIG could be very newsworthy and powerful. But again, this was a one way street. This could bring very negative publicity to AIG and perhaps put downward pressure on the stock. Maybe such a public allegation could force a settlement from AIG but it would also destroy whatever was left of my career. And I still was not convinced I had a provable case, nor was I aware of how enthusiastically the DOL would pursue my case.

It was clearly this point of indecision, and the constant stirring of my frustrations that lead to the first full-blown case of anxiety I had ever experienced. Sure I had experienced temporary anxiety prior to public speaking or college exams but this was different. This was the constant playing and re-playing of the same tapes in my mind. The way things were versus the way they were supposed to be. These were the tapes of humiliation, embarrassment, frustration at the childish behavior of AIG, shame, guilt, remorse, and indecision. It was an all consuming form of anxiety that permeated every waking moment. I tried to take quiet walks along the Hudson River and I savored my weekends with my beloved family but nothing, absolutely nothing could put an end to this anxiety and the accompanying deep sense of sadness and loss. This anxiety became debilitating. I was suffering from chronic headaches, I had no energy, and my overall interest in life was fading. This couldn't go on. I had to find a way out of this toxic environment.

Chapter 16: Brewer's Yeast

By now it was September of 2005, and the warm and humid New York summer was giving way to the cooler, crisper days of Fall. The atmosphere of AIG was still toxic and oppressive. My depression was growing. Every day—every hour—I pursued my mental countdown. "Six more months of this hell. Only six more months. Six more months." I wasn't sure I could make it to February. Convincing myself that I could became a personal mission.

I fought back with my feet. Getting out of the office and walking was a simple, pleasant distraction. It helped me feel normal again, if only briefly. The rush of traffic and throngs of people in the streets of lower Manhattan felt warming to my soul, reminding me of the way life was before all this sadness. New York was so vibrant, so busy and diverse. There was so much about the city to enjoy and appreciate: the festive Seaport Plaza with all the historic ships at harbor, the quaint shops and secluded cafes, the street merchants and tourists, ancient buildings and interesting landmarks. I would walk streets like Liberty and Fulton, gazing through shop windows and enjoying the hubbub of human activity. Or I would stroll over toward the site of the World Trade Center. There, for a brief moment, my sadness was replaced by the knowledge of how much others had lost at this same site only four years before. Standing at Ground Zero in silence, gazing into that great cavernous hole in the ground, always helped me to put my own loss in perspective. Almost without fail I would be asked by some giddy tourists to take their photograph in front of this catastrophic backdrop. Looking at their happy faces through the viewfinder I thought, life does go on. We can forget our hurts, forget our sadness.

At AIG my workload had been reduced to little, if any, meaningful work. Seventy percent of my responsibilities were gone. The silence in my empty corner of the world was deafening. My day began with my morning coffee and a thorough reading of a borrowed copy of the *Wall Street Journal*. I checked my emails, maybe returned a phone call or two. Nothing else relieved the silence and the empty schedule. Nobody ever strolled by or initiated a conversation. It was as if I had become invisible. After three months of initiating lunches with others, who rarely reciprocated in any way, I stopped trying. I would take an early lunch by myself, adding an hour or so for my midday stroll. Yes, I felt guilty about it, but I would be no more productive just sitting back at my lonely desk. Returning to the office after my walk, I would check emails again, return another few calls, find ways to squander the rest of the afternoon. Any experience of strategic disagreement or personal conflict was gone. In its place was . . . nothing. The humiliation I had endured had failed to drive me out. There now seemed nothing else they could take away from me. Now perhaps the tactic was "Let's bore him to death." If so, it was working. I told myself that I could take this boredom for another six months, but it was driving me crazy. I had been a busy and productive person all my life, and this emptiness was nearly impossible for me to endure. But from boredom can come creativity, and I was formulating my legal options.

During this period I received a phone call from an old friend, Leon Wagner. Leon was a new principal in a successful investment management/hedge fund called Goldentree Asset Management in New York. Goldentree had been managing about $50 million in high-yield bonds for Sun America at the time I was asked to assume responsibility for the Sun high-yield bonds, and I became

Goldentree's principal contact at AIG. I had actually known Leon many years before, and this new business arrangement allowed us to renew our friendship.

Leon's business partner at Goldentree was Steve Tannenbaum, who had a reputation in the high-yield world as something of a hothead. Back during my AGC days, when Tannenbaum was managing a large high-yield mutual fund for Mainstay Funds, I had a most unpleasant confrontation with him during a bondholder meeting. Steve and I had opposing views on how to vote on one of the issues at hand, and he was less than tactful about expressing himself. "You may have been in the high-yield bond business for a long time," he said in a conference call with many other investors, "but you haven't learned a goddamned thing about it." I was furious at his comment, and when I learned that I was to be responsible for the Goldentree relationship with AIG my first thought was to immediately settle the score and to terminate Goldentree as an outside manager of Sun's high-yield bonds. Just to get even. But when I learned that Leon was now his partner, I decided to try to build a better relationship with Tannenbaum and see what he could do for us at AIG. Steve and I ended up getting along very well, which in turn strengthened my longer-term relationship with Leon. I often had occasion to be thankful that I'd not acted rashly, as knowing Leon proved to be one of the true bright spots during my stay in New York.

Leon was an avid fan of major league baseball, and he called one bright September day and asked if I wanted to join him for an evening Mets game at Shea stadium. "Yes, absolutely," I said, and thought, *anything* to relieve this boredom. We agreed to meet at Goldentree's midtown offices late in the day and drive to the game from there. I met Leon in his office, where he told me some news. He had recently bought a minority stake in the Milwaukee Brewers. Baseball was Leon's first love. You could see the eyes of a child light up as he went over the "Brew Crew's" off-season trades, explaining which ones were working out and which had been a bust. He then presented me with my very own Brewers baseball cap, royal blue with gold trim and a prominent, white script M on the front.

Then we were off to Shea. On our way to the ballpark Leon and I talked of old times and new times, of our families, of life in New York, and business in general. It felt so good to be in the presence of someone I could call a friend. It seemed I had lost all such relationships at AIG in New York. There was nothing threatening about my friendship with Leon. As the minutes slid by I felt almost normal, the pain and sadness of my treatment at AIG taking a temporary back seat.

Leon and I enjoyed the customary ballpark fare of hot dogs, popcorn, and beer. The cool evening air felt soothing. Our conversation was mostly lighthearted as we enjoyed the early New York evening. The roar of the crowd and the on-field exploits of the New York Mets reminded me of my youthful happiness in simpler times. But then, almost out of the blue, Leon turned to me. "You don't seem like your old self, Gordon," he said. "I can't quite put my finger on it, but is anything wrong?"

So he could tell. I was touched at his concern, but also cautious at first. After all, ours was in part a business relationship. I was worried about confidentiality. Did I know Leon well enough to really trust him with my personal unhappiness? I said something about losing some responsibilities, but Leon continued to probe. He seemed to know that I was deeply troubled, and he wasn't the kind of guy to just blow it off as "not my problem." He really seemed to want to know what was happening to me. He actually seemed to care. God, it felt so good to actually talk with someone who wanted to understand.

Over the next two or three innings my reluctance faded, and I unfolded my sad tale to Leon, including all the indignities and humiliations I had suffered at the hands of those in power at AIG. "Those bastards," Leon growled. He had known me during my many productive years and he seemed amazed and deeply saddened at AIG's behavior. Then he flipped open his cell phone. "Hold on a minute," he said. "I have just the person you need to talk to." A few seconds later Leon was on the phone with Jonathan Sack of the midtown law firm of Sack & Sack, summarizing my tale of woe. Five minutes later he hung up. Jonathan had done some human-resources legal work for Goldentree, he explained. "Jonathan would love to see you tomorrow after work. Call him during the day to confirm the exact time."

The evening Mets game was well along by now, and I was surprised that Jonathan would be working so late. That's normal for Jonathan, Leon explained. I wasn't sure what to make of this conversation, but at least Jonathan was willing to see me after hearing the highlights of my story. Perhaps I could get a legal opinion as to whether my case qualified as retaliation or not. Either way, it might at least help to clarify my situation and relieve me of this incessant anxiety.

Soon my evening with Leon drew to a close. I thanked him from the bottom of my heart for his friendship. We shock hands and I thanked him for his interest and his referral to Jonathan. That evening I rode all the way back to Battery Park on the New York subway wearing my Milwaukee Brewers cap. I figured if anybody asked, I could say that I knew the owner. To this day I am still the proud owner of this cap. One thing has changed, though. To my eyes, the big white M on the front stands less for Milwaukee than for *mensch*, the Yiddish word meaning a person of integrity and honor. Leon had been my *mensch*. It didn't matter to him that he had a business relationship with AIG. He was going to do the right thing for a friend. A true *mensch*.

On the evening of the next day I left work a bit early for my meeting with Jonathan. We weren't meeting until 7 p.m., but I was still new at the Manhattan subway system. I figured I would find Jonathan's office building first, then have some dinner in the area and be right on time for our meeting. Being on time was always important to me, and in this case I certainly didn't need anything else to heighten my anxiety.

The law firm of Sack & Sack occupied some modest, nondescript office space on the 19th floor of a midtown high rise. By 7 p.m. only Jonathan and a single assistant were there to greet me. We shook hands and began to chat. I quickly saw that Jonathan was a true "piece of work." If I were a Hollywood film director and I had asked central casting to send me someone who looked and acted the part of a young, cocky, loud, brash, obnoxious, midtown New York,

Jewish lawyer, Jonathan would have gotten the part, hands down. He was all of that and a real no-bullshit kind of guy—just the kind of guy who was in no way intimidated by AIG. I had walked in with a Goliath and found my David.

Jonathan saw a steady stream of disgruntled employees who had all kinds of reasons to feel bitter enough about their treatment to want to "sue the pants off" their employers. Only trouble was, they had no case. In their own minds, yes. Perhaps even in reality. But not in court. Retaliation can be very difficult to prove. In retrospect, I am sure I was initially just another one of Jonathan's many non-clients who felt mistreated by their bosses. But I had one thing going for me, and that was Leon's introduction. Jonathan went way back with Leon, and he was smart enough to know that Leon wouldn't waste his time. And so for three hours Jonathan and I reviewed my history with AGC and AIG. I discussed in great detail all of my accomplishments, my whistleblower memo, and all of the subsequent retaliation. Jonathan asked one probing question after another, as though I were a witness in court. In fact that was exactly what Jonathan wanted to know. Does this guy have a case? Would he hold up under cross examination? He took copious notes. He just wanted the facts. No emotions please. Stay focused only on the facts.

Could I substantiate my accomplishments?
Yes.
Could I substantiate the retaliation?
Yes.
Did I have e-mails?
Yes.
Would I be willing to wear a wire and go into Richard's office
    for a one-on-one conversation?
A wire? Gee. Uh, yeah. I think so.

After three hours Jonathan wrapped up. He closed his notebook and leaned back in his chair. He ran his fingers through his dark brown hair. He seemed like a man in deep thought. "I think you have a compelling story," he said finally. "And I think you'll make a great witness." Assuming everything I told him was true, he said, this was perhaps "the most egregious case of corporate retaliation I have ever seen." Wow, that was powerful!

But, Jonathan stressed, we needed to find a smoking gun. We needed tangible proof that AIG had willingly and knowingly carried out this retaliation against you. We had good *circumstantial* evidence of retaliation, but we had no *direct* evidence. AIG, he cautioned, was no easy target. If this case was to go to trial it could cost a bundle and take years. "That's why we want to have just the right evidence to convince AIG to settle out of court," Jonathan said. He stressed again the possibility of me bugging a conversation with Richard Scott, hoping to get him to admit to some form of retaliation. The mere thought of trying such a cloak-and-dagger maneuver sent a new rush of anxiety through my very soul.

Jonathan had one more message before I left. Act quickly. From his experience he could see a very predictable pattern, and he did not think I had much time left at AIG. It was crucial, he said, that I pursued any case of retaliation against AIG while I was still employed there. To file a case *after* termination would make it look like the case was filed because of the termination and not necessarily because of any retaliation. "Our case is much more powerful if you are still employed by AIG," Jonathan repeated—and AIG, he predicted, was about to fire me. "They'll find a reason."

I explained that I was leaving the next day for a weeklong motorcycling vacation in Colorado. That would give me some time to think this over, I told him. I'd get back to him upon my return to New York.

"Don't wait too long," were Jonathan's parting words. "They're just about to can you."

Talk about a no-bullshit kind of guy.

As the elevator sank me nineteen floors back down to the street, my doubts began and my anxiety returned. I liked Jonathan. I knew he was perfect for the job. And he sure seemed ready to move ahead with the case. He had all but licked his chops. "I just love big, dumb companies like AIG," he had said. But I had just met this fellow three hours before, and I wasn't sure I could trust his opinion. Jonathan, I knew, had very little to lose. If we won, he would get a hefty cut of whatever settlement we came to with AIG. If we lost, he lost some work time, nothing more. It was my career, my reputation, my self-esteem that were at stake, not his.

Nor was I convinced now that I had a solid case. Circumstantial evidence, yes, Jonathan had said. But direct evidence, no. Could I get the evidence we needed? The thought frightened me. I hated the thought of wearing a wire into Richard's office. It was like a bad detective movie. Had my life really deteriorated that far? But what else could I do? Sneak into Richard's office at midnight and rifle through his files? Surely Richard would not be so stupid as to put down anything in writing. Mercante or Neuger, maybe, but not Richard. Richard was an attorney from a prestigious Houston law firm. Wasn't he smarter than that?

That's how my internal dialogue went. Over and over and over.

I called one other trusted friend. David Zerhusen was a former neighbor who had worked as the head of human resources at a prominent Houston manufacturing company. He was also a practicing attorney and a former partner in a Houston law firm. Fortunately, I was able to contact David and get a second opinion on my legal case against AIG. David agreed with everything Jonathan had said. It's retaliation all right—if you can prove it. Without direct evidence the outcome of my case would still be very uncertain. "AIG is huge," David said. "They will drag this out for years. There are just so many games they can play, and they're pros at it. They'll be great at explaining away all of their actions in such a way as to try to avoid any liability."

David left me with a piece of advice. "Bad press for AIG is your strongest threat," he said. "With all of the bad press they're already getting, and given your tenure and senior position, they are not going to want this fight to go public." Wise words indeed.

But my internal dialogue continued, all my questions and uncertainty playing and re-playing constantly in my head. What should I do? Who could I trust? Why was I so anxious? I had challenged my superiors before. Why was I so afraid to challenge them again? Because now I knew their power. They would pay a guy seven figures just to hang him up to dry. They had kept me on to humiliate me, and now they were going to throw me away. With each replay, I relived all the pain, all the hurt, all the sadness, all the loss. Could I rely on Jonathan's opinion? Was I really about to be fired, or might I yet last until February? I knew in my heart that this couldn't last much longer. I simply did not have the strength to endure it. My anxiety level was skyrocketing. My anger and grief had plunged me into a depression I felt I'd never recover from. I felt like I was falling apart, shattering into a million little pieces. In twenty years with AGC and AIG I had always felt so proud, so self-confident. What had happened to me? I felt so powerless and small, so timid and weak.

For now, at the very least, I could look forward to a week of riding with my buddies. I was sure the time away would help stem my anxiety and depression. Motorcycling had always been my all-time favorite form of recreation, a relaxing and wonderful separation from all of my cares and worries. I would be traveling with Bill Greenwade and Thomas Heinkemeier, two of my favorite riding buddies. We were to meet Saturday morning in Abilene, Texas, then drive on through New Mexico and into the mountains of Colorado. Surely the fellowship, the beautiful country, the sweeping mountain roads, and the time and distance away from AIG would combine to help me sort out all of this information and opinion. When I returned, I thought, I'll be able to make the right decision.

Chapter 17: A Bunch of Grown Men on the Verge of Tears

The plan was to all meet for lunch in Abilene. "Abilene, Abilene, prettiest town I've ever seen," as the old George Hamilton song goes. In fact the entire central Texas region from Houston to Abilene was something less than spectacular. My great-grandfather had been a cattle rancher in Abilene around 1900, and I didn't imagine the arid landscape has changed much in the last hundred years: very gently rolling plains and pasture land, with the occasional meandering creek and isolated stand of pines or scrub oak trees. The farther west you went, the drier the landscape became. It was not yet the magnificent country of Colorado, but bucolic and peaceful enough, and I hoped it would be soothing to my tortured soul. Riding through scenery like this on my bright, red Ducati motorcycle, I normally would just let my mind wander. The miles and the day would roll on, the stresses of my life would fall behind me, and I would settle into a peaceful, thoughtful time of introspection.

Not today. It was as though my motorcycle helmet was a pressure cooker, keeping all my destructive thoughts imprisoned inside me, unable to get free. Instead of the peace and tranquility I so desperately sought, all I could concentrate on were the limitless humiliating events of the last four months. As I was later to learn, this reviewing of the past is the psychological equivalent of re-experiencing it, reliving the events, the anger and humiliation, over and over again. The emotional centers of our brain don't know the difference, and all this stress brings on chronic anxiety and depression. So it was for six lonely hours, with all the past agonies recirculating in my head. I realized then that it didn't matter where I was or what I was doing. As long as I was alone with my thoughts, I was trapped, trapped in a world of hurt and pain with no hope for distraction. I began to check my watch and mileage. How many more miles to Abilene? Give me some human contact, I thought. Something— anything—to get my mind off of this torture.

The sight of that pre-designated Kentucky Fried Chicken in Abilene was indeed the "prettiest I've ever seen." There in the parking lot was Bill Greenwade's sporty new red BMW touring motorcycle; there was Thomas Heinkemeir's trusty blue BMW Roadster, both loaded to the hilt with a week's worth of luggage. I was so happy to see these guys. I needed time with my buddies, just as I had needed the time with Leon back in New York. But I didn't want to share any of my tales of woe with Bill and Thomas. This was time for joy and fellowship. All I wanted was to forget about AIG, if only for a while. We dined on plates of the Colonel's chicken and got caught up on each other's news. It was great to be among friends again, and I was starting to feel better. "How are things going in New York?" they asked. "Oh, fine," I lied.

From Abilene we headed across the plains of West Texas to the garden spot of Lubbock in the Texas panhandle. Many of my kids' friends attended Texas Tech University in Lubbock, and I used to tease them about how much fun life must be out there on the Great Plains, which are flat as far as the eye can see except for a few grain silos. But the scenery held no humor for me now. Mile after mile my thoughts retraced the same old patterns, reliving the past and trying to make sense of my future—*Why was this happening? What had I done so wrong? What should I do?*—over and over and over again. My anxiety became so overwhelming that I started taking huge, deep breaths of air and very slowly exhaling to calm my nerves. At one point we stopped for gas. The few minutes of company didn't help. I was as nervous and jittery as I can ever remember. *This isn't supposed to be happening,* I thought. *I'm with my buddies. I'm supposed to be relaxed, and here I am about ready to jump out of my skin.* I even committed the cardinal sin of having a beer during the break. Never, ever in the past had I combined any alcohol with motorcycles, but I was desperate to do something to quiet my anxiety.

We were out past Lubbock on our way to Clovis, New Mexico, out in the middle of nowhere, when I had a flat tire. Nothing like losing air pressure in your front tire at 60 miles an hour to pique your anxiety. Once you stop, though, fixing the flat isn't much of a problem if you come prepared, as we had. You just hoist the bike up on its centerstand, find the hole, clean it, plug it, and refill the tire with air. But faced with this minor challenge I simply froze. I felt emotionally spent. I just couldn't handle any more anxiety. Sitting by the side of the road with my head in my hands, I watched Bill and Thomas fix my flat tire, something they'd seen me do a half-dozen times before. They knew then that something wasn't right.

We eventually made it to Clovis and stopped at one of those roadside steak joints for dinner. We were road-weary and ready for a break, especially me. I was hungry for some human interaction to distract my thoughts. Dinner conversation began in the usual manner, with casual comments about the ride that day.

"How's your tire?"

"How's your butt?"

"What's the weather look like ahead?"

"Aren't you glad we made it out of Texas?"

Soon, though, the talk turned to our beloved friend, Steve Wenger. Steve was the common thread of friendship that had brought Bill and Thomas and me together many years before, and we had enjoyed many years of motorcycling together. I'd met Steve back when our daughters were in the same Indian Princess tribe at the YMCA. Steve reminded me of my father. He always had a story to relate or a new joke to tell. He could walk into a room full of strangers and walk out everybody's new best friend. As a biker, though, Steve always rode way too fast. "Take it easy," I would tell him. "Slow down. You've got too much to lose." But Steve seemed addicted to speed, which his Ducati ST4 motorcycle could certainly deliver. A few months before our trip, Steve fell off his Ducati near Louisville, Kentucky, and slammed into a guardrail at fifty or sixty miles per hour. He suffered massive internal injuries, including a pancreas that had been split it two. He was still in intensive care, and his doctors were very guarded about his prospects of recovery. We all said a silent prayer for Steve that evening. Thinking about him and praying for him helped me put my own pain in perspective. At least I had my health and my future. Steve's were in considerable doubt.

Then Thomas and Bill wanted to know what that flat tire episode was all about. "That's not you, Gordon," they said. "What's going on?" So over my rib eye steak and Texas toast I gave them the Reader's Digest version of my woes at AIG. They listened, they asked questions, they sympathized. I asked for their understanding of my odd behavior, and they wished me the best in my fight. This was all I could ask, and it felt a bit better to let some of it out.

And then it was Bill's turn. "My son just left for a thirteen-month tour of duty in Iraq. He is a medic in the Marines. We're just not sure what his future holds. He'll certainly see combat, and my wife and I are just so distraught that we can't bear to watch the evening news." We listened, we asked questions, we sympathized, and we said a little prayer for Bill's son.

And then it was Thomas's turn. "My teenage daughter has left home again, and we haven't heard from her in three weeks. We think she is in California with that derelict boyfriend of hers, but we just don't know." We listened, we asked questions, we sympathized, and we said a little prayer for Thomas' daughter.

That supper was a special one for me, one of the most unique meals I've ever experienced: a trio of grown men all on the verge of tears, sitting around sharing the all-too-real challenges in their lives. There was a true sense of shared sadness. They say misery loves company, and it's true. We were reminded that life can really be a bitch sometimes, but that we are not the only ones with trouble in our lives—and that friends can always help. We each left that funky New Mexico steak house with a better sense of proportion on our own personal problems.

That evening we stayed at a KOA campground in Tucumcari, New Mexico. There was no motorcycle shop in Tucumcari, so the next morning we rode straight to Albuquerque on Interstate 40 to find me a new front tire. No one wants to ride a motorcycle for long with a plugged tire. From Albuquerque we rode north through Santa Fe and then along Highway 84 to a campground in Chama, New Mexico.

All that time alone with my thoughts wasn't healthy. My anxiety was still out of control. That evening in Chama I was so lost in my thoughts that I left my watch in the men's room at the campground. Later I left my cell phone at a restaurant. I had to wake the owner of the restaurant the next morning at dawn to get it back. I'm losing it, I thought. It's as if I just can't function any more. I began to worry about being so absent minded while riding a 100 horse power motorcycle on twisting mountain roads. Better slow down.

At least in New Mexico it was cooler and the scenery was far more spectacular than west Texas. From Chama we headed north along Highway 84 into Pagosa Springs, Colorado. There we headed along the fabulous Highway 160 over the 10,850-foot Wolf Creek Pass and then on to the old mining towns of Creede and Lake City. This was the part of Colorado we had traveled so far to see: crystal-clear mountain streams, dense evergreen and aspen forests, magnificent mountain vistas, the colors of autumn in the Rockies, and the never-ending twisting mountain roads of Colorado. At last, some relief from sadness and anxiety!

All the while, weaving through the scenery before me and my sadness and confusion within, I had this John Denver song floating through my brain. It was the one about the guy from New York City who wanted to live in Colorado: *I guess he'd rather be in Colorado / He'd rather spend his time out where the sky looks like a pearl after a rain….* I couldn't help but be distracted by the overwhelming grandeur of those Rockies, if only for a while. Great roads, great vistas, and great friends all reminded me that my life wasn't so bad. *I guess he'd rather be in Colorado / He'd rather play his banjo in the morning when the moon is scarcely gone....* Hey, if worse came to worst, I thought, I could always live right here in Colorado. Maybe operate a ski lift in the winter. Be a fishing guide in the summer. Yeah, and make $8 an hour. *I guess he'd rather work out where the only thing you earn is what you spend . . . .*

That evening we camped in Gunnison. The following day we headed east, then north, through Buena Vista and Leadville and on to Kremmling and Granby, our final stop for the day. The temperature dropped into the twenties that night, just a bit cool for our Texas sleeping bags, so we holed up in a motel. We got up the next morning to find ice on our bikes. *In the dawn I hear him humming / Some old song he wrote of love in Boulder Canyon....* As we left Granby and headed toward Estes Park via Grand Lake, I felt that life in Colorado was slowly starting to heal my sadness. Oh, it was still there, but there were enough other joys and distractions to help. By now I had even perfected my deep breathing exercises, a way to at least partially mitigate the constant, nervous, edgy gnawing of anxiety.

In the end up in his office / In the end a quiet cough / Is all he has to show / He lives in New York City.... This song felt so close to home. So perfect for my situation. I knew I had to break free of AIG before I had my own last quiet cough in New York City. John Denver must have been living inside my head with all of those awful thoughts.

In Grand Lake we stopped for a roadside breakfast. I was just about to bite into a toasty pecan waffle when I got a call that would change my life.

It was Tim Janszen, the new High-Yield Bond Head for AIG.

"Hi Gordon," he said. "Are you sitting down?" Quietly, almost sheepishly, Tim told me that he was leaving AIG to set up his own distressed-debt fund, with substantial sponsorship from a prominent northeast private equity group. Not only that—he was taking four other top employees from the High-Yield Group with him. The catalyst for their leaving had been AIG's response to my plans to set up specialized funds within the High-Yield Group and to bring in outside investors. Three key potential managers of these funds were so disgusted by AIG's rejection of my proposals that they, and a couple of others, were now leaving to set up their own fund. Tim was apologetic. He had worked for me for many years, he understood my present woes, and he felt this mass departure would be a blow to me. I, on the other hand, was absolutely elated. This was my first bit of good news in five months.

Why? Because, I realized, this was the event that would finally break my mental and legal logjam. I was well beyond the point of caring about AIG and the very real blow of losing these very talented people. What I cared about was the choice that Richard Scott and Rich Mercante would now have to make.

How and with which people were they going to fill this huge new void?

The road from Grand Lake through the Rocky Mountain National Park and on to Estes Park has got to be the most spectacular mountain road anywhere in the United States. The mountain pass rises above 12,000 feet, well above the timberline. The views and vistas from this road are nothing short of overwhelming. They were the finest moments of our Colorado ride. But I didn't see a thing. I was completely lost in my thoughts about what to do next. How does this change my future? Will they bring me back to Houston? How can we replace these guys? Will we lose outside investors? Am I now more important to AIG—or less? The entire magnificent ride to Estes Park was completely lost to my memory as I hashed and rehashed what this latest news meant for my future.

The logical choice to come back to Houston and to run the High-Yield Group again was me. I had built the department; I had hired the team; I had brought in the outside investors; and I had run the group for nearly twenty years with outstanding results. If they wanted me to return to Houston to help fill the void, I would be out of New York City, have something of my old job back, and certainly be able to stay well past my 55th birthday. If they did *not* want me to return—then who would they promote? The next two most eligible managers in Houston were Greg Braun and Bryan Petermann. Both men combined did not have anywhere near my years of experience in high-yield bonds. So the trap was set. Either return me to Houston and a life of some normalcy; or bring in someone with woefully inadequate experience—and I would have my smoking gun. Yes! True, it was still only circumstantial evidence. But if AIG didn't bring me back after the departure of these five employees, the evidence, circumstantial as it was, would be irrefutable. How could they say no? Only if they still wanted to retaliate against me. It would be so obvious, so perfect. Maybe there *was* a light at the end of my dark tunnel. I couldn't wait for Richard's next move. By the time we got to Estes Park, I knew what mine would be.

Since I was still Head of Leveraged Finance, High-Yield still reported to me on the organization chart. Under any normal circumstances, I would have certainly been a part of the decision on how to respond to the loss of so many key employees. So I called Richard's secretary and set up a three-way call for that afternoon with Richard Scott, Rich Mercante, and myself. I made certain to say exactly why I was calling. I wanted to discuss how we were going to fill this void in Houston. We set up a conference call for 5:00 p.m. Eastern, 3:00 p.m. Mountain time. I knew that I would have to find a pay phone, since my cell phone service was so spotty in the mountains. The last thing I wanted was to miss any of Richard's and Rich's bullshit due to a poor connection. But I had traveled these roads before. Looking at our maps I knew of a set of phone booths outside a convenience store in Pine Junction, Colorado. I made sure I was there promptly at 3:00 p.m.

My recommendation to Richard and Rich was simple and straightforward. I did not believe that anyone remaining on the High-Yield team was yet ready to run the group. I therefore recommended that I return to Houston to manage the group until someone emerged as my likely successor. Richard asked my opinion of Bryan Petermann and Greg Braun. I said I thought they would be good future candidates. If I returned, Greg and Bryan would be my top two lieutenants. But they needed a great deal more management experience. Both men had always been high-yield bond analysts or portfolio managers and had never been in a position of managing people. Richard then said that no decision had been made and that he wanted to sleep on it. He thanked me for my input and told me that he would make his decision in a few days.

Hmm, I thought. Since Richard's lips were moving I suspected he was lying. I wasn't sure what the truth was, but I suspected the decision had already been made without my input. AIG always filled these kinds of voids immediately. Waiting did not make any sense. What was Richard going to learn in the next few days that he didn't already know? He already knew Petermann and Braun well, since they had worked with Richard as far back as 1999 at AGC. Hiring someone from the outside would take too long and worry our employees and outside investors. I knew in my heart that the decision was made. I was not going to be asked to return to Houston. "Those bastards," I said to myself.

That evening we camped outside the Royal Gorge near Canon City, Colorado, rode into town, and found a Village Inn for dinner. Again, as soon as my food arrived, I received another phone call from Tim Janszen. Had I heard?

"They announced that Bryan Petermann was the new Head of High-Yield this morning." This morning. In other words, before my call with Richard and Rich.

"It was a bit odd," Tim went on to say, "because later in the afternoon"—after my call—"they announced that Greg Braun would be a Co-Head of High-Yield."

I guess Richard didn't sleep on it for very long.

Now I knew I had a fight ahead—but I had my smoking gun. Denying me the Houston job had raised the retaliation to a level that would be virtually impossible to deny. I was just too obvious a choice. Richard had blown it, and I didn't think he was even smart enough to realize AIG's potential liability. I had one worry left. Jonathan's parting words that I was about to be axed. Could this high-yield reorganization accelerate the firing process? I didn't know, but I wasn't going to wait around to find out. We had to file a letter alleging retaliation, and right away. Time was of the essence.

No one, not even AIG, can fire someone after they submit allegations of retaliation against a whistleblower, at least not until those allegations are fully investigated. Filing my grievance with AIG would preserve my income and support my belief that my case was about retaliation, not termination. I had to get Jonathan working on a letter to submit to—in Leon's elegant phrase—"those bastards."

No more indecision. No more endlessly churning thoughts. I saw the path ahead clearly. The next thing I had to do was get Jonathan on the phone. It was too late now for even Jonathan to be working, but the next day was Friday, and I called him first thing.

"I'm sorry Mr. Massie," his secretary told me, "but Mr. Sack is in court all day. I can try to get him a message, but he asked not to be disturbed. Can he call you on Monday?"

Araaagh! "Listen, I really need to talk to him before the weekend. It is very important. Can we set up a call for, say, 8 p.m. Eastern time?" We were headed home now and were back in Texas and the Central time zone. By nightfall we were back in beautiful Lubbock, and I was ready for my 7 p.m. call with my new best friend, Jonathan Sack.

I will forever remember that Denny's restaurant in downtown Lubbock. My cell phone was dropping calls for some unknown reason, so I elected to use Denny's pay phone in the back hallway on the way to the restrooms. There, amid the clanking of dirty dishes, the barking of dinner orders, and the flushing of toilets, I placed my all-important call.

Jonathan was giddy with the news that I was moving ahead with my case against AIG, and he saw the high-yield shake-up the same way I did. "It's about as close to direct evidence as we can get," he said. "And we can also sue them for age discrimination!"

Whoa, I thought. Down, boy. First things first. Since I would be back in Houston on Sunday, we agreed that, rather than flying to New York, I would just report to work in Houston on Monday morning. First thing that morning Jonathan would fax me a draft of his allegation letter. If everything looked okay it would be couriered to each recipient in the afternoon. Then we would wait and see what happens.

How I would love to have been a fly on Richard's wall when he opened that letter, I thought. But most importantly my income would be safe, at least for a while, and we could start our legal proceedings against AIG. Sure AIG could draw this out forever but I would still be on their payroll. My anxiety was lifting. My mental logjam was breaking up. I knew the biggest battles were still to be fought, but I was confident that AIG was vulnerable. Nor had I forgotten David Zerhusen's remark that my greatest threat to AIG was negative press. What were my choices here? How could I at least threaten to do the most damage? Jonathan's main focus was on the legal issues and making sure I had a strong case—but he did say he had an editor friend at the *Wall Street Journal*. I had been AIG's most senior investment professional in Houston. Perhaps my public outcry would be noticed.

Finally, I thought, the shit was going to hit the fan.

Chapter 18: "Pack Your Things"

My commute that Monday morning into Houston felt somehow peaceful and comforting, part of my old routine. I knew that by closing time today we would submit our retaliation allegation letter. That mere piece of paper, I suspected, would trigger such a firestorm of anger from Richard Scott and others that my hours at AIG were truly counting down to zero. Regardless, the hour of introspection that I gained amidst the thick Houston traffic on Interstate 45 reduced the churning of my negative thoughts and put my anxiety under better control. Very simply, I knew what had to be done. Besides, while I had loved walking to work in lower Manhattan, I also loved being back in the seat of my Jaguar convertible. It was a throwback to happier times.

The Jaguar XK8 had caught my eye in late 2001. Long and sleek, with those perfectly curved lines, it was, in my opinion, the sexiest car on the road, bar none. I knew that Jaguars had frequent mechanical problems. I knew about their exorbitant repair bills. None of that mattered to me. I was in love. On the other hand, I had always been careful about spending money, and a list price of $85,000 was not my idea of a value proposition. So I began looking for a good used model. Houston dealerships didn't have the right combination of price, miles, and looks—black on black was essential—so I turned to eBay. Before long I found the perfect car, offered by a dealership of good repute in Dallas. The car had twenty thousand miles on it, an extended, two-year, bumper-to-bumper transferable warranty, and it was offered at the "buy it now" price tag of $37,000—less than half the original price.

Even lovers, by the time they reach middle age, have learned to be cautious. I called up the dealer, got a salesman on the phone, and made him walk around the car and do a complete visual inspection for me. I got the vehicle history report from CarMax. Everything checked out. I called the salesman back, paid the "buy it now" price to shut down the bidding, got a certified check from my bank, and flew out to Dallas to pick up my new baby.

Our honeymoon was short. Before long I grew to appreciate firsthand the agonies of owning a Jaguar. Sure I had my warranty, but almost every month brought some new problem: strange engine noises, windows that wouldn't close, blown stereo speakers, two new thermostats, transmission glitches, front-end alignments seemingly every five thousand miles. Jaguar must be the only automobile brand that can manufacture a rear view mirror that needed to be replaced—at $350 plus labor. I always babied that car, but four years had passed, it was 2005, and my sexy Jaguar was well out of warranty. One thousand dollars for a standard oil change and service! I truly loved to drive this car, but it was becoming a real pain in the ass to own and repair.

As I drove into Houston that sweltering morning, feeling the transmission slipping on me, I couldn't help but see the similarities between my Jaguar and my career at AIG. Both had started out with so much promise. Both had come with guarantees—in AIG's case, a three-plus year contract, with guaranteed minimum bonuses, stock option grants, and restricted stock grants in each year. And both had come with advanced warnings. I had put so much of myself into building and maintaining both relationships, but both had let me down. Maybe I should have known better.

Finally I reached the AIG employee parking lot. Having left the Houston office, I no longer had my parking pass, a violation that would normally earn me a nasty little note on my windshield from some earnest security guard. The thought made me irritable, a reminder that I no longer really belonged here. I'll park wherever I damn well please, I thought. What are they going to do—fire me? Yet as I passed through the enclosed walkways to my office, casually nodding to familiar faces walking in the opposite direction, I felt like I was home again.

A hello and squeeze from my blessed St. Jude made me feel at least partially welcome. Judy had been my personal secretary and the senior administrative assistant for the whole High-Yield Bond Group in Houston. "This place just isn't the same without you," she said. But that was the last of the warm greetings from my staff. Word had traveled fast since Thursday's announcement promoting Bryan Petermann and Greg Braun. A few peeked in my door to say hello, but most kept their distance. This puzzled and troubled me at first, but then I realized that most people did not know how to approach me. It was as though I had a grave illness, or had been recently divorced, or experienced a death in my immediate family. What does one say? What do you say to someone who had been passed over so publicly—to someone who was, in effect, being forced out? Do you bring it up? Offer condolences? Or take the easiest route and ignore the whole thing? In those hours, I realized that ignoring someone's loss is perhaps the cruelest treatment of all. No, you can't really fix anything. But just letting the person know that you care, expressing some sympathy, will often mean the world to them. Just as Thomas and Bill did for me in New Mexico. Just as I had done for them in turn.

I found my old familiar office surroundings as I had left them. The desk and shelves in my palatial space were bare, with no sign of human occupation. Tim Janszen, who had been promoted to the new Head of High-Yield when I left for New York, would have been entitled to move in but for some reason he had never chosen to do so. Maybe he thought the room was cursed, I thought glumly. After a while I closed my office door. I wanted to be alone and hidden, to have time alone with my thoughts. I knew that my career, at least with AIG, was over. *Twenty years.* It seemed like a lifetime to me. I had grown up here. I had flourished here. And, apparently, I had failed here. Thoughts came back of all the people, all the characters I had worked with and enjoyed. Julia Tucker, my old boss. She was always good for a laugh—or an insight. Yes indeed, I had lived in interesting times, as the old blessing recommends. I had managed so many people in those tumultuous years, and yet had only once fired a subordinate. There always seemed to be better alternatives available.

I gazed down from the spacious windows. The view was stunning. Below, almost at the foot of our building, the slow-moving Buffalo Bayou wound its way through a wide green belt of bike paths, trees, and hiking trails. A mile to the east, I could see the grand panorama of downtown Houston. Memories of working there years before with Prudential came flooding back to me. Those were simpler and better times, I thought. Now my life felt as stripped and bare as the office where I now stood. Although thankfully I had never been through a divorce, this is how I imagined it might feel: staring out from an empty space, recalling all that was promised, all that was lost. I felt so very sad at that moment.

Later that morning Jonathan Sacks called. Our allegation letter was ready, he told me. He was faxing it over. I asked Judy to stand guard by the communal fax machine. The letter was short and crude, but it made the points we needed to make, claiming "a campaign of retaliation" and demanding that AIG "cease, desist, and refrain from engaging in any further retaliatory actions" against me. This time I wasn't going to worry about the tone of my letter, which Richard had so complained about in my original whistleblower memo. The main objective—to establish a claim of retaliation before I was terminated—was all that counted. I called Jonathan back and instructed him to release the letter to Richard, Rich Mercante, AIG's general counsel in New York, and a handful of other names. Just like signing divorce papers, I thought.

My office door was open now, but lunchtime came and no one came by to ask if I was hungry. All alone, just like New York. These were people that I had hired, trained, promoted, fought for, and worked with. Now I was damaged goods. Richard's cancer had spread so fast. In the afternoon I was invited by Bryan Petermann to attend a credit review meeting. I attended, but my heart and mind were elsewhere. Returning to my office, I puttered around for a while and then left, though it was still the middle of the afternoon. What was the point in staying?

My teenage son, Hunter, was surprised to see me. "Dad! Why are you home so early?"

I swallowed. "Well, uh, I'm ... not going to be working at AIG anymore."

"Great! Since you've been working in New York I feel like I don't have a dad." Hunter was blissfully uninterested in the details. His teen-level reaction made me feel better.

That night I slept surprisingly well, considering all that was on my mind. My main feeling was one of relief that my letter had been sent out before I was fired. Anxiety and depression were still my demons, but they did not seem so overwhelming. I felt like a soldier resting quietly before battle, taking comfort in whatever sureties I could. Knowing that I would remain on the payroll and keep my benefits during whatever legal proceeding was going to ensue was important to me.

Returning to work the next day, I found a note from Judy placed prominently on my desk. *Call Richard Scott immediately.* Richard took my call and spoke calmly. "You are being placed on paid administrative leave pending the outcome of our investigation of your allegations of corporate retaliation. Please pack your things and leave immediately." Click.

Jonathan had been right all along. If my experiences of retaliation had just been a figment of my imagination—if AIG had in fact *not* been looking for a reason to fire me, if I did indeed have real work left to do—they would have responded very differently. Receiving such a letter out of the blue would have caught them unaware. The reaction would have been one of confusion and inquiry. *We don't understand. How could you feel this way? We have always valued your work, and we continue to do so.* Instead their response had been swift and certain. My firing was imminent. They were just looking for a reason to get me out of the picture, and I had beaten them to the punch. They could not now brush off my case as that of another terminated employee. Oh, the wisdom of Jonathan's experience. God bless you, Leon Wagner.

As for the idea that Richard was going to investigate my allegations, I really had to laugh. The idea of AIG and Richard Scott looking into their own behavior in any genuine way was unthinkable. What was he going to do, appoint a blue ribbon panel? Maybe AIG would find itself guilty, pay itself a large fine, and everything would be okay? Richard was so full of his own bullshit that hearing his voice almost made me ill.

I called Jonathan and told him what Richard had said. Jonathan's response was kind and thoughtful. "Take a few days and calm yourself down. If you're not going to work, you might as well relax and enjoy it. You've been through hell, and you need a break. I'll get back to you in a couple of days, and we'll talk about our next move."

I quickly packed up the few things I'd brought with me that day. The one thought in my mind was *I didn't want to see anybody, I didn't want to talk to anybody. I wanted to be invisible. I wanted to be gone.* The humiliation was just too great. I told only Judy, sitting at her desk as always, right outside the door to my empty office. If anybody calls, I told her, just give them my home number. I gave her a big squeeze and saw the tears welling up in her kind eyes.

"Goodbye, Gordon. You have been a great boss, and I'll miss you. Thank you for everything."

I picked up my briefcase, walked past the large, windowed conference room where I'd presided at meetings so many times, past the receptionist and out the front door, never to return. That was my last moment with AIG. As I rode down the thirty-seven floors to the lobby, I thought. *It's done. My path is to home. There's nothing more that can be salvaged.* My fate was now largely in the hands of the lawyers, and I was just going to follow Jonathan's orders. Much work remained in my battles ahead, but I believed that I'd done the right thing and that my case was solid.

I made my last drive home and walked into the loving arms of my wife, Barbara. There I broke down and began to sob. I don't cry very often, but this was a good, honest cry that seemed to last quite a while. I can't ever remember such hurt.

Over the next few months I was to discover a simple truth that many had discovered before me. You can put a man out of work with one dismissive command. Taking the work out of the man, on the other hand, can require invasive surgery, and without the benefit of anesthetic.

Wednesday morning I awoke at my usual time, 6:30 a.m., overwhelmed by a feeling of dread. *What now? How do I fill my day?* I was used to working seventy-hour weeks. As far as any form of domestic life was concerned, my calendar was empty. Barb was in theory a stay-at-home mom—our son Hunter was still in high school—but she was heavily involved in charity and school activities and had a very active social life. She was rarely home. None of my friends were out of work. I had no idea what to do with myself. The man looking back at me in the bathroom mirror was nothing like the successful executive I had once known.

Washed up.

Put out to pasture.

Kicked to the curb.

The phrases stumbled around in my mind like little daggers of self-destruction.

Working people—*productive* people—enjoy having time off. Retirement seems like a just and logical reward for a working life well spent. After decades on the job we start looking forward to the end of our careers. At 60 or 65 or even 67 years of age, if fate has been kind to us, we can anticipate a busy life of leisure, full of plans and friends and travel. While some may never reconcile themselves to the transition, others eagerly anticipate those golden years.

I was fifty-four years old and emotionally depleted. I had nothing planned and few inner resources left to plan with. This was all happening too fast. The script was all wrong. The days and weeks stretching out in front of me already felt like a total loss, a massive, unfillable void. *What do I do? How can I stay busy? What happened to my self-esteem? Am I worth anything anymore?*

I didn't have any answers. I had no idea what to do with myself. All I felt like doing was going back to bed. Maybe I would wake up and realize this was all a bad dream.

Sometime in the next few days somebody from the L.A. office called. Maybe it was John Lapham, the bank loan manager I'd inherited from Sun America. I don't remember.

"What's all this about you resigning?"

I didn't know that I had resigned. *Gee, Richard, what happened to your investigation of my allegations of retaliation?*

Oh, yes, he said. AIG had issued an announcement. Others called as well. In due course I received a copy of the announcement. I don't have it any more, and I've forgotten the wording. But I remember the essence. For twenty years of service, some faint praise. The kinds of lukewarm phrases reserved, in corporate-speak, for a laggard, a burden they're pleased to be rid of. Nothing like being damned by faint praise.

Then Jonathan Sacks called. He wanted me in New York right away. I needed to come up anyway, I said. I had to collect my things at my apartment, negotiate an early exit on my lease, and retrieve my stuff from my office. But Jonathan wasn't interested in my personal effects. He wanted evidence. Documents, e-mails, notes, anything I could find in writing to substantiate my accomplishments and the subsequent retaliation by AIG. Everything you can put your hands on. The sooner the better.

I still had a pile of frequent flyer miles on Continental Airlines, I told him. I'll fly out tomorrow.

The preparations for battle were about to begin.

Chapter 19: The Whistleblower's Binder

The next day found me aboard a flight bound from Houston to La Guardia airport in New York. The physical flight was uneventful. My spirits, on the other hand, experienced a good deal of turbulence.

At first my thoughts rose with the aircraft. Jonathan had submitted our letter before I'd been fired. I'd been home with my family for a few days in Houston. I had some idea what our game plan was. The clouds of uncertainty and indecision, the bullying and buffeting of negative thoughts, had to some extent lifted. I could focus on the task before me: get to NY, pack up my stuff, get the lease taken care of, go to AIG, get my files, meet with Jonathan. My "to do" list and the prospect of being proactive cheered me up.

Still, I felt the need to resume my career. Anywhere but AIG. *I'm only fifty-four years old*, I thought. *I'm not going to believe all this negative self-talk about being washed up. I'm too young to retire. Let's get going on this!* Finding a job at my age would not be the easiest of tasks, but I had industry contacts and a good long-term reputation. I began to formulate a list of people to call in beginning my search for a new job.

The big unknown, of course, was how I was going to explain to a potential employer why I was out of work. At that point I had no idea how I was going to relate what had happened. Nor did I have any idea how far out the ripples were going to go. Would I be black-balled from the industry?

"Mr. Massie, who can I contact at AIG for a reference?"

No one.

That didn't sound like a good answer. And I was aware enough to know that my self-esteem was low and my emotional state fragile. I suspected that job interviews and all the work they entailed would only exacerbate my situation further. My anxiety and depression might not be apparent in the first few minutes, but I knew I couldn't fool anyone for long. A mind running on negative thinking is like a laboring engine. A person seeking a new job needed energy, passion, enthusiasm. How could I possibly convey those things in a job interview when all I felt like doing was sleeping all day?

Still, I had my list underway. *I do have options*, I told myself. *Life will go on after AIG. Who needs that dysfunctional behemoth anyway?*

But the turbulence continued and my mental engine churned on, gears grinding. Anger. It wasn't losing my job that troubled me so. It was the way I had been treated by AIG. I felt like a rape victim. If AIG had wanted me gone, we could have met like mature adults and negotiated a peaceful and mutually agreeable settlement and severance. Instead? Pain and humiliation for me. A waste of time and money for AIG management and shareholders. Ill will from my staff about the way I was treated, with a pile of subsequent resignations. And now here we were, arming ourselves with lawyers and preparing for war. Why did it have to happen this way?

The answer was simple. This was AIG's way. It began with Hank Greenberg's famously confrontational style and trickled down from there. My college friend, the insurance broker, had told me that AIG almost always contested any sizable claim, fighting like hell to reduce or eliminate their payout, wearing down their adversaries. I feared this would be my final fate. More churning of bad thoughts. More anxiety.

Finally, as my flight descended into New York, I made a decision. Now was not the time to be initiating a job search. I was still on the AIG payroll. I still had my AIG benefits. I was emotionally spent already, and this legal battle could take a lot of time and energy.

Pursuing another job at the same time would be doubly difficult and distracting. October had just begun, and the holidays would soon be here. Jonathan was right. The time off would do me good, and I'd be able to pursue my case against AIG with a clear mind. I would do nothing on the job front until at least the beginning of 2006. I needed a break from the working world.

Being back in New York City was eerie and strange. I felt as if I was operating in a foreign land, behind enemy lines. Throughout my flight I had remained relatively relaxed, even upbeat for a moment or two. Then, as if on cue, just as the plane's wheels touched the runway at La Guardia airport, I felt that familiar rush of anxiety and depression, a torrent of angst rushing through the groundwater of my very soul. I was alone again, without my support system. I had to begin waging war against AIG, a formidable opponent by anyone's reckoning, with only Jonathan Sack at my side. I could only hope and pray that he was really as good as Leon said he was.

It's odd the way New York City can often magnify whatever feelings a person arrives with. In happier times a visit to New York City could be a joyous occasion, the bright lights and elegant stores and the city's rich heritage reflecting and enhancing my already elated mood. Sometimes the city could even cheer me up when I felt low. But today, as I gazed out of my cab on the ride to Battery Park, the city seemed unappealing and filthy. I saw only dirty streets and dour faces, mirroring my own sadness.

I let myself in to my lonely apartment and began to pack up my few remaining personal items in the two empty suitcases I had flown in with. One source of anxiety, though minor in comparison to AIG, was my lease. By contract I was liable for eight months of rent at $6,000 a month. When I explained to my agent that I needed to terminate my lease immediately, eight months early, he let me out of the lease with no payments or penalties whatsoever. At first I was stunned. Then I realized that they could now re-rent my space in a heartbeat, and at $7,000 a month. But it was one less thing to worry about, and I was very pleased.

By now it was the end of the working day. From the window of my restaurant I watched the throngs of commuters rushing home to their families. The faces seemed sad and lonely to me, but again, it was probably a reflection of my own loneliness. I wished I was rushing home to my family. Instead, there I sat at a table for one, quietly brooding over all of the information I needed to gather once my supper was over and I was back in my tiny office—an office that, for all intents and purposes, was no longer mine. I needed access to my files, both electronic and paper. For the last four months I had been documenting everything that was even remotely related to my case for retaliation, but I needed to get into my office—if my passcard would still let me into the building. Richard was my nemesis, through and through, but he was not a detail nemesis. He just didn't focus much of his energy on the small stuff of life. Presumably these things were beneath his status. He had sent me home from Houston, and I didn't think it had occurred to him that I might pop up again in New York. But what if I was wrong and my passcard was inoperative? How could I retrieve my files and be prepared for my meeting tomorrow with Jonathan? Richard had said "pack your things," after all, and that's exactly what I would be doing. Didn't I have a right to my own files? More negative thoughts churning, more anxiety. I looked at my watch. 7:45 p.m. Time to steal my way into AIG's offices.

Wending my usual way through the canyons of Wall Street, I noticed that the throngs of exiting commuters had dwindled to a slow trickle. I did not want to attempt my entrance until sometime after 8:00 p.m., when I felt certain that few if any of my former colleagues would be around. Approaching 70 Pine Street in the gathering darkness of the evening made me feel as though I was some kind of secret agent, or perhaps a second-story burglar looking to steal some precious gems or military secrets. As I entered the lobby my heart was racing. Would I get in? Would the security guards recognize my face from some "Wanted" poster Richard had circulated?

Calm down, you idiot, I told myself, as I swept my passcard through the turnstile slot.

Nothing happened.

I tried again.

Nothing.

Shit. What now? Maybe I could just casually leap over the damn turnstile. Would anybody notice?

Don't let anyone tell you that New Yorkers lack kindness. One of the security guards came over and asked if he could help me. He had a soft voice and a very kind face.

"Yes, thank you. My card doesn't seem to be working." I handed him my card, which included my photograph, and he scrutinized it carefully.

"Let me check our records," he said finally. "Give me a couple of minutes."

Those minutes seemed like an eternity. What would happen if I could not get in? Would I then have no case, no written evidence for Jonathan? More crazy thoughts, heartbeat racing, anxiety level shooting off the charts. But then my kind security guard returned. My passcard only allowed entrance to the building between the hours of 6 a.m. and 6 p.m., he explained, and it was now 8:10 p.m.

Oh, shit, I thought again. Would he tell me to come back in the morning with everyone else? I explained that it was a matter of some urgency that I get into my office, and perhaps my kind friend saw the panic on my face and the anxiety in my soul.

"I'm going to go ahead and let you in, Mr. Massie," he said. "All we ask you to do at this hour is to sign in with us before you enter. We need to keep track of all late-night visitors."

That's all! Signing my name was something I still remembered how to do, and I was granted immediate access. Elation! My thoughts started racing again. *What an idiot I can be*, I thought with relief. Now I knew how drug smugglers must feel once they've crossed that international border with their stash. Minutes later I was back in my tiny office, rifling through all of my glorious files.

In the next four hours I put together one of the most impressive three-ring binders of my life. Mentally I blessed the thoroughness I had acquired thanks in part to my MEM/Modelnetics training. The first section of my binder was entitled "Accomplishments." It documented the performance of AIG's high-yield bond portfolio over the last four years, the growth in third-party assets and fee income during the same period, the results from the Bank Loan Group, the three-day agenda of the Credit Conference I had organized, my Wall Street marketing efforts, the results of our Distressed Debt and Emerging Market portfolios, and even a full description of the staff family picnics I provided for at my home in Texas.

Section Two was entitled "Recognition;" all of my annual reviews, my bonuses, my promotions, my invitation to participate in the rarefied circle of the Starr International (SICO) partnership. The third section, "My Internal Memo," was simply a copy of my actual whistleblower memo.

The fourth section, "Retaliation," was the most important and the hardest to assemble, requiring a thorough review of my e-mails and personal notes to document all the subtle and not-so-subtle forms of retaliation that were used against me during the last four months. The fifth and final section was entitled "Miscellaneous": before-and-after organization charts, timelines, my internal memo describing "25 Positive Attributes of AIG," and every other e-mail I could possibly find to support my claim that I had been a positive force within AIG.

By midnight I had assembled two impressive and identical binders—one for me, one for Jonathan—each almost an inch thick: my whistleblower's binder. My work here was done. I walked out, with a friendly nod to my security guard buddy. I felt great. This was real, positive progress in documenting my case. It was a badly needed boost to my ego and my pride.

That night was my last lonely night in my stark Battery Park apartment. I would spend the following morning with Jonathan, return later in the day for my two suitcases, then take a cab back to La Guardia for my 6 p.m. flight back to Houston. I hoped never to return. New York City was indeed a magical place, but it held far too many bad memories for me.

My second meeting with Jonathan took place at a large table in his conference room. I handed him a copy of my binder. "Take a look at this and tell me what you think." In the space of about thirty minutes Jonathan devoured its contents. He flipped page after page with voracious enthusiasm. He broke the silence with a couple of clarifying questions, but otherwise he never lifted his eyes. As I scanned his facial expressions and watched his body language, I felt better and better. Finally he finished his first read of my binder and pushed his chair away from the table. One good thing about Jonathan: he was an extrovert, not inclined to keep his emotions to himself.

"This is absolutely beautiful. This is the most complete and compelling material I have ever read about a case. You were totally dead-on with everything you told me. Thank you for all of the work you must have put in to this. We're gonna fry these bastards."

Our meeting continued for another hour or so. With my nice fat binder in hand, Jonathan understood my case better. He grilled me again, testing my ability once more to hold up under cross-examination. Then we turned to strategy. Jonathan's first piece of news was that an in-house AIG attorney had already called him to respond to our original allegation letter. This attorney would be representing AIG in future discussions and had requested a personal meeting with Jonathan at AIG's offices "to discuss Mr. Massie's allegations." It was a predictable response, with one surprise. AIG's attorney attended the same Temple as Jonathan did in Rye, New York. The two were old friends.

"Is that a good thing or a bad thing?"

Jonathan seemed surprised by my question. "Gordon. You are my client. My first and foremost loyalties are to you." In fact, he thought this was a very positive development. "I can handle this guy, no sweat, and I have credibility with him." Jonathan told me he would meet with the AIG attorney in the next couple of days. He would not bring my binder yet, he said. This was just a casual meeting between friends to discuss a case. He wanted to try to feel out AIG's position without appearing as too aggressive or threatening. This sounded fine to me. At that point, tt seemed our discussion had come to its logical conclusion for now, and I got up as though it was time for me to leave.

But Jonathan wasn't through. For the next fifteen minutes he put business aside and talked to me like a friend. Once again, I saw a different side of a man I had judged too quickly to be loud and brash. Jonathan had a softer side, and his years of experience gave him a lot of insight into the tremendous stress his clients were under.

"Gordon," he said. "Listen to me. You have been through hell. I'm sure you feel as though your life has been shattered. But we will get through this together. I want you to hold your head up high. You did the right thing. You have a great case. All of this agony will pass. When it does, I'm going to come down to Houston. I want you to buy me a giant plate of barbecue, and we are going to celebrate our victory over big, dumb AIG." He looked me in the eye. "Okay?"

Jonathan's honest attempt to give me some peace moved me so much that my eyes welled up with tears. I could barely trust my voice. "Thank you, Jonathan," I said. "Thank you." We hugged in parting, and I left his office and headed home for Houston.

Three days later Jonathan phoned. His voice sounded troubled. "I met with my AIG attorney friend. AIG is taking the position that you have been a perennial malcontent for many years and that simply because you do not agree with AIG's re-organizations there is no basis whatsoever for your allegation of retaliation." What was AIG prepared to offer me in the way of a settlement? Jonathan had asked.

Six weeks' severance pay, the AIG attorney replied. He had spent considerable time with Richard Scott discussing this matter, he said. Six weeks' severance was standard and it was AIG's best and final offer.

Six weeks? Six weeks' severance was what you got if you had worked for two years at a minimum wage job, not if you spent twenty years in a senior investment management position and had a compelling case for retaliation as a whistleblower.

Upping the ante a little, Jonathan had summarized the highlights of my binder. The AIG attorney seemed unimpressed but agreed to discuss some of the specific allegations with Richard Scott. He would get back to Jonathan in a couple of days, he said. In other words, said Jonathan, they are going to play hardball.

Three days later Jonathan called again. More bad news. His AIG attorney friend had spoken again with Richard Scott and reviewed some of my specific allegations. Richard had utterly dismissed them. There were many very plausible explanations for the events that Gordon had specified, he said. None of them seemed even remotely retaliatory to him. Based on this information, AIG reiterated their offer of six weeks of severance. Oh, could Richard ever twist the truth!

"We are AIG," Jonathan's attorney friend had added caustically. "We can drag this out forever if you wish to pursue this further. This is what we do best."

I was devastated. "Okay, Jonathan. What do we do now?"

Jonathan was not deterred. "This is the standard opening bullshit I always hear, Gordon," he said. "Don't worry. They're just positioning. The six weeks is bait. They want to see if we'll take it." For a moment, I hesitated. Six weeks wasn't much for twenty years of service, but at my current salary it was still almost $50,000. AIG had standard language in their severance agreements precluding any future litigation, which I would have to agree to if I accepted their offer. If instead I sued AIG and lost, I'd walk away with nothing—less than nothing, actually, since suing AIG would be expensive, stressful, and difficult to prove. Most people, as they well knew, would back down and accept even this paltry offer rather than go into battle.

But Jonathan didn't think the AIG attorney realized what we had. He wanted to meet his friend again, go over our evidence page by page, and show him exactly what our case was all about. "This guy is no dummy," Jonathan said. "As far as he knows, we're bluffing. We have to hit him right between the eyes." The two set up another meeting, and I waited with nervous anticipation from my home in Houston.

I tried to find some kind of distractions. I drove to nearby Lake Conroe and took our family ski boat out on the lake alone for a mindless cruise. The lake was the source of so many wonderful memories of family outings during the hottest of Houston's sweltering summer days. Recently I had asked my now adult daughter about her fondest memories of growing up. "That's easy, Dad," she answered promptly. "Being out on the boat, swimming, and listening to your

Jimmy Buffet music all day." A couple of beers didn't hurt my mood, but I still felt an overriding sense of sadness and loss. Maybe we could get some more money out of AIG, I thought. So what? That wasn't going to fundamentally change my depression. I needed some kind of convincing monetary victory, I needed heartfelt apologies from a bunch of people, and I didn't expect any of the above.

While I was out on the lake, Judy called. "Hi Gordon," she said. "Just wanted to hear how you're doing."

How am I doing? I felt completely empty inside. Out to pasture. Kicked to the curb. Irrelevant. Useless. "Oh, great," I said. "Just great. Hey, I'm out here cruising on my boat while the rest of you are working! Thanks for calling, Judy. I really appreciate it."

When I returned home from the lake Barbara greeted me at the door. "Jonathan tried to reach you on your cell phone, but he couldn't get you to pick up, so he called here. He sounded excited."

I called him back right away. "Jonathan, it's Gordon. What's up?" Jonathan was giddy again. He couldn't wait to tell me about his latest meeting.

"I gotta tell you, Gordon, I felt a lot of hostility when I entered that room. But I can be charming. I asked my friend to take the seat next to me so we could go over your documents together. He seemed reluctant, but he sat down, and we got started. So I brought out this big, fat binder, right? As soon as I opened it, I could see his mood and his body language change. We went through page after page of the evidence you collected. It was compelling, it was complete, and he knew it. He was blown away. Finally we finished the whole book, and by now he was overwhelmed. He had this incredible 'Oh, shit' expression on his face. I could just tell he was thinking media. More bad press for AIG. He was thinking liability. *He knew.* At the end of our meeting he said, 'What does your client need to settle?'"

We got 'em just where we want 'em, Jonathan told me. They know they've screwed up. "So Gordon," he said. "What do you want? How much do you need to settle?"

I had thought about this question carefully. I had lost my salary and cash bonus for the foreseeable future, at least until I could find another job. On top of that, I had lost my unvested stock options and restricted stock. Plus all this needless pain and suffering. I gave Jonathan my dollar figure.

Jonathan choked. He sputtered. He seemed both staggered at my number and dismayed that I would be so unreasonable.

"Gordon," he said finally, "you'll *never* get that. AIG will fight you for decades before they agree to that!"

"Now, wait a minute," I said. "Yes, it's a big number. But AIG has very deep pockets—and they are vulnerable. We know it and they know it." Once again I remembered the advice of my friend, David Zerhusen.

"We may not win this in court, if it comes to that," I said, "but what about your editor friend from the *Wall Street Journal?*"

So we hatched a plan. Jonathan and his attorney friend would meet again, in person, just as in the first two meetings, to discuss what I wanted to settle. Jonathan would deliver my exact dollar figure. He would give his friend a few minutes to be dumfounded, then Jonathan would propose a more reasonable offer. "Give Mr. Massie eighty percent of his dollar number, and I believe he will settle," he'd say. At the right moment, he'd turn up the pressure. "If you do not agree within 24 hours, we will immediately release a full news story to the *Wall Street Journal* containing all of Mr. Massie's allegations of retaliation. Remember, he has twenty years with this company and he was the most senior investment professional in AIG's Houston office. This is a one-time, non-negotiable offer by Mr. Massie. Take it or leave it."

And this is exactly what Jonathan did and said in his next day meeting with the AIG attorney. "Our man swallowed real hard," Jonathan reported. "But he promised to get back to us within 24 hours."

Twelve hours later Jonathan got a call from AIG. "Will Mr. Massie agree to a suspension of AIG's contributions to his 401K plan during his severance pay period? If he gets another job he cannot have two simultaneous 401K contributions from different employers."

My 401K plan? Oh, joy. For once God, not the devil, was in the details.

AIG had cratered.

Chapter 20: Finding Some Sanity

And sure enough, within 24 hours AIG agreed to our alternative proposal, and the weight of the world was lifted off of my weary shoulders. The promptness of AIG's response was also noteworthy. Based on my prior experiences with AIG, I knew that any expenditure of this amount required Board of Directors' approval. How did that happen? What did Richard Scott tell the Board? How could he have possibly explained his actions when his attorney had so quickly and painfully seen our case? Was Richard's head now on the chopping block? How could AIG possibly have seen fit to keep him around? What about Win Neuger or Rich Mercante? They were certainly willing accomplices. How could AIG be so stupid as to let this all happen?

The answer was again quite simple. This was AIG's way. This was the cost of doing business the way AIG did business. I was sure they figured that for every Gordon Massie style victory there were ten other schmucks that took the six weeks of severance and ran home with their tails between their legs. There were no ethics or moral issues at stake here. Just raw business. The impact on human beings was irrelevant. There was not going to be any apology. There was not going to be any admission of guilt. Just an impersonal severance agreement and the silent exchange of big dollars. There was no remorse, no recognition of any wrongdoing, and no looking back by

AIG. In fact, I was the one who, oddly enough, began to feel the remorse. I felt remorse for agreeing to take their money and to agree to maintain the confidentiality of our agreement. My silence was being bought and AIG would be free to repeat these offenses again and again. Shouldn't I have stood my ground and gone public with my allegations? Shouldn't I have allowed the public to truly see inside AIG the way I had? Wouldn't the world be a slightly better place if I had filed my case with the Department of Labor and the whole world could know of AIG's dirty secrets?

I have tortured myself over these questions for quite some time now and I really do not have any great answers. But the truth was that when I was finally offered my settlement I was a complete emotional wreck. Anxiety and depression had depleted my will to fight. The idea of a media battle and all that potential publicity was most unappealing to me. Also, extending out for what could have been years of legal conflict would have been far too emotionally scaring for me and the outcome would have still been uncertain. Perhaps had I been emotionally stronger I would have taken a longer term approach and really waged war against "Those Bastards."

While these were my immediate concerns at the time, I soon realized that there was nothing in my settlement agreement with AIG that precluded me from telling my story publicly, as long as I did not reveal any confidential AIG information or any of the dollar terms of my settlement. Hence, I have the ability and freedom to now write my story.

Another factor was that I truly expected some heads to roll inside of AIG once the Board became aware of how I was treated. My settlement cost AIG a big number and for this amount to be so flagrantly wasted by Win Neuger, Richard Scott, and Rich Mercante had to reflect badly on their status at AIG. But sadly this never happened and all three continued in their roles as senior members of AIG's Investment Department for several more years to come.

Only at AIG. Only at AIG could such inhumanity be tolerated. How did this organization become so corrupt? Did they honestly believe that their piles of cash were there simply to bail themselves out of their illegal activities? Were these people not human beings with families and feelings and sensitivities to others? Apparently not.

You would have thought that my elation over my settlement would have permanently lifted my mood and self-esteem. It did for a while but gradually I slipped back into a steady state of deep anxiety and depression. Why was this happening? With my other assets I had more than enough funds to take the rest of my life off. I was free! I didn't have to ever work again unless I chose otherwise. How many people can walk away from corporate America at the ripe old age of 54 and, if they choose, never work again? No more commuting. No more stress. No more office politics. No more coping with inhumane "superiors." This was supposed to be a happy, momentous time in my life and yet I was gripped in sadness and a deep sense of loss. Why? I had no answers. No explanation for my unhappiness. Perhaps time will heal me. I did not know.

As 2005 drew to a close, my thoughts returned to the matter of perhaps trying to find a new job. Since the settlement in October, I was continuing to battle my emotional demons and these were undoubtedly made worse by my idleness and lethargy. Inside I sensed this innate urge to be busy, productive, and important again and yet I had absolutely zero motivation. Ever have one of those dreams where you are trying so hard to run at something but you can't make any progress whatsoever? That was me. My feelings of irrelevancy and uselessness made it almost impossible to take any positive steps to start feeling any better about myself. What do you do when you are suddenly and unexpectedly dropped into a world of retirement much earlier than you ever planned? Combine this with the reality that my kids were mostly grown and gone and life began to feel too quiet, too boring, and too lonely. All of my friends were still working and Barbara had a full and busy calendar of her own. So going back to work began to seem like the best alternative. A frequent comment that was made by my close friends was "You're too young, you'll want to go back to work." This bothered me somewhat. How did they know what I needed to do? They had not experienced the torture that I had experienced. Were they not being a bit presumptuous about what I needed to do?

Regardless, I decided to make a few phone calls to people I knew in the investment business to see what might be going on. Houston was not a big investment management town, big oil yes, but not a lot of jobs in my specialty. So my calls were mostly to cities like Chicago, Boston, and even New York. Yes, there were certainly jobs available but I would have to uproot my family and relocate. Our youngest child was still a junior in high school and the thought of moving him to a new school and community was not in any way appealing. Hunter was a shy and quiet young man who was just beginning to open up and thrive socially. We didn't want to do anything to change his momentum. Relocation was a major negative and I also came up with the following other reasons why a new job did not make sense to me at the time:

- My emotional state was still so tentative that I may not interview well
- I didn't need additional income
- We did not want to leave our good friends in Houston
- Re-entering the corporate world had limited appeal to me
- I wanted to see what retirement was all about, if only for a while.
- We loved where we lived, except in the summertime

So it was not a hard decision to remain unemployed, at least for a year, I told myself. It was important to me to try this retirement business out and see if I could grow to like it. There simply had to be more to life than the working world and all of the stress and routine it required.

But I was still battling my unrelenting anxiety and depression. Sometimes I would sleep most of the day. Anything to stop all of these destructive churning thoughts.

It was as though I had received this gaping wound from my battle with AIG and it would not heal. I was living with a constant open sore that just festered deeply on my body. So Barbara insisted that I see our family physician for a medical check-up. Before I went to see our family doctor I pulled up one of those internet lists of "The 25 Most Common Symptoms of Depression" and I think I checked the boxes of about 20 symptoms. Dr. Rogers immediately put me on an anti-depressant and gave me additional prescriptions for my anxiety. Dr. Rogers added, "Don't just take these pills and expect everything to be fine in a week. I want you to see Jerry Devine at Devine Family Counseling and work on some emotional therapy. You need both drugs and therapy if you hope to have a full recovery."

To me my depression was strictly situational. My situation had changed and so it was only logical that my depression would lift. It was only a matter of time. What I needed to do was to get busy at something and to start having new and positive experiences now that I had entered my retirement year(s).

I needed to do something grand, something bold, and maybe even something extravagant. Our daughter was in graduate school in Denver and she, along with her two brothers, had become avid skiers. For me Colorado was always a wondrous place, especially in the summertime when the Houston heat was unbearable. So I convinced Barbara that I wanted to drive to Colorado to see our daughter and I was going to drive around and check out some areas in the mountains for a second home. "Just don't buy anything" were her parting words. But, of course, I did.

Yes, without Barbara seeing anything more than a few photos I went ahead and bought a 2400 square foot home near Breckenridge, Colorado, in the dead of winter. The elevation was over 11,000 feet and it had a panoramic view of the Continental Divide. It was my Rocky Mountain High moment. The words to that John Denver song were never truer than on that day.

This was all exciting and very distracting for a period but now I was back in Houston trying to figure out what in the world I was going to do with all of my idle time when I was not in Colorado. One of the joys of my job with AGC and AIG had been the opportunity to meet so many successful people in business. There was one individual I met on a high-yield bond roadshow in Houston that had successfully started and managed a very profitable manufacturing company in the upper Midwest. He was actually selling his company to a leveraged buyout firm and he came along on the roadshow to help the new owners market the company's new issue of high-yield bonds. Sitting next to this man, I asked what his personal plans were going to be after the sale of his company. "Oh, now its my time to return." I paused in the hope that he would explain where he was returning to. "No, no, I mean return to society. Give back. Philanthropy." He clarified. He went on to explain his personal view of the three phases of a successful life. "Learn, earn, and return." The first third of your life should be all about learning and getting your education. The next third of your life should be focused on earning a living. Hopefully a good one so that you can take advantage of the last third of your life, returning. Taking all you have learned and earned and really giving back to society for the benefit of those less fortunate." Wow, I thought. That was profound and his generous words have stayed with me for many years. So here I was perhaps facing the last third of my life and maybe it was time for me to return. Helping others, I had always heard, was a great way to help yourself.

Habitat for Humanity was always a volunteer organization that had interested me. I was a bit of an amateur carpenter and the idea of building simple and affordable housing for the working class was appealing to me. So I called. "I am sorry Mr. Massie but we really do not need any more help on our home construction. But we really need some volunteers to work at the Restore," said the voice on the phone. Restores represented a new concept at Habitat where individuals and businesses could donate construction materials and household items and these items would be resold to the public to help support the local Habitat affiliate. The Conroe, Texas affiliate was currently in the process of setting up their own Restore and that was where I could volunteer. "As long as it is mindless, physical, and without stress, sign me up," was my answer. The next day I reported for my new "job."

Restore was grunt, physical, warehouse work pure and simple. Pick-up and receive donated items, sort through everything, and put the good stuff into the store and sell it. It was mindless, back break-ing lifting and moving. No wonder they needed people. But it helped me. I needed low stress, physical work to at least keep my mind somewhat occupied. Returning home I was physically spent and aching all over, but the work helped me to relax, and I felt bet-ter knowing that I was helping a worthy cause. But the work did lit-tle to enhance my self-esteem. I wasn't wheeling and dealing in the world of corporate finance. I was shifting through a lot of donated junk and trying to salvage what we could sell. My self image was under considerable pressure as I sorted through the salvage of my own career.

Coincidentally, Jeff Skilling of Enron fame was also donating his time at the Houston Habitat Restore affiliate about 35 miles south of my location. Yes, apparently Mr. Skilling had developed a bit of a drinking problem while he was awaiting his insider trading and fraud trial. He was convicted of public intoxication in Houston and ordered to perform a certain number of hours of community serv ice and he ended up at the Houston Restore doing the same work I was doing. How ironic, I thought. A corporate fraud artist and a corporate whistleblower working for the same good cause. Anyway, just before his trial began, Skilling was asked in a media interview how he enjoyed his time volunteering at the Habitat Restore. When he said, "I found it very rewarding," I knew he had the same ability to bullshit people as well as many at AIG did. For a while I thought of traveling to the Houston Restore to meet Mr. Skilling, but no, I had already been with enough crooks recently.

My Restore work was occupying about two days a week for me so I had some extra time to fill. One of our neighbors was on the Board of the Montgomery County Women's Center, also in Conroe, and she encouraged Barbara and me to become volunteers at this organization which provided shelter and counseling to victims of rape and domestic violence. Becoming a volunteer required that we take a 40-hour training program and go through a full background check. Many of my guy friends thought I was really losing it when they discovered my interest in volunteering at the Women's Center.

But I was curious. Domestic violence was something I could never begin to comprehend. My father absolutely worshipped the ground that my mother walked on. I was raised to honor and respect all people and I had multiple strong female role models in my life. The idea of violence against women was appalling to me and I thought that maybe as a male volunteer I could set a better example of "maleness" to these unfortunate women and children. So I answered the Hot Line, made repairs around the shelter, helped with some fundraising, and even had the opportunity to visit on occasion with some of the women and children at the shelter. This experience was profound in terms of helping me understand that in spite of my demons and my angst, my life in comparison with these unfortunate women and children was pretty good.

Over the course of the next few months I dabbled in a few other things. I had discussions with a few local people who were looking for seed capital to start new businesses. With my carpenter skills I studied the residential real estate market looking for fixer-uppers to remodel and flip. New contacts in Colorado also spoke with me about investing in a real estate development near our Colorado home. I even initiated conversations with BMW Motorcycles about restarting a failed dealership near my home in Texas. But nothing ever seemed to make sense. Lots of great ways to lose money. I would look at the numbers in these business plans and quickly lose interest. The stock market seemed less risky with more upside so I followed it actively.

There were highs and lows during this period but mostly lows. The anti-depressant drugs did not seem to alleviate my depression and my overall enthusiasm for life was waning. My working world had been filled with so much before it all blew up. I was the big cheese. When I walked into rooms other conversations stopped. I controlled billions of dollars of capital. My decisions had pronounced ripple effects on people, companies, and AIG. I flew first class, stayed in the best hotels, and ate at five star restaurants. As noble as my volunteer work might have seemed, it was still mostly menial work with little intrinsic reward. But it still did get me out and I was always among a very kind and compassionate group of other volunteers.

Another area of some enjoyment for me was the opportunity to re-connect with long lost friends and family members. I became active with two cousins in doing some Massie family genealogy work and that is how I learned about my great grandfather's Abilene roots. Looking up and surprising old friends was always a great but temporary distraction. But sometimes I felt sad as these old friends had to rush off to work amid their busy lives and I went back to my semi-emptiness. Seeing new and old friends gave me a sense that most people were uncomfortable talking with me about my experience at AIG, just as my co-workers had been before my departure. Again it felt like death, divorce, or grave illness in their minds and they seemed ill at ease in probing me for more details about my loss. It felt good to talk with friends about my experience but I always seemed to sense a lack of interest or a lack of comfort in the topic.

Why was I still so sad? I had everything that so many people dreamt of and yet I was still so unhappy. There was no enthusiasm. Nothing got me as excited as before. Even my motorcycle trips seemed routine and boring in my retirement world. It was as though every day was cold, gray, and overcast. Staying in Colorado helped for short spells but there was no real relief. I had thought I wanted to travel in retirement but even that felt like far too much effort. Barbara and I both knew I was still deeply depressed and it was now time to visit my therapist, Jerry Devine. Yes, it was time for devine intervention. Sorry about that.

We had known Jerry and Helen Devine over the years and they both had great reputations in our area for working with people just like me. So I heeded the long ago advice of Dr. Rogers, and I made my first appointment with Jerry.

Jerry was an older man, maybe in his late sixties, and he had loads of experience in dealing with chronically depressed people like me. He brought me in to his dimly lit and comfortable suburban office. "Please, have a seat. Would you like some coffee?" he asked. I noticed several boxes of Kleenex tissue strategically placed around his office. Apparently I could have a good cry in any seat in the house. Jerry started by just getting me talking about my experience. What happened? Give me the timeline? How did you feel? How did you cope? What are you doing now? For probably 45 minutes out of my first hour with Jerry I just spoke and answered Jerry's probing questions. It almost felt like a rerun of my first meeting with Jonathan except it was a great deal less intense. Talking about my experience was always a source of some relief to me. Gauging the reactions of others was always the challenge. But Jerry was a pro and I could feel him really trying to focus on what I was saying.

After my 45-minute semi-monologue Jerry seemed to have grasped the essence of my story. He then spoke. "You know what I think? I think the way you were treated was the same as being raped. They caught the guy and he is in prison now, but that doesn't take away your pain and sense of violation. You are suffering something akin to Post Traumatic Stress Syndrome." Wow! That pretty well explained how I felt. "But why do I feel so low all the time, even several months after my settlement?," I asked. Then Jerry went on to explain how the brain doesn't know the difference between the actual bad experiences I had and my constant reliving of the experiences through my churning negative and self-destructive thoughts. "Every time you think about AIG you pile on a little bit more stress, more anxiety, and more depression. What we have to work on is changing your thinking about your experiences." Sounded like a tall order to me.

Cognitive Behavior Therapy is all about trying to change one's self-defeating and negative thoughts. If you can change your thinking patterns you can actually begin to change how you feel about past and future experiences. Its like the shy boy who convinces himself that no girl would ever dance with him. But by changing his negative self-talk about being unattractive he can begin to see his positive attributes and begin to gain the confidence he needs to ask a girl to dance. So for the next couple of months I met weekly with Jerry and we worked on Cognitive Behavior Therapy to try to get me to control and divert my thinking. "Think about all the good that you experienced. Think about your excellent results and your excellent relationships over the years. You have to convince yourself of the good.

Maybe you should write a book!" In fact Jerry strongly urged me to draft a letter to Richard that I could later choose to send or not. "Tell Richard how great you were and what a prick he was. It will at least make you feel better. You don't have to send it. And your mind will start to think about all of your accomplishments again."

I knew Jerry was right and I took a few stabs at this letter to Richard but it never went anywhere. The time spent with Jerry was very helpful and it helped me to understand my illness and what it was going to take to make me healthy again. I began to feel a touch better in the days ahead but I still retained that underlying sense of sadness and loss. Sure I could force my brain to think positive thoughts for a while but the old habits and churning thoughts just wouldn't completely leave me.

Writing this book has really brought home to me what Jerry was saying. There is much I have to be proud of and sometimes it takes years and lots of concentrated effort to bring that pride back to its rightful place in my mind.

While during this period I choose not to write my memoirs and not to write Richard Scott, I did read a number of books on the subject of retirement. Most books on retirement deal with the financial aspects of accumulating enough assets so that you can kiss the working world goodbye. These books did not appeal to me. Thanks to my historic frugality, my settlement with AIG, and a lucrative pension from AGC, I was set for life. But I tried to focus on figuring out how to best allocate my time and how to exert my energies in order to start feeling better about myself. With all of my choices and all of my freedom there had to be someway that I could begin to feel passion and enthusiasm again. And so I read and read. I asked and I investigated. And here were my simple conclusions about what it was going to take for me to have a rewarding and self-fulfilling retirement:

- I had to have and maintain my good health.
- I had to have a reasonable amount of income and reserve assets.
- Everyone needs a close circle of family and friends.

- Each of us needs a lengthy list of activities and endeavors that we wish to vigorously pursue.
- Each of us needs the energy, passion, and enthusiasm to pursue the items on the above list.

The television commercials from the financial institutions that wanted to manage my retirement dollars always made me laugh. Pictured strolling hand in hand on some Caribbean beach was an older couple savoring the warm tropical air as the clear blue surf washed up on their sandy toes. Oh what bliss retirement must be! Well the reality is different. I might spend one or two days a year on a beach with Barbara but that left 363 other days to fill. Therein lies the challenge. For me this was a huge challenge. I had the top four items on my list but not the fifth. My fragile emotional state and underlying sadness left me without the energy, passion, and enthusiasm to pursue any of my life's dream or goals. I thought of my own ten basic concepts of how I wished to manage my High-Yield Bond group. The second concept on my list was "Give AIG your full commitment. Do your work with energy, passion, and enthusiasm" Shouldn't I be practicing what I had been preaching? Yes, but I could not figure out how to do it. How could I regain my energy, passion, and enthusiasm for life?

Chapter 21: The Great Collapse

During the years 2006-2008, my curiosity about the people and events at AIG would not wane. Since I was following the stock market and watching the financial news networks, the topic of AIG seemed to often come up in the news of the day. Maybe it was just quarterly earnings reports or some mundane new addition to management, but regardless, my interest was always piqued. I read the Wall Street research reports, talked with my old friends still at the company, and even kept regular tabs on the financial blogs. Part of the reason for my keen interest was that I still owned a fair number of AIG shares that I had received as part of my settlement. The other reason, I guess was simply morbid curiousity. Was anyone getting fired? Had Martin Sullivan (the new CEO) blown the place up yet? What was Greenberg up to? I was drawn like a moth to a destructive flame.

My immediate curiosity following my termination was about the future of the personnel within the High-Yield Group in Houston. There had been those five immediate departures that had occurred during my trip to Colorado but was anybody else going to leave? Of the 24 or so analysts, traders and portfolio managers in Houston, nearly half left soon after I was terminated. Did they leave because of AIG's treatment of me? No, there were far too many other considerations for these people. But I could not help but wonder if maybe in some subtle way my experience may have been at least considered by these departing employees. Did they ever want to be treated like Gordon? Maybe they watched in silence but maybe they also knew my pain and humiliation. Twenty years of dedicated service and treated so badly. Maybe they truly knew. But the real reason for the departures was that most had become disillusioned with AIG and they had found better opportunities with other organizations. Some people had told me that I was the glue that held the group together but I don't think so. Morale had deteriorated and people were simply tired of the chaos and dysfunction of the organization.

Perhaps one of the most startling and interesting resignations from AIG was that of Greg Braun. As you may recall, Greg had been appointed one of the co-heads of the High-Yield Group after Tim Janszen's departure. Greg's departure had actually occurred some time after my termination and was reportedly due to an issue of strong disagreement among Greg, Richard Scott, and Rich Mercante. Now Greg was a very private person and he did not convey much of his experience directly to me. But I had my sources and I milked them for all they were worth. What I had been able to gather was that Greg had accused Richard and Rich of inappropriately allocating new high-yield bond purchases to some investment grade bond portfolios directly managed by Rich in New York. Oftentimes when there was a hot new high-yield bond issue the bonds had to be allocated and limited by the originating Wall Street broker to all of the interested buyers. Since the buyers did not receive as many bonds on the new issue as they wanted, many buyers in the secondary market emerged, bidding up the price. For example, a new issue was priced at par or 100 and yet may be bid up to 104 in the secondary market. For this and many other reasons, AIG operated under strict guidelines to make sure these new issues were appropriately and fairly allocated to all of the accounts that AIG managed (both AIG accounts and the accounts of outside investors). AIG could not arbitrarily allocate these new issues to certain favorite accounts. But apparently this was what Greg accused Rich of doing. He was reportedly trying to "pump up" the performance of a couple of key portfolios he was managing.

I had always admired Greg during the time that he worked for me. He had incredibly high moral and ethical standards and would sometimes bring up ethical business issues and questions to me that I had not even considered. So I knew that Greg had very high standards. Anyway, the conflict among Greg, Rich, and Richard boiled over and Greg eventually resigned in disgust because of the alleged dishonestly of Rich's activities and Richard's apparent willingness to tolerate these activities. Greg had later contacted me and requested Jonathan Sack's phone number and I offered to help in any way I could. Greg kept his cards close to his vest so I was still somewhat in the dark with regard to his experience. Later I heard from another source of an incredible quotation from Rich Mercante that had occurred during his dispute with Greg over these portfolio activities. "I thought we (AIG) had gotten rid of all the whistleblowers when we fired Gordon." Could anyone be as stupid as Rich Mercante?

The news wires were buzzing in February, 2006 when AIG was levied a $ 1.6 billion fine by various regulators who had alleged that AIG had participated in bid-rigging schemes and paid insurance brokers to steer business its way, used fraudulent insurance transactions to bolster the quality and quantity of its earnings, and underreported to state insurance departments the amounts of workers' compensation premiums it had collected. Of course, the AIG spin doctors did their level best to try to convince the public that this was a one-time occurrence and that AIG had truly cleaned house. For nearly a week, AIG was very prominent in the news and there were regular and repeated updates on such stations as CNBC and CNN. I believe it was CNN that showed a film clip of the AIG lobby at 70 Pine St. in New York while the announcer gave the latest news update on AIG. This film clip actually showed Richard Scott and Rich Mercante smiling broadly as they walked across the AIG lobby and entered through that same damn turnstile that I had struggled with before. And all the while I heard the announcer's words, "AIG has been levied the largest fine in corporate history." "Look mom, dad is on TV!" My how proud their children must have felt.

Poor, poor Rich Mercante. It wasn't very long after his episode with Greg Braun that Rich really found himself in hot water. Rich was by then one of the highest ranking executives within AIG's Investment Department and he had reportedly entered into a "Clinton-esque" relationship with one of his female subordinates. Now I had met Rich's wife and two children and this sort of news always made me sad. For me this was always a reflection of one's true character. But the relationship was not Rich's actual mistake. Reportedly, Rich was using the AIG internal e-mail network to send his female friend some "inappropriate e-mails" which resulted in his immediate firing. I was so impressed that AIG had vehemently adhered to its stringent employee "Code of Ethics" and shown Rich the door! It was comforting to me to know that AIG did, in fact, have some ethical standards and that email violators were given the same swift boot that was given to whistleblowers.

Another poor unfortunate soul at AIG was Martin Sullivan, the new CEO who had replaced Hank Greenberg in 2005. Martin had joined AIG right out of high school and he had no college degree. He began his career as a clerk in the mail room and 31 years later was appointed as the next CEO of AIG. Now by all reports Martin was a very decent human being. This engaging and somewhat chubby Englishman was described as the polar opposite of Hank Greenberg: calm, approachable, and witty. Martin had worked all of his career in AIG's commercial property and casualty insurance operations. I am sure that he worked very hard under Mr. Greenberg and had been considered very competent in the property casualty end of AIG's vast business empire. But no one could ever be another Hank Greenberg. No one could ever know, or understand, or manage AIG the way Hank did. Hank had built his AIG empire and had been in charge since 1962, the year I graduated from sixth grade.

Remember Greenberg ran his empire with an iron hand. He did not tolerate much in the way of disobedience. He wanted submission and complicity on the part of his top management team and he effectively surrounded himself with "yes" men. Hank was always in charge and everyone knew it. So into the massive void left by the departure of Hank walked Martin Sullivan. Martin didn't know much about AIG's vast operations of airplane leasing, financial products, consumer finance, life insurance, investments, derivatives, structured financial products and so on and on. He was a property casualty insurance guy and he had to completely trust the wisdom and business experience of all the other heads of all the other departments within AIG. As I have suggested before, these various departmental heads were in these positions in many cases because they were willing to defer all critical decisions to Mr. Greenberg. They saw a rookie in Martin Sullivan and perhaps an opportunity to finally now "Do their own thing," once Hank had left AIG.

The whole successor question had been asked of Mr. Greenberg for many years while he was the CEO of AIG. Remember he was 80 years of age when he stepped down as the CEO of AIG in 2005. Financial analysts almost always asked the successor question of Hank whenever there was an opportunity during AIG's quarterly conference calls. Hank's answer was almost always the same, "I have no plans to retire and when I do there will be strong managers at AIG to succeed me," was how I would paraphrase Hank's constant response. But there never were these strong managers at AIG, at least in my opinion. The strong, the talented, and the able all left as soon as they could experience the "joys" of working with Hank. As I have written before, Hank did not want independent, free thinking upstarts on his team of top managers. This thinking became painfully obvious in 2005 when Martin Sullivan was named as Hank's hand-picked successor. Greenberg had years to build a strong team of new managers and poor old Martin was his best choice? AIG needed a solid team of well functioning, intelligent, and visionary new managers to replace the strong personality of Hank. But now AIG had Martin Sullivan, a decent, hardworking human being who was way over his head and with an impossible task ahead, especially when it came to dealing with a strange new type of mortgage instrument called sub-prime.

Sub-prime mortgages were the brainchild of the residential mortgage industry and really gained popularity beginning in 2005. Virtually everywhere in this country residential home prices were rising on a steady annual basis. Whether it was new construction or old, city or suburb, or rich or poor neighborhood; home prices seemed to defy gravity and consistently rise year after year. So the mortgage industry decided that this market should be opened up to a much larger world of home buyers than had historically been able to meet the requirements to qualify for a home mortgage. Sub-prime lenders loosened these requirements dramatically. Buyers would "qualify" for home loans based upon artificially low "teaser rates" which kept mortgage payments very low for a few years but then escalated to higher market rates in the future. In addition to these low teaser rates, the documentation that prospective borrowers had to produce in order to qualify for a sub-prime mortgage was dramatically reduced. No verification of income, employment, credit history, nor other assets was required in many cases. The term used in the industry was a NINJA loan. No Income, No Job or Assets. The naive logic behind these sub-prime loans was that home ownership should be available to more people and if some of these people couldn't meet their mortgage obligations there was no problem because inevitably their homes had appreciated in value and could be resold for more than enough proceeds to pay off their mortgages.

So from about 2005 on, AIG began to dramatically increase its exposure to sub-prime mortgages, underneath the not-so-watchful nor informed eyes of Martin Sullivan. Martin had to trust his new lieutenants since he could not be expected to be an expert on these new mortgages. But by late 2007, sub-prime mortgages were beginning to become real problems for the capital markets. Quite simply, many teaser rates were expiring and borrowers were seeing as much as a doubling in their monthly mortgage payments. Add to this the spotty credit history and limited income or assets of many sub-prime borrowers and you suddenly had a brewing storm of rising mortgage defaults and falling home prices. Financial analysts became increasingly concerned about the sub-prime mortgage exposure of all financial institutions. Since Richard Scott had previously been the Head of Fixed Income at AIG he frequently was asked this sub-prime exposure question. Early in 2008 he publicly announced that he was confident that AIG could very easily manage its balance sheet exposure to sub-prime mortgages.

Flashing red lights, buzzers, and alarms are all going off all at once inside my feeble brain! If Richard said it, it must be true, right? I would have felt better with a simple "no comment" from Richard, but since he spoke openly and publicly it had to be false, at least in my mind. I felt confident that Richard was valuing his sub-prime mortgages in about the same way AIG had valued all of those toxic high-yield bonds owned by Sun America in 2001. Did Richard know any other way to think or act when faced with pressure from another human being? So the very next day I sold all of my remaining shares of AIG stock (that had formerly been restricted stock) for a price of $58 per share and, other than my AGC pension, that was the last of my financial exposure to AIG.

Several months later I was visiting an old friend in Austin, Texas, where I had been doing some Massie family genealogical work at the libraries of the University of Texas. My friend was employed by the Texas State Insurance Commission and was charged with responsibility for, in part, monitoring the credit quality of the investment portfolios of AIG's various life and annuity insurance companies that were domiciled in the State of Texas and subject to regulation by the State of Texas. I asked my friend about AIG's sub-prime exposure and his response was "We are getting increasingly worried about the AIG companies. Richard Scott continues to visit us in Austin on a regular basis and he has finally come off of his high horse and become a lot more humble and apologetic about the sub-prime problems." Imagine that. My instincts about Richard were dead on.

In the meantime, AIG's earnings continued to decline quarter after quarter due in part to continuing losses in the sub-prime mortgage portfolio. For the year 2007, AIG reported net income of $6.2 billion which was down 56% from 2006 net income of $14.05 billion. Virtually this entire decline was attributed by AIG management to losses related to sub-prime mortgages both in AIG's investment portfolio and through the sub-prime related credit default swaps written by AIG Financial Products, which was not part of AIG's

Investment Department. Credit default swaps are basically insurance policies underwritten by AIG to insure others against losses in their sub-prime related holdings. As these sub-prime losses in others' portfolios mounted, AIG had to cover these losses through the insurance liabilities they incurred as a result of selling these credit default swaps.

For the first quarter of 2008, AIG reported a net loss of $7.81 billion compared with net income of $4.13 billion for the first quarter of 2007. Again, nearly all of this decline in net income was attributed to losses on AIG's credit default swaps and losses in AIG's sub-prime related securities portfolio. These losses were reported to the public on May 8, 2008, and AIG simultaneously announced its intent to shore up its balance sheet by raising $12.5 billion of new capital in the very near future. At that point AIG's common stock had fallen in value to $44.15 per share. After the announcement that AIG would raise new equity, AIG's share price fell to $40.28 the next day.

Eventually, on May 20, 2008 AIG was successful in issuing $20 billion in new equity and debt capital, but at this time the shares sold for a price of $38 each. By now poor old Martin Sullivan was really feeling the heat from AIG shareholders about these credit default swap and investment losses that seemed to get bigger and bigger in spite of Sullivan's earlier pronouncements to the contrary. Finally, after months of speculation, Martin was dismissed by AIG's Board on June 15, 2008, almost exactly 39 months after he had replaced Hank Greenberg in the wake of an earlier accounting scandal. During this 39 month period, AIG's common stock declined from $51 to $34 per share but somehow Martin still walked away with a severance package of over $25 million for his noble work. Just how out of touch could AIG's Board of Directors have been at the time? Shareholders be damned!

On August 6, 2008, AIG reported that for the second quarter of 2008 it had incurred a loss of $5.36 billion as compared with net income of $4.28 billion during the second quarter of 2007. Just like clockwork, this decline in net income was almost entirely due to losses incurred by AIG in its credit default swap and sub-prime investment portfolio. On the date of this announcement AIG shares closed at a price of $29.09 and for the next month there were rampant rumors of liquidity problems and further catastrophic additional losses at AIG. By September 9, 2008, AIG's share price had fallen to $18.37 per share and the price seemed to be in a daily state of collapse. The management team at AIG had no remaining credibility with its shareholders who seemed to be bailing out of the stock at any price.

Finally, on September 16, 2008, the federal government announced that it was providing an $85 billion loan to AIG and the government would also receive warrants to purchase nearly 80% of AIG's stock at a very low price. AIG's share price subsequently fell to $2.69 per share on September 18, 2008. AIG was effectively bankrupt. AIG was only kept alive through a lifeline of temporary credit provided by the Federal Reserve Bank. Oh how the mighty have fallen! AIG had once been a financial behemoth with shareholder equity worth over $200 billion, and now its shares were almost worthless. Anyone could buy a share of AIG for about half the price of a gallon of gasoline at the time.

I knew AIG had some massive problems but I had never anticipated back in 2005 exactly how severe those problems would become. My heart went out to all of my former colleagues who were still employed by AIG. They were hardworking and ethical people (with a few exceptions) and they deserved better. The tragic collapse of AIG was devastating to its shareholders, its employees, and to the U.S. economy in general. Before too long AIG top management became the modern day poster children for corporate greed, fraud, arrogance, and mismanagement. Move over Ken Lay, Jeff Skilling, and Andy Fastow, the public has some new people to hate now!

Chapter 22: Vindication

By middle September there is no more gorgeous or majestic place on Earth than in the Rocky Mountains of Colorado. The lush summer foliage is falling prey to the cold midnight air and the deep greens are changing into bright yellows, shimmering golds, glossy oranges, and shining reds. As the forests rise up to the snowy peaks, all of these colors are in bright contrast to on another as far as the eye can see. Colorado had become a healing place for me. Its beauty and majesty never failed to touch my soul and gave me a renewed appreciation for life. Just being outside in the fresh mountain air was almost enough to drain me of my continuing underlying sadness. Mountain biking, river rafting, fly fishing, and hiking were all consuming to me during my summer stays at our cabin near Breckenridge. But regardless of how engaged I otherwise was, I was still dealing with my bouts of depression and feelings of loss and grief. It made no sense. I had a wonderful life and yet, somehow I kept reliving my experience. I simply could not leave well enough alone and my mind would not allow me to forget. In spite of all outward appearances, I was still troubled on the inside.

Barbara and I had plotted a two day driving route that would take us from our cabin to Buena Vista, over Cottonwood Pass to Crested Butte, then over Kebler Pass and into Glenwood Springs for the night. The following day we would rise early to see the Maroon Bells outside of Aspen, then into Aspen for lunch, followed by a drive over Independence Pass, and then onto Leadville and home. We have never in our lives been so absolutely spellbound by such overwhelming natural beauty. Barbara opened up her new camera and I don't think there was an aspen tree or rushing mountain stream along the entire route that she did not photograph. On our first day of this two day trip we had arrived at Crested Butte and enjoyed a delightful lunch on a terrace overlooking the distant slopes of a mountain ski resort in late summer. After lunch Barbara wanted to do her usual shopping and browsing in the local stores. For me, enjoying a good book while seated on a Main Street park bench was a better distraction, so we parted ways in Crested Butte for about an hour.

How glorious was the day. Majestic fall colors, a nip in air, clear blue skies, and a peaceful and historic Colorado, once mining, and now resort village. The only sight on the horizon to detract in any way from my serenity was the distinctive shade of brown patches of dead pines now sharing so much space in the otherwise gorgeous landscape. Yes, the pine bark beetles had come to central Colorado and they were beginning to destroy much of the ubiquitous population of Lodgepole pines. But as the locals would always rationalize, "This is nature's way. There really isn't anything that man can do to stop the beetles." The truth was that mankind had a lot to do with making this forest so vulnerable to the beetles in the first place. This forest was over 100 years old and yet man's influence had weakened the trees. Fire had been suppressed, depriving the forest of its nature source of rejuvenation. Climate change was also suggested as a potential source of problems since warmer winter nights did not provide the cold temperatures to naturally kill the beetle population. Whatever the reason, the loss of so many lush evergreens was a difficult burden for all in this area to bear.

In a way these dying forests were similar to dying AIG. It wasn't sub-prime mortgages that really caused the death of AIG anymore than the beetles could be blamed for killing these forests. Investment risks have always been part of life at AIG just as pine bark beetles have always been present in our forests. What really mattered was what had made the forests and AIG so vulnerable to outside attacks in the first place. Not every financial institution was collapsing from subprime exposure and not every forest was dying due to out of control pine bark beetles. AIG's problem was that years and years of poor management had weakened it from within. It had become like a sick forest, waiting for a colony of pine bark beetles to get to work. In my mind there were four key factors that weakened AIG to the point where it became so vulnerable to outside forces and risks:

- AIG was far too large and geographically and operationally diverse.
- AIG was too disorganized without reasonable systems and controls.
- Within AIG there was a culture that tolerated fraud and corruption.
- Weak management depth caused by years of domination by Hank Greenberg.

In my opinion, these were the true underlying causes of AIG's death. These were the factors that made AIG so unhealthy and so vulnerable to disease. In this case the disease was the advent of the sub-prime mortgage.

As I was resting peacefully on my park bench my cell phone rang and I saw that it is Tim Janszen. Little Timmy, as I used to call him. Tim was now running his own distressed debt fund and he had recently hired my oldest son, Stewart, as a financial analyst. So I always looked forward to my chats and updates with Tim. "Are you sitting down?" Oh that question again from Tim. "Guess what? The Big Dick just got the axe. One of the first to fall at the hands of the Feds," Tim explained. The Big Dick was our code name for Richard Scott and it had always seemed to fit his character. Wow! How the mighty had fallen, again! We chatted on about the unbelievable tragedy that had befallen so many of the innocent at AIG, and soon Barbara had returned and I said goodbye and thanks to Tim.

"Richard Scott just got dumped! First one to get axed by the Feds," I explained with a touch of glee in my voice. "Really! Wow! I can't believe it! Barbara shrieked with delight for all the genteel boutique shoppers in Crested Butte to clearly hear. "The Big Dick just got the axe! He really got the axe!" And I thought to myself, "How sweet is this news?" Lorena Bobbitt would surely be proud!

Richard Scott got the axe because he had been the driving force behind AIG investing upwards of $50 billion in sub-prime mortgage related securities with the proceeds of AIG's securities lending activities. Companies like AIG have huge amounts of securities in safekeeping as a result of all the investments they buy and hold. Rather than just simply idly holding these securities, AIG could loan out these securities on a temporary basis to other institutions or funds that, oftentimes, wanted to "short" these securities. A "short" sale is when you borrow a security that you do not own and sell it in the market hoping the price will later fall. If it does fall the short seller can buy the security back later in the market at a lower price and return the security back to where it was borrowed and make a profit. Companies like AIG that lend out their securities receive a small fee for their trouble but also the temporary use of the cash collateral that the securities' borrowers have given them during the borrowing period.

What AIG did so "brilliantly" was to invest these cash collateral flows in long term, collateralized sub-prime mortgage obligations (CMOs consist of debt obligations sold to investors which are backed by pools of mortgage loans), most of which were rated AAA by the bond rating agencies. The problem was that the rating agencies had slapped AAA ratings on these CMOs based strictly on the historic performance of similar but different mortgage securities and their underlying assumptions about the strength of the U.S. residential real estate market. What the rating agencies had not taken into consideration was that the rapid and recent escalation in the use of sub-prime mortgages had fundamentally changed the nature of the residential real estate market in the U.S. Historical default rates of more traditional, higher quality mortgages were no longer relevant and never should have been used in the granting of the original AAA ratings to these CMOs. Simply put, the sub-prime borrower was far weaker than the historical home loan borrower and defaults were rising faster than anyone had predicted. These were the reasons why we in high-yield never fully trusted the rating agencies. They made mistakes just like everyone else. We never ever bought a security based only on its rating, but we always did our own analysis. Just as Rich Mercante had naively fallen for General Motor's Baa2/BBB rating, Richard Scott had naively fallen for the AAA ratings of his CMOs.

In time, as AIG's financial condition became more tenuous, security borrowers decided to return their securities to AIG and they wanted a full and immediate return of the cash collateral they had previously posted with AIG. In order to comply, AIG had to liquidate some of their holdings of these now deeply depressed (in price) CMOs, resulting in enormous losses to AIG. I really don't know the exact losses attributable to Richard's inane securities lending strategy but it had to be well into the billions. And so Richard was shown the door and there were very few mourners, certainly none who were sitting on a park bench in Crested Butte, Colorado.

I have thought a lot about the whole process of originating and holding a sub-prime mortgage in the financial markets and I have tried to assess who I believe is most culpable for this disaster. Some working class guy innocently and naively thinks that he can afford to live in a very nice home and he wants to enjoy the benefits of real estate appreciation. Some mortgage company wants to profit from the origination of this mortgage to my working class guy so they grant him the mortgage with a teaser rate and little, in any, documentation. The mortgage company sells the mortgage to some Wall Street banker who will package all of these sub-prime mortgages into a CMO and sell off interests in the CMO at a nice profit. It is the institutional bond buyer, like AIG, that ultimately buys the CMO debt and holds it for, presumably, a long time.

Who along the way is taking the most risk and should have known better? That's easy. The institutional buyer. He is the one who has to live with the consequences of a really dumb idea and a bad AAA rating. He is the one left holding the bag when many of these sub-prime borrowers default and his CMOs plummet in price. What is also astonishing is that these institutional buyers have the most training and experience in analyzing these risks. This is what they are hired and paid to do. If they had simply said "No, we are not buying any more of this crap," the whole sub-prime factory would have shut down and the U.S. financial markets would have been spared all of this grief. Any financial analyst worth his or her salt should look well past the bond ratings and critically examine all of the assumptions and risks inherent in a particular security well before its purchase. Apparently, this was too much to ask of the folks at AIG.

Once again the level of complete incompetence within AIG continued to startle even a grizzled old veteran such as myself. How could Richard and others have possibly been naive enough to see value in these sub-prime mortgages? The AIG Financial Products Group was similarly fooled by the sub-prime market and effectively lost billions in it through credit default swaps (discussed in more detail in Chapter 23). Where was the basic credit analysis, the sensi ble aversion to excess risk, or the critical thinking of these highly paid investment professionals? Were they given the wrong financial incentives? Had they simply taken their collective eyes off of the ball? Were they simply too dumb or just extraordinarily incompetent? My answer to you is "all of the above."

Throughout the balance of my Colorado stay I began to feel my mood lift. Now when my recurring thoughts focused once again on AIG, it wasn't so much about me anymore. Certainly I continued to feel remorse for people like my St. Jude, but now I began to see AIG differently. I saw its frailty and its immense vulnerability. I could disengage from my historic sadness and almost view AIG's collapse in the same way I had viewed the Enron collapse nearly seven years before. It just wasn't about me anymore and I was letting go. I didn't want to see myself as a vengeful person but, my god, I enjoyed thoughts of Richard suffering the same type of humiliation that I had suffered only three years before. AIG had blown apart and come crashing to the ground in full view of the entire world and, as much as I hated to admit it, I was enjoying this.

Upon our return to Houston, I had the opportunity of watching Hank Greenberg being interviewed by Charlie Rose on our local PBS affiliate TV station. Mr. Greenberg can really be charming when he wanted to be. It was Hank's contention that "None of this (AIG's collapse) happened on my watch." If he had been in charge none of this would have happened because Hank believed in good financial controls. I thought back on the lack of controls which led to the billions of losses at Sun America. But regardless, maybe Hank was right. Maybe if he had been in charge nothing like this would have ever happened to make AIG collapse. But that is not the point. Hank had run AIG for 43 years and he was 80 when he was terminated. He had every opportunity in the world to build a solid and competent management team to succeed him and he failed. To wash your hands of the collapse and say "It didn't happen on my watch," is the same as parents abdicating all responsibility for their children once they leave home. It just doesn't work that way.

Later in early 2009, I saw the list of Forbes' Richest People in a recent issue of *Forbes* magazine. Conspicuously absent from the list was Hank Greenberg. It was noted that Hank had apparently hung on to all of his AIG shares and consequently seen his personal net worth plummet from over $2 billion at the end of 2007 to a measly $100 million at the end of 2008, or a drop of 95%. I thought about my own decision to sell half of my AIG shares after the AGC acquisition and the resulting criticism I had indirectly received from Hank. Apparently Hank had still failed to master the art of investment diversification. He was a true believer until the bitter end. This captain certainly went down with his ship. I also thought of the criticism I received from Richard Scott for my declining the coveted participation in the SICO private partnership. Of course, now all of those SICO shares were not only inaccessible but the AIG stock backing these shares was now virtually worthless. By contrast the once restricted AIG shares that eventually became fully vested to me were sold much earlier at average prices of around $65 each. Richard's dream of hob-nobbing with the mega-rich of the East Coast, financed by his massive holdings in C.V. Starr shares, was all now just a sad reminder of his own greed and hubris.

But I had grown weary and tired of this vengeful thinking. It was time for me to completely let go of all of my remorse and negative thoughts. Now I could see myself differently. My pride and my self-esteem began to blossom and I began to notice a different reaction from people I met when the subject of my history with AIG was broached in conversation. Instead of my sensing that people feared even the discussion of my AIG past, now there was a tremendous interest in my experience. People did not perceive my experience as a whistleblower at AIG as something akin to death, divorce, or disease any longer. My experience suddenly became something of great interest to friends, family, and new acquaintances. As I told my story more often my pride and self-esteem were heightened even further. In their eyes, the collapse of AIG had vindicated me and I could take renewed pride in what I had done.

Suddenly I was no longer feeling the same intensely negative emotions of shame and humiliation of the last four years. As the history of AIG was being written by the news of the day, I could begin to see my part in this corporate drama differently. Back in 2005, I had attempted to be a force for positive change within AIG. In my own way I had made an effort to re-direct the AIG culture into an ethical world. I had confronted the monster and, while battered and bruised, I had survived while AIG had effectively died. Yes, I was a survivor and I could now hold my head up high and proudly proclaim that I had, in fact, seen "the train wreck coming."

My life was definitely getting better. My moods were much more upbeat. I could be alone with myself and my thoughts and there was no remorse, whatsoever. Finally, after nearly four years of unrelenting sadness, I was cured. I was healthy again. Now I had my renewed energy, passion and enthusiasm to really and truly enjoy and savor the last third of my life. Life was good again and it was good again for Thomas Henkemeier ever since his daughter returned home and their relationship improved. Bill Greenwade's son returned from Iraq unharmed and is now working happily as a paramedic in Dallas. Even Steve Wenger, the guy who was only given a 5% chance of surviving his motorcycle accident, is today alive and thriving in Louisville, Kentucky. Yes, the world had become a better place and I could be part of it again.

Without question, I had been vindicated by the implosion of AIG. Some friends proudly told me that "Revenge was mine." But it wasn't about revenge or imagining the pain of my tormentors at AIG that aided my recovery. Revenge rarely makes one ever feel good about themselves in the long run. No, it was about being able to recall all my history, all my childhood years, and all the pressures I had to endure in my career, and realizing that in spite of all my pain, all my humiliation, and all of my loss, I still did the right thing.

Chapter 23: Rolling the Dice

The September 2008 federal bailout of AIG marked only the beginning of a series of increasing amounts of U.S. government aid to this beleaguered company. After three additional bailouts through April, 2009, the U.S. government had now provided AIG with a total aid package of $183 billion and the government effectively owned 80% of the common stock of AIG. What was happening here? How was it possible for this aid package to more than double in such a relatively short period of time? The answer lies in AIG's ungodly exposure to credit default swaps and sub-prime mortgages, and in the continued decline in the U.S. economy since September, 2008.

Think of a credit default swap (CDS) as an insurance policy issued by AIG to an investor that owns an investment like a CMO or a mortgage. This investor has become increasingly concerned about the ability of the sub-prime mortgagees (who are making the monthly interest payments that he receives) to continue to make their mortgage payments. So this investor contacts his Wall St. broker and arranges to purchase insurance against the possible loss of principal and interest payments on his CMO or mortgage investment. AIG is in the business of selling CDS and so our investor agrees to purchase a CDS contract from AIG for, say, ¼ of 1% of the principal amount of the investment each year. So if the investment amount is $1 million AIG will receive $2,500 per year to insure this investor against the loss of his investment. Doesn't sound like much does it? But if you are AIG it looks like found money. AIG was insuring AAA rated securities with, presumably, a minute risk of default. Even if the mortgagees default the homes backing the mortgages could certainly be sold to cover the mortgage, right? So the Financial Products division of AIG sold CDS contracts with insured amounts in the hundreds of billions, and raking in millions of dollars of income on the sale of these CDS contracts. This income, of course, was directly used to calculate year-end bonuses for key members of the Financial Products team at AIG.

The Financial Products division at AIG is not an insurance company and not subject to any type of insurance regulation even though the CDS contracts are effectively a form of insurance. Apparently, what the financial wizards at Financial Products either forgot to do or refused to do was set up any reserves for future losses on their CDS portfolio. Recall that establishing these reserves would have had the accounting effect of reducing current income and therefore potential bonus income. Since no regulation or reserves were required they just assumed that AIG would have no future losses on its CDS portfolio. This is like Allstate deciding to pump up their income by assuming that auto collision claims will disappear in the future so no more reserves will be necessary.

Another way to look at AIG's foray into CDS is to compare it with gambling. Traditionally the market for CDS and other financial derivatives has existed as a way to hedge one's investment, or a means to reduce risk. In the prior example, the CMO holder wanted to reduce his risk of loss so he bought a CDS contract to insure against his potential loss. What AIG should have been doing when it sold its CDS contract was to protect its own position by also owning securities which would have risen in value if the sub-prime market fell, or hedging its own exposure to the sub-prime market. Not AIG, which somehow looked at the sub-prime mortgage market and saw no risk, whatsoever, and effectively gambled the entire company on their assumption that the sub-prime market was indeed solid. AIG was unhedged and effectively each new CDS contract written added to AIG's sub-prime bet. AIG's future was now going to be determined by the next roll of the sub-prime dice.

By September, 2008, the perfect storm of rising sub-prime defaults, falling home prices, rising unemployment, and a weakening economy had already put AIG effectively into bankruptcy. Now add to this mix the virtual collapse of the U.S. financial system and perhaps one can understand AIG's continued deterioration and need for additional bailout funds. The sub-prime cancer had spread quickly throughout the financial system. Bear Stearns, Fannie Mae, Freddie Mac, Lehman Brothers, Washington Mutual, Indy Mac, and Wachovia Bank were among the larger financial institutions which failed and were either liquidated or absorbed by other institutions. The other major banks such as Citibank, Bank America, Wells Fargo, and Chase were all in a state of chaos and federal bailout funds were eventually required in order to shore up their balance sheets and the public's confidence in these institutions. Commercial and personal lending by the banking system effectively ground to a halt and the U.S. economy was gripped by fear and paralysis. All of this was due to the widespread exposure of these institutions to sub-prime mortgages and the resulting depletion of their capital bases. After September, mortgage foreclosures soared and home prices fell at unprecedented rates, further aggravating the already precarious financial conditions of the banks.

AIG's two main objectives following the initial September, 2008, bailout were to reduce its exposure to the sub-prime mortgage market and to sell off assets to repay the federal government. In the free-fall post–September U.S. economy these objectives were impossible to achieve. The collapse in the home mortgage market only increased AIG's exposure to losses and the collapse in commercial lending significantly reduced the worldwide demand for and value of AIG's assets which were available to be sold. Effectively, AIG could only sit there and hemorrhage cash as it covered its sub-prime losses and honored its CDS liabilities. This hemorrhaging of cash could only be financed by more and more federal aid.

As discussed previously, another factor contributing to the depletion of cash at AIG was the unwinding of AIG's securities lending portfolio. As the bad news about AIG spread, anyone or any organization that had borrowed a security from AIG and posted cash collateral with AIG wanted to return the security and get back their cash as soon as possible before AIG potentially filed bankruptcy. So AIG's cash balances were further depleted by huge demands for the return of cash collateral. Again, only federal aid could finance this cash drain.

There has been much public debate about whether or not AIG should have been saved or simply allowed to fail. This is an extremely difficult question to answer and we will probably never have a clear answer. But one way of looking at the federal bailout of AIG was that it effectively contained the AIG disaster to AIG. If AIG had been unable to honor its liabilities all of those losses would have been scattered around the U.S. and the world. Everyone who bought CDS protection from AIG (or posted cash collateral) would have been out of luck and their losses would have been substantial. Plus the collapse of AIG's other businesses would have created untold losses throughout the world economy. By bailing out AIG the federal government effectively quarantined the AIG losses and kept them from spreading around the world and potentially leading to a global financial collapse. My gut tells me that bailing out AIG was the right thing to do, although I would expect that AIG may be unable to fully repay the federal government for its bailout. In all likelihood, AIG will be sold off into many smaller pieces to buyers and investors around the globe. AIG will certainly raise cash from these asset sales but maybe not enough, in my opinion, to fully repay the government. Within AIG, there will probably be a core group of traditional insurance companies which will be retained and reorganized under a new name. In essence, AIG as we have known it, will cease to exist, except in the history books of failed business enterprises such as Enron, Worldcom, and Drexel Burnham.

Why did this have to happen? What can we learn from AIG's collapse? Can similar collapses be prevented in the future? Certainly there will be plenty of new regulations for financial institutions to adhere to in the future and, if properly drafted, these will help. But there will always be business failures in our future since these are tied into the web of capitalism and are difficult to prevent simply through additional regulations. In the prior chapter I tried to summarize the four basic causes that I saw of AIG's failure. But now I want to boil these down even further to something very basic. Something that applies not only to AIG but also to other fallen giants such as Enron, Drexel, and HealthSouth. The basic cause and common thread of all these corporate collapses has been the unbridled human greed and arrogance displayed by the senior managements of these companies.

To repeat, in my opinion, AIG failed for the following reasons:

- AIG was far too large and geographically and operationally diverse.
- AIG was too disorganized without reasonable systems and controls
- Within AIG there was a culture that tolerated fraud and corruption
- Weak management depth caused by years of domination by Hank Greenberg

It is within this environment at AIG that the greed and arrogance of AIG's senior management flourished. Corruption thrived in this environment. The incompetent and dishonest easily went about their work with little fear of detection or accountability.

While AIG was in the midst of a massive federal bailout its executives were throwing a lavish party for themselves and clients at a posh seaside resort in Southern California. After AIG had finalized its recent $183 billion bailout in April, 2009, management of the Financial Products Group received hundreds millions of dollars in bonuses. After they bankrupted the company! All of these actions were symptomatic of a management team that was completely self-absorbed by its own greed and arrogance to others. AIG was the corporate equivalent of a sociopath.

The fatal flaw at AIG was senior management's inability to deal with and arrogance toward its shareholders, employees and regulators. Management at AIG was all about self-enrichment and the preservation of their power. This was the common theme that connected AIG, Drexel, Enron, Worldcom, and HealthSouth. Unbridled human greed and arrogance were at the core of all of these collapses and will be at the core of future collapses unless shareholders, employees, and regulators consistently demand and receive the respect and ethical treatment they deserve from the senior managements of our institutions and corporations. Senior managers must be held accountable for their actions. There must be full disclosure of management's actions. Shareholder rights and interests must be protected. Regulators must be dealt with openly and honestly. Codes of Ethics must truly stand for something. Employees must be allowed to challenge and debate their senior management. And, of course, retaliation of any kind against the whistleblower should not be tolerated under any circumstances.

Epilogue

The writing of this book has indeed been a cathartic and thera-peutic experience, just as my therapist, Jerry Devine, had recom-mended three years before. I sat down in earnest in January, 2009, and by the end of April, I had completed the first full draft of this book. Not only had the collapse of AIG vindicated me but my emo-tional outpouring in this book had, in effect, provided me with the final cleansing of my ill will toward AIG. Once again I was now able to approach my life with renewed energy, passion, and enthusiasm. So, of course, come May 1 it was time for a road trip.

Taking an extended solo motorcycle trip is both a geographic exploration and an exploration of one's own soul. The geography that I wished to explore included the states of Texas, New Mexico, Arizona, California, Nevada, Utah, and Colorado. The time alone and the experiences along the way would certainly test my mental state and emotional stability. Joel Segel, my writing coach, had my full draft and I would stay in contact with him along the way. There was a welcome break in my volunteer activities and Barbara was OK with my three week departure. And Houston was now getting hot and humid so it seemed the perfect time to leave.

The trip began with me crossing the great plains of West Texas and riding through the rugged mountains of Big Bend National Park all in 100+ degree heat. About 200 miles outside of El Paso I blew a front tire on my Triumph motorcycle and, thanks to the help of a couple of locals, the bike and I were trucked to a motorcycle dealership in El Paso for a new tire. From El Paso I headed north and crossed the Continental Divide in the spectacular mountains of Southern New Mexico. My route took me through the Indian reservations and mountains of Northern Arizona and into the deserts of Southern California. There I explored the ecological disaster known as the Salton Sea, crossed the Anza Borrego desert, and rode into San Diego to visit the University of California campus I had attended for two years back in the 70's. It was then up the coast to have lunch with my buddies from the Bank Loan Group with AIG/Sun in Los Angeles.

From L.A. I traveled north along the coast to visit my brother in Santa Barbara whose hillside home had just been miraculously saved from the recent Jesusita fire. I camped the next night in Big Sur and was able to repair a clogged fuel filter on the Triumph in spite of totally inadequate tools and light. In the San Francisco Bay Area I visited with my extended family and soon was headed east across the Sierra Nevada mountains. From there I crossed the surprisingly beautiful mountainous region of Southern Nevada and then through the canyon lands of central Utah. By now it was May 22 and my trip ended the following day when I rode into Denver with the principal objective of helping my daughter and her fiancé purchase their first home.

All in all this was perhaps the most memorable motorcycle trip of my life. The roads, the scenery, the people I met, and the opportunity to explore so much of the Southwest made this trip a truly wondrous experience. But perhaps more important was my own state-of-mind. I was at peace and my mind was quiet. The anxiety, depression, and grief were now all completely gone. My mind could be open to the wondrous beauty and exciting challenges of this trip. All of the experiences of traveling the open road could be savored and enjoyed to the fullest. Even the occasional hardship along the way could be dealt with without undo anxiety.

However, my trip did end on one sad note. My daughter's new puppy, a pointer mix, was going to carry the name "Hank" for the rest of his life. Oh, where had I gone so wrong?

For more information please log on to
www.aigwhistleblower.com